Mishnah and the Social Formation of the Early Rabbinic Guild

A Socio-Rhetorical Approach

Studies in Christianity and Judaism /
Études sur le christianisme et le judaïsme : 11

Studies in Christianity and Judaism / Études sur le christianisme et le judaïsme publishes monographs on Christianity and Judaism in the last two centuries before the common era and the first six centuries of the common era, with a special interest in studies of their interrelationship or the cultural and social context in which they developed.

GENERAL EDITOR:	*Peter Richardson*	University of Toronto
EDITORIAL BOARD:	*Paula Fredriksen*	Boston University
	John Gager	Princeton University
	Olivette Genest	Université de Montréal
	Paul-Hubert Poirier	Université Laval
	Adele Reinhartz	McMaster University
	Stephen G. Wilson	Carleton University

Studies in Christianity and Judaism /
Études sur le christianisme et le judaïsme 11

Mishnah and the Social Formation of the Early Rabbinic Guild

A Socio-Rhetorical Approach

Jack N. Lightstone

with an Appendix by Vernon K. Robbins

Published for the Canadian Corporation for Studies in Religion /
Corporation Canadienne des Sciences Religieuses
by Wilfrid Laurier University Press

2002

We acknowledge the financial support of the Government of Canada through the Book Publishing Industry Development Program for our publishing activities.

National Library of Canada Cataloguing in Publication Data

Lightstone, Jack N.

　　　Mishnah and the social formation of the early Rabbinic Guild: a socio-rhetorical approach

(Studies in Christianity and Judaism = Études sur le christianisme et le judaïsme ESCJ; v. 11)
Includes bibliographical references and index.
ISBN 0-88920-375-X

1. Mishnah—Socio-rhetorical criticism.　2. Judaism—History—Talmudic period, 10-425.　I. Canadian Corporation for Studies in Religion.　II. Title.　III. Series.

BM497.8.L54 2002　　　　　　　　296.1'2306　　　　　　　　C2001-903140-8

Cover design by Leslie Macredie. Cover image: Title page of Mishnayot Seder Qodashim. Lemberg: Avraham Yosef Madpis (Printer), 1875; photo-reproduction of the volume from the Jacob M. Lowy Collection, National Library of Canada / Collection Jacob M. Lowy, Bibliotheque nationale du Canada.

The author and publisher have made every reasonable effort to obtain permission to reproduce the secondary material in this book. Any corrections or omissions brought to the attention of the Press will be incorporated in subsequent printings.

Printed in Canada

Mishnah and the Social Formation of the Early Rabbinic Guild: A Socio-Rhetorical Approach has been produced from camera-ready copy supplied by the author.

Order from:

Wilfrid Laurier University Press
Waterloo, Ontario, Canada　N2L 3C5
http://www.wlupress.wlu.ca

Dedicated to the memory of my father,
Emanuel Lightstone
זכרונו לברכה

Table of Contents

Preface and Acknowledgments

This book concerns a set of related questions which drove me to pursue graduate studies and an academic career three decades ago. At that time, I was intensely intrigued with the question, Wherein lie the origins of the rabbinic movement, and how might the evidence from the early rabbinic movement be made to speak of those origins? As a graduate student of Professor Jacob Neusner and his colleagues, these questions became increasingly compelling to me. I learned to perceive the difficulties and complexities of so defining the questions themselves that the limits and possibilities of pursuing meaningful research toward answers were apparent. In other words, the questions themselves were problematized. Since there is no one indisputably valid way of articulating with precision the questions, there is no one manner of pursuing research to seek answers. At the same time, one cannot flee to methodological and theoretical relativism; there are arguably better and worse ways of dealing with these issues. The current volume represents my latest, but undoubtedly not my last, attempt to address them.

My approach continues to be informed by the insights and methods of several cognate disciplines, encompassing literary analysis, sociology and anthropology, and history (including, in the last chapter, the history of material culture at the core of the archaeological enterprise). The conceptual and methodological realm of socio-rhetorical analysis, the driving force of how this volume conducts its business, is itself the result of a mélange of several of these traditions of inquiry. Socio-rhetorical analysis, as more recently articulated by scholars of early Christianity and its literatures such as Burton Mack and Vernon K. Robbins, has provided me with the basis for redefining, once again, how I articulate the questions with which my scholarly career began. And yet professors Mack and Robbins may find my own idiomatic adaptation of socio-rhetorical analysis to be foreign and transformed in their application to Mishnah, related texts, and the question of the social formation of the early rabbinic guild. Perhaps, and this is my hope, they would find something new and compelling in socio-rhetorical analysis, its theoretical and methodological underpinnings, as adapted to the current study. It is, therefore, altogether fitting that this volume includes an appendix authored by Vernon K. Robbins.

Who is the intended audience for this work? The answer is as difficult to articulate as it was for my previous book, *The Rhetoric of the Babylonian Talmud: Its Social Meaning and Context* (Lightstone, 1994), of which the current volume is a complement. Because I have benefited in an ongoing way from many different scholarly circles (sociology and anthropology, history and history of religions, Judaic studies, biblical studies, classical history, etc.), my writing is geared to all of them at once and none of them in particular, even though this book could hardly be classified as a "general" work obviously intended for a wide readership. The fact is that different parts of the work will be compelling to different audiences–sometimes the student of rabbinic literature, sometimes the scholar of the history of Ancient Judaism, sometimes the social anthropologist, sometimes the biblical scholar and historian of Early Christianity. Therefore, something of a readers' guide for different intended readerships is in order. Those who are not primarily interested in the study of early rabbinic literature will find the detailed textual analyses and charts of rabbinic texts less compelling, even if they are essential to argue the theses of the book and demonstrate the use of socio-rhetorical analysis with respect to rabbinic literature. For them I suggest that greater attention be paid to chapters 1, 2, and 5, with a cursory reading of chapters 3 and 4 (with attention to the beginning and end of the latter two). The anticipatory sections toward the end of chapter 1 and the deliberate "recapping" provided at the outset of the other chapters is specifically designed to allow the book to be read in this selective manner. So, too, expeditiously widening the discussion in chapter 5 to deal with what we know of the Palestinian Patriarchy, to inquire of any impact of the rabbinic guild upon the material remains of late second- and early-third-century Galilee, and to hint at the relation of our questions to the processes of Roman-style urbanization in the Land of Israel in the period reflect not only the diverse scholarly traditions that have influenced the author but also the desire to have the work speak about Mishnah and the social formation of the early rabbinic movement to the aforementioned range of, I hope, interested readers.

Translations of passages cited from early rabbinic literature are my own. They are based upon standard scholarly editions of the original (when available), with attention to *significant* variations in the major extant manuscripts. For Mishnah, I have used the Hebrew text of H. Albeck (vocalized by H. Yalon). My translations of passages in Tosefta are based upon the edition of S. Lieberman (for tractates covered by Lieberman's edition); for other tractates, I am dependent upon the text of M.S. Zuckermandel, with attention to S. Lieberman's *Tosefet Rishonim*. For Semahot, I have used the Hebrew text published by D. Zlotnick.

For each of the principal rabbinic passages analyzed in depth in chapters 2, 3 and 4, I have produced a detailed, rhetorically "scored" chart of the translated text. In order to serve subsequent analyses, individual segments of the charted translations are designated by *capital* letters. When, therefore, in my discussions I refer to m. Gittin 2:1C, I am designating a segment of the Mishnah text in my scored chart. However, for the convenience of the reader, I have also provided before each rhetorically scored chart a translation of the same passage formatted in a more simple manner, in the expectation that this will prove more conducive to some. The latter too is segmented for ease of reading, but the system of segmentation is not as complex as that in the rhetorically scored charts. In these more simple presentations of the principal texts under discussion, I have used *small* letters to identify segments, in order to avoid confusion with references to sections of the rhetorically scored charts. In the appendix, all of Professor Robbins's references are to the Mishnah text presented in the more simple form.

This work has been completed over a protracted six-year period, most of which has coincided with my duties as provost and vice-rector at Concordia University in Montreal. My office staff, and my senior administrative colleagues have all been patient with me as I struggled to find time, often at their expense, to complete this work. Their forbearance is much appreciated. My graduate research assistants, Ms. Mayjee Philip, Ms. Kelly Menchick, and Dr. Maria Mamfredis have made important contributions to this book. I appreciate too the work of Ms. Heather Adams-Robinette, who proofread and corrected the final copy. My colleagues in the Department of Religion at Concordia continue to provide constructive criticism coupled with moral support. Colleagues at the Society of Biblical Literature, at the annual meetings of which initial versions of chapters 2 and 3 were delivered as conference papers, impelled the original research. In this regard, I have already mentioned the inspiration provided by the works of Vernon Robbins and Burton Mack. An engine of my research for over 20 years, including that resulting in this book, has been my colleagues in the Canadian Society of Biblical Studies. I cannot think of a single group, in addition to my immediate departmental colleagues, which has so informed what I have done and how I do it over the last two decades. Particular thanks go to professors Peter Richardson, Stephen Wilson, Terry Donaldson, Michel Desjardin, Harold Remus, Wayne Mcready, and Bill Klassen, to name several of the Society's members, who year after year have listened to, commented upon, and encouraged pursuit of this work. Wilfrid Laurier University Press, its current and former directors, have been immensely supportive over the years as I have pursued new avenues of scholarly inquiry. Their faith in my work has helped me sustain my efforts. Vernon K. Robbins's continued interest in my work has also been an inspiration, and I am most appreciative of his having agreed to write this volume's appendix.

A preliminary version of chapter 5 was published in S.G. Wilson and M. Desjardins, eds., *Text and Artifact in the Religions of Mediterranean Antiquity: Essays in Honour of Peter Richardson* (Waterloo, ON: Wilfrid Laurier University Press, 2000) for the Canadian Corporation for Studies in Religion. I wish to acknowledge the Corporation and the Press allowing me to include this previously published material in this volume.

On the basic human level, no one provides me with more support and encouragement than my family, my wife Dr. Dorothy Markiewicz, and my children, Jennifer and Etan. There is no expression of gratitude possible that equals my sentiments toward them.

The research and publication of this book was made possible by grants from the Social Sciences and Humanities Research Council of Canada and from Concordia University; the ongoing support of these institutions has been key.

My father, Emanuel Lightstone, Menahem Mendel ben Michael veLeah, died in September 1999 (5760 *anno mundi*) and was buried on the eve of the Day of Atonement. He was a man who trully combined *torah* and *derek eretz*, the love of learning for its own sake and unquestioned humanity. It is to his memory, may it be a blessing to us, that this book is dedicated.

Jack N. Lightstone

1

Introduction:
Focusing on the Social Meaning
of Mishnaic Rhetoric

The Mishnah derives its importance from the fact that this late-second-century document was the first text produced and promulgated as *authoritative* by the early rabbinic guild. This book examines the social meaning of the rhetoric of the Mishnah. The saliency of studying Mishnah's rhetoric stems from my definition of the term. I take rhetoric to refer to the formal modes of speech socially defined as authoritative or persuasive by some community or group. This first chapter of the book comprises two major sections. In the first, I describe what I mean by "the social meaning of rhetoric" and argue how the analysis of the social meaning of Mishnah's rhetoric contributes something distinctive and new to our knowledge of Mishnah and of the guild of rabbinic masters who produced it. In order to place this approach in context, in this first section I also recount several other methodological and theoretical approaches to the study of Mishnah and of Rabbinism's origins. Some of these approaches were my own waystations en route to this book, and this volume's results are meant to complement or supplement results garnered by these other approaches. Other methods I have circumvented or rejected outright en route, for reasons that I make clear. The chapter's second principal section looks at rhetoric as a priestly-scribal virtuosity, and the final section outlines this book's structure and previews its findings.

I
Methodological and theoretical issues:
Ways taken and forgone

My path to this book on the social meaning of mishnaic rhetoric began with an interest in the origins of both the earliest rabbinic movement and rabbinic Judaism in the historical, social, and cultural context of the late first through early third centuries CE. This century and a half of the emerging rabbinic movement immediately followed upon the destruction by the Romans of the Jerusalem Temple, its cult, and its national administration of Judean and Galilean Jewry (Goodblatt, 1994: 6-30). Yet the path through this rather straightforward research agenda has led me radically to redefine the ways and means, and the whys and wherefores, of going about the work. I questioned at a number of junctures the working assumptions not only of the work of others but also of my own enterprise. Indeed, I have abandoned altogether the notion that there could be some methodological or theoretical route to analyzing the relevant evidence that would produce a comprehensive picture of rabbinic origins. That is not to say that all approaches are equally appropriate. I do not propound a kind of methodological and theoretical relativism. Rather, each *defensible* approach reveals and makes sense of some aspects of the evidence, insofar as the approach is rigorous, appropriate to the defined task, and not founded on untenable, *a priori* assumptions. To use a metaphor from the biological sciences, consider the staining of a tissue specimen with different solutions in a medical laboratory. Each type of stain makes some things highly visible while occulting others. Each stain offers quite a different take on the same tissue sample.

To better situate the take produced by this book's methodological and theoretical approach, and to justify its value with respect to antecedent and parallel approaches, let me briefly address in turn several questions.

> Why focus specifically, even if not exclusively, on Mishnah, in shedding light on the earliest rabbinic guild and its origins?
>
> What is occulted by, or what problems are inherent in, approaches other than that adopted in this book in illuminating that guild and its origins?
>
> What methodological and theoretical perspectives are antecedent and have contributed to our focus on the social meaning of Mishnah's rhetoric?
>
> What does it mean to examine the social meaning of Mishnah's rhetoric and what is thereby illuminated?

I.i. Focusing on the Mishnah in understanding the origins of the rabbinic guild
At first glance, among the documents produced by the rabbinic guild up to the end of the sixth or beginning of the seventh century, evidence from Mishnah would appear to be the least enlightening of the character and origins of the guild. For those readers not familiar with Mishnah there is little narrative evidence in Mishnah. One finds far more in other rabbinic documents produced in the first six centuries CE.[1] Mishnah, meaning roughly "(The) Teaching," comprises 65 individual tractates, grouped into six major subject divisions called "Orders." The content of Mishnah is primarily legal. However, it is quite unlike the *Didache* or the *Didaskalia Apostolorum* (two works offering rules for conduct in and the organization of early Christian communities), the *Community Rule* (a Qumran scroll purporting to offer rules for the community that produced the document), or the surviving fragmentary "constitutions" of some Greco-Roman voluntary associations or guilds; Mishnah's legal dicta do not concern the organization of, and life within, the rabbinic guild. Rather, Mishnah's laws encompass a wide range of quite different topics: agricultural tithes to the priesthood and the central Temple; laws concerning the Sabbath and Judaic festivals; family law; aspects of civil and criminal law; sacrificial practices; laws pertaining to uncleanness. In general, Mishnah's laws pertain to a social world in which the Temple and its

---

1.   This being said, no rabbinic documents from this era may be classified as narrative or historical in genre, even if they contain narrative or history-like sections. Late Antique Rabbinism produced nothing like the early Christian gospels or Eusebius' *Historia Ecclesiastica*. The first (known) rabbinic document which could be classified as historical in genre, *Iggeret Rav Sherira Gaon*, dates from the 10th century CE.

cultic, administrative, judicial, and legislative institutions still stand. Yet the rabbinic guild that produced Mishnah operated in the aftermath of the real Temple's destruction, along with its associated institutions. The fact that some of Mishnah's laws taken in isolation can and have been practised within rabbinic Judaism without the Temple does not change the fact that the primary focus of Mishnah's legal dicta is a Temple state, now reconstructed "in the imagination" in lieu of the one destroyed "on the ground." That is why, as stated at the outset of this section, Mishnah appears a most unlikely focus for our purposes, the elucidation of the character and origins of the early rabbinic guild.

For quite other reasons, however, it is not as counterintuitive as it first appears to look to Mishnah and its formal patterns of speech for evidence relevant to understanding the nature and origins of the earliest rabbinic guild. Those reasons have, foremost, to do with three claims about Mishnah.

(1) The Mishnah is a remarkably self-consistent work with respect to literary characteristics.

(2) Scholars generally agree that Mishnah, edited between 190 CE and 220 CE, is the oldest surviving, and probably the first, literary work produced by the early rabbinic movement.

(3) Almost immediately upon its production and promulgation within the rabbinic guild, the study of Mishnah became the principal act of becoming, and then being, a rabbi within the life of the guild circle. Not even the study of the books of the Judaic Bible, sacred to all Jews (and early Christians), sufficed to fulfill this.

These three observations or claims–Mishnah's self-consistent "shaping," its date, and its privileged place within the guild where it originated–make Mishnah a key "artifact" of the group that produced it. Therefore, notwithstanding the difficulty of interpreting an artifact to shed light on its fashioners, Mishnah provides a privileged point of entry to questions of the nature and origins of the early rabbinic guild. The challenge is to spell out a theoretical and conceptual framework and an attendant methodology that will help us move from the traits of the artifact to propositions about the group that produced it.

Yet, as intimated, most scholars who wish to tell the (hi)story of the earliest rabbinic movement and to describe its features will include Mishnah as a prominent element *in* their accounts, but will turn largely to other, later rabbinic documents, with greater narrative content, in fashioning that account. To account for the difference between them and me brings us back to the first question articulated earlier, namely, What methodological and theoretical take have I adopted, and why? As indicated in the questions posed earlier, to broach these issues I shall have to say more about the current state of Mishnah studies, its successes and shortcomings, as I see them. Afterward and in light of that discussion, the place and utility of this book's methodological and theoretical approach will be more easily described and more readily understood.

I.ii. Terminological boobytraps and tacitly enshrined agendas

Using several relatively recent "mainstream" works as examples will provide a speedy entrée to the issues by describing what I deem some *terminological boobytraps* (to use Morton Smith's term) in evidence in these works. As we shall see, these terms are telltale clues or surface symptoms of deeper problems, namely, inherent *circularities* in the methodological and theoretical constructs that inform the studies in question.

D. Weiss-Halivni, S. Safrai, and A. Goldberg are all prominent, first-class scholars of early rabbinic literature. Yet recent works by them (Weiss-Halivni, 1986; Safrai, 1987a, 1987b; Goldberg, 1987a, see also 1987b) aptly serve the claims I wish to make in this section. The two theses I argue are quite simple. First, with few exceptions,[2] the academic study of Mishnah continues even in the last two decades to be driven by questions that not only are extraneous to, but also seriously bias the study of the document itself. These biases preclude addressing such questions as, What is the character, context, and meaning of Mishnah, and what may Mishnah, the earliest rabbinic document, reveal of the processes of social formation of which it was both a reflection and an agent? My second thesis, which I will take up subsequently, is that the study of the earliest social formation(s) of the rabbinic guild and the study of that guild's earliest literature have tended to be caught in a mutually self-validating circularity. It is difficult to discuss these two theses entirely separately, for the realities which they try to capture do not operate independently of one another. Still there is considerable advantage in trying to do so.

What our examples will show is that questions of what Mishnah is and about the group(s) that produced it have been confounded, in whole or in part, by other related questions. And the terminology and agendas of these latter questions have migrated into the former, where they are misplaced. These "misplaced" agendas and terminology are encapsulated in questions such as:

> Where did "Rabbin*ism*" (as opposed to the rabbinic movement) come from; what are its origins in pre-mishnaic times?
>
> How did "*the* Sages" operate before and after the destruction of the Second Temple?
>
> What are the origins of "*the* halakah" (rabbinic law) or "*Oral* Torah," in what forms were they transmitted by "the Sages" before the editing of *their* Mishnah, and by what literary processes did they *come to be preserved in* their Mishnah?

or even in

> What were Jesus' or the earliest Jesus movement's stances toward the Sages and their Oral Torah or halakah, and how did that stance shape what early Christianity was to become?

All of these queries seem quite legitimate in themselves. They may not directly address the question What is the nature, context, and meaning of Mishnah? But, in addition to their own *prima facie* legitimacy, these questions appear not to preclude addressing the questions central to this book.

In fact, the opposite is true. First, the litany of queries as formulated above begs central questions about Rabbinism before 200 CE (the approximate date of

---

2.   Prominent among the exceptions is the work on Mishnah of Jacob Neusner, whose contributions will be discussed later.

Mishnah's redaction) and about ancient Judaism generally. Second, and of considerable concern to this book, precisely that which is begged in the questions as formulated provides *a priori* answers to questions about the origins and redaction of Mishnah and its content. This is so because these queries assume a particular historical scenario of Rabbinism's development and social location, including the origins, provenance, transmission, and agglutination of earliest Rabbinism's legal tradition. As a result, the evidence of Mishnah, the first written work produced by Rabbinism, can only be understood and interpreted as the product of these developments. What, then, is the question that is begged, and how so?

The questions as formulated are replete with what Morton Smith would have called "terminological boobytraps," a term he used to describe a similar phenomenon in the modern study of Gnosticism. I understand terminological boobytraps as words from specific contexts with specific referents that are then used to refer to things outside of their original contexts. Outside of their home contexts, terms become terminology which, as opposed to descriptive words, create powerful methodological tides. When used outside their original specific settings they may come to carry a more generalized meaning or have a more general referent than in the initial usage. Alternatively, the specificity of the original meaning may then be painted onto the new referent. The user may or may not be forthright about, or even aware of, whether he or she intends to identify the new referents with the original. What transpires is of methodological import, because what is begged is whether the new referents are or are not substantially the same as the original ones, and the scholarly interpretation of data is inextricably tied to heuristic perceptions of *degrees of similarity* and to how and by what heuristic criteria one initially *groups data* for analysis. Moreover, in many instances what is begged is whether there is a direct *historical connection* between the new and original referents.

The more glaring problematic terms in the aforementioned questions are set off in quotation marks or italics: (the) Sages; (the) halakah; (Oral) Torah. Each term, especially with the definite article specified or implied, has a precise referent within a particular context, provenance, and era.

"(The) Sages" is used in Mishnah as an attribution for a legal ruling when that ruling is assigned to anonymous rabbinic authorities or simply to rabbinic authorities generally, specifically in contrast to opinions attributed to a single named rabbinic authority, such as Rabbi Aqiva or Rabbi Meir. The term continues to be used thereafter in rabbinic literature as the preferred term for the rabbis as a group–this apart from passages contrasting the view of a single rabbi with the opinion of many. To use the term (the) Sages to designate any group, class or movement of Judaic authorities who functioned before Mishnah's redaction is to assert, willy-nilly, that these authorities are in some serious sense rabbis in the rabbinic sense and that their movement and religion might legitimately be called rabbinic Judaism. Hence, if one asserts, that the Sages of the "Second Temple Period" legislated for the Israelite nation in Judea, Galilee or beyond, then one implies that in some serious sense rabbis and rabbinic Judaism were phenomena of the Second Temple Period, that their rulings defined normative Judaism of that period, and that these rulings first attained written form in Mishnah at the end of the second century. Such claims, in essence, establish the history and provenance of Mishnah's content even before one has examined a single passage of Mishnah.

"Halakah" (literally, "the Way"), is first, the term adopted by rabbinic texts to refer to agreed-upon rabbinic law, in the singular, as in the formulaic talmudic phrase, "and the law [in this case] is in accordance with [the opinion of] Rabbi x" (והלכתא כרבי...). An undoubtedly derivative, second sense of halakah is the entire body of rabbinic law as accepted by the rabbinic movement at any one time–the Halakah. This usage appears frequently in the writings of post-talmudic, and especially modern, authors, but less often in early rabbinic texts themselves. When modern scholars use the term in either sense to refer to Judaic law or laws prior to Mishnah, they imply wittingly or unwittingly that consensually validated rabbinic legal rulings or a consensually validated *body* of rabbinic law existed before the authorship of Mishnah, the first rabbinic document. So to imply suggests that a rabbinic movement existed in pre-Mishnah times. Moreover, the notion of an *accepted* body of pre-Mishnah law is equivocal and ambiguous, for it intimates acceptance or authority within the pre-Mishnah Jewish community at large. Wedding the latter to the former notion of consenual validity among a group of pre-mishnaic rabbis (in my view an oxymoron) predisposes the student of Ancient Judaism toward the implicit perception of a pre-mishnaic normative Rabbinism in some form or another. Sectarian law, such as is represented in the Community Rule or the Damascus Covenant, or Jesus' critique of the law as portrayed in the Synoptic Gospels is then seen as sectarian or critical with respect to the Halakah. In all, the use of the term halakah in reference to Judaic law before Mishnah's authorship and the application of the expression (the) Sages to anonymous pre-mishnaic Judaic authorities reinforce each other in rendering self-evidently appropriate and affectively satisfying a reconstruction of Judaic religion and society during the Second Commonwealth in which a "rabbinic" movement defined and continuously refined a normative system of cultic, social, and economic law. This evolving system was the standard from which others, like the early Jesus movement or the Qumran community dissented, and which Philo or Josephus sanitized for hellenistic sensibilities.

Furthermore, to use the term "Oral Torah" as a near synonym for (the) Halakah or halakah before Mishnah's authorship is, first, to adopt later Rabbinism's self-serving apologetic about the origins of its teachings and evolving legal system and, second, implicitly to render plausible talk of Second Commonwealth halakah and pre-mishnaic Sage-Rabbinism in the absence of any written evidence dating prior to Mishnah's authorship *ca.* 200 CE.

It is obvious that these terminological malapropisms seriously affect the selection, categorization, and interpretation of evidence deemed to be related to the history of Judaism and Judaic society during the Second Commonwealth and in the century or so following the Commonwealth's demise in 70 CE. These, however, are not the issues of this book. My focus is the effect of their use and of the picture of Judaism and Jewish society that use imposes upon the study of Mishnah. For while it is perhaps clear how, on this basis, mishnaic evidence may be anachronistically and uncritically used to reconstruct pre-mishnaic Judaism, less often considered is how such usages and related, implicitly conveyed perceptions affect the study of Mishnah itself. We stated earlier, for example, that the notion of a pre-mishnaic group or movement of (rabbinic) Sages biases one toward viewing Mishnah as the gathering together and consigning to writing of a pre-existent rabbinic tradition. In similar fashion, the (pre)disposition *prima facie* so to view Mishnah inclines one to diminish or overlook the differences among early rabbinic compilations, for Mishnah then tends to be seen as one such gathering and agglutination of antecedent sage-rabbinic tradition among others, such as those appearing in Tosefta, allegedly pre-mishnaic (tannaitic) traditions in the Palestinian and Babylonian Talmuds, and the (so-called) tannaitic midrashim (Sifra, the three Sifres and the two Mekiltas). For all of these documents it is their character as repositories that is implicitly stressed. What is veiled from active, systematic inquiry, even recognition is each document's character as a distinct, idiomatic literary *ouevre*, *authored*, not simply compiled, by some person or persons with their own agenda, outlook, style, purpose, and social provenance.

I submit that most scholars currently working in the field of early Rabbinism and its literature would find nothing unusual, inaccurate or, perhaps, incomplete in briefly characterizing Mishnah as (simply?) the gathering together in organized fashion and consigning to writing of a pre-existent rabbinic tradition. Indeed, even the more recent adoption and adaptation in Mishnah study of form and redaction criticism and tradition history, with their roots in the study of the history of the Synoptic *tradition*, have, in effect, predisposed students toward such a view, because all of these methods inherently portray a text as the agglutination of fragmented parts. It is only with great effort that J. Neusner, who pioneered the application of such methods to the analysis of Mishnah, sought to overcome what I believe to be this strong bias inherent in these methodological approaches. While he has managed to do so more than any other scholar of the last two decades, I believe that these methods' gravitational pull in the other direction, toward the fragmentation of a text and toward the pre-history of its allegedly pre-existent parts is inexorable. For others, like Weiss-Halivni, Goldberg, and Sanders, who are far less conscious of the terminological boobytraps described earlier and perhaps less self-conscious methodologically, the predisposition to view Mishnah primarily as a repository of pre-mishnaic "halakic Sagism" is largely unchecked.

A blatant case in point is Goldberg's essay, "The Mishna–A Study Book of Halakah" (Goldberg, 1987a) and its place among other essays in S. Safrai's *The Literature of the Sages. First Part: Oral Tora, Halakha, Mishna, Tosefta, Talmud, External Tractates. Compendia Rerum Iudaicarum ad Novum Testamentum* (1987). The volume's title from beginning to end is in itself a revelation. First, the use of the term the Sages rather than the rabbis expresses the blurring of historical boundaries and the effacing of differentiation between the period in which the literature of the *rabbis* was produced and the previous centuries in which that literature's content was (allegedly) produced. Second, as the volume's subtitle intimates, essays on "Oral Tora" and "Halakha" (both by Safrai, 1987a, 1987b) precede those on the major documents authored by the earliest rabbinic movement. What is here implied is also confirmed by what is explicitly stated in those essays. Sage-rabbinic processes of Oral Tora and a rabbinic-like conception of a normative halakah go back to well before the Hasmonean Revolt. Moreover, in the volume's view, these processes produced the Mishnah and subsequent rabbinic texts, rather than the opposite, namely, that halakah and the (rabbinic) doctrine of Oral Tora are defined and produced in the documents of early Rabbinism, beginning with the earliest such document, Mishnah. Almost every page of the first several essays of the volume offers material substantiating my characterization of the book's *Tendenz* as I have described it. The opening paragraphs of Goldberg's essay nicely captures what I allege to be going on. He writes (Goldberg, 1987a: 211):

> Following the destruction of the Second Temple, the amorphous corpus of teaching of the Sages, while remaining oral, began to take on definitive literary form, culminating, after a century and a half of growth and development, into the literary works, which go by the name Tannaic literature. The most important part of this literature, and the first to be edited in accomplished form, is the Mishna. Other Tannaic works are the Tosefta and the Tannaic midrash collections. Since the Mishna serves in many ways as the foundation for these other works, which were also later, it is generally described as the basic work of Oral Tora.
>
> The Mishnah is the carefully worded literary formulation of Pharisaic-rabbinic law as it developed in the late Second Temple period and some generations afterwards.

Later (pp. 211-13), he continues his characterization of Mishnah and of its origins as follows:

> In this perspective, Mishnah marks a definite turn in the literary form of Oral Tora. Historical necessity here again called for a sure way for the preservation of the Oral Tora in this time of crisis. A process of set formalization began which was to continue for over a century and would result in the Mishnah as we have it today. In this there was gain and loss. The obvious gain was that now the Oral Tora could be memorized by rote and its preservation made easier ....
>
> As stated, the Mishnah is the rote formulation of Pharisaic-rabbinic halakha.

Later in the article Goldberg documents the topical outlines of Mishnah's tractates and considers organizing principles that seem to have governed the redactor's juxtaposition of antecedent traditions. Goldberg allows that Mishnah's editor has "smoothed out" the language of pre-existent constituent elements. But his overall tendency in what he is able to perceive Mishnah to be is set at the outset of the essay in the sections that I have cited.

    David Weiss-Halivni's *Midrash, Mishnah and Gemara: The Jewish Predilection for Justified Law* (1986) provides another, most interesting case in point, because the self-conscious problematic of the work is the relationship of literary form taken by rabbinic law in various venues at different times, and factors which affected that form, including their social, intellectual, and political history.

But notwithstanding his greater subtlety and care, Weiss-Halivni does not extricate himself from the baggage which in a far more overt way affects the work of Goldberg and Safrai. One need only begin with the discrepancy between the book's title and its chapter headings: (1) The Biblical Period; (2) The Post-Biblical Period; (3) The Mishnaic Period; (4) The Amoraic Period; (5) The Stammaitic Period; (6) The Gemara as Successor of Midrash; (7) The Legacy of the Stammaim. A book, then, which defines its problematic as the meaning and significance of the literary forms taken by (legal) Midrash (a body of post-mishnaic rabbinic literature), Mishnah (a particular rabbinic document) and Gemara (that is, the Babylonian Talmud) quickly becomes reconfigured as the reconstruction of the literary history of pre-mishnaic (Jewish?/rabbinic?) law commencing centuries before the authorship of the first rabbinic text, Mishnah. As the chapter titles indicate, the focus and *starting point* is not the idiomatic character of documents but the history of legal-literary processes of which the documents are simply the epiphenomenal effects. Again Mishnah is the repository of materials. These materials exhibit a certain literary character in common, because during the "mishnaic period," which for Weiss-Halivni *preceded* the production of Mishnah, Jewish (*sic!*) legal materials were expressed in this fashion. Weiss-Halivni is far more careful and discriminating than others in his use and, at times, avoidance of terms such as the Halakah, the Sages and Oral Torah, but has not really escaped their gravitational forces.

Before continuing, let me summarize the problem with such studies of Mishnah and of other early rabbinic documents. By commencing with a reconstruction of the pre-mishnaic, social history of Judaic law, paradoxically as represented largely in Mishnah itself, before considering the character of Mishnah in its own right, they prejudge much of what one would ask about the "what" and "wherefores" of Mishnah. They in fact steer one's attention away from much of the evidence of Mishnah, specifically any evidence of the literary unity and coherence of the document, determining the character of both the whole and its individual units and sub-units. In this respect, such works cannot in the final analysis establish what Mishnah is and what significance may lie in the evidence of Mishnah's character. And, as an aside, without answers, complete or incomplete, to such questions one cannot reliably apply data culled from Mishnah to any other purpose, whether to reconstruct the social history of a nascent rabbinic movement or of pre-mishnaic Judaism and Judaic society, or for that matter of Judaism contemporaneous with Mishnah's authors, all of which are overriding and biasing interests of authors like Weiss-Halivni, Safrai, and Goldberg.

Even this, however, only describes the problem at its surface level–one of steered agendas and prejudged or begged questions. There is, as noted earlier, a deeper level to the problems evidenced in this terminology and its use. In the studies discussed above, words like the Halakah, the Sages, and the Oral Torah have come to play the role of theoretical and conceptual constructs. That is, in a subtle fashion they provide the framework for the choice of relevant evidence and for the explanation or interpretation of that evidence. Mishnah is explained with reference to the activity of the Sages and their need to preserve the Oral Torah and especially that Torah's halakah. Thus, before we have ever opened Mishnah and examined any of its particular traits, an entire theory of Mishnah, and indeed a theory of the rabbinic guild's earliest literary activity is given. This state of affairs results from a circularity that has haunted much scholarship on early rabbinic literature and the question of the origins of the rabbinic guild.

I.ii.1. Circularities – In a paper on paradigms for social descriptions of early Christianities, Burton Mack describes two phenomena (Mack, 1995). The first is a circularity that has haunted the study of early Christianities: the New Testament literature provides the primary evidence *and theoretical paradigms* for the reconstruction of early Christianities, and these reconstructions form the basis for understanding the New Testament. In Mack's words, "Catch-22!" The second is what Mack dubs the scholarly game of "Gotcha!" It is the pursuit of finding the fundamental flaw in someone else's reconstruction or in the adoption and use of a theoretical paradigm on which a reconstruction is founded. By calling Catch-22 when we see it, we may hope to break loose of problematic, self-validating, and tautologous scholarship. Through calling Gotcha, we revise ways of reading the evidence. In time Gotcha produces ever more refined paradigms and social/cultural reconstructions.

Almost everything Mack says of the scholarly study of the New Testament and of related reconstructions of early Christianities holds for the study of early rabbinic literature and the social reconstruction of early Rabbinisms. For many scholars, the question of the origins of the rabbinic guild seems not to be a vexing unknown. Witness *The Literature of the Sages* (Safrai,1987c). It is apparent that the principal contributors to this volume (Isaiah Gafni, 1987; Shmuel Safrai, 1987a, 1987b; and Avraham Goldberg, 1987a, 1987b) all share a common view of the origins and fundamental character of early Rabbinism, and they do not see this shared view as subject to serious doubt or debate. Their analyses assume a context in which worthwhile scholarly debate continues about the details only. And they seem to admit that, with respect to a number of specifics, the available evidence may not permit the emergence of a broadly based consensus. Nevertheless, as far as this significant faction of scholarship is concerned, the main lines of the emergence, history, and nature of the early rabbinic movement are well established and clear.

However, here we see Catch-22. The same circularity that Mack identifies in New Testament studies and social descriptions of early Christianities is mightily at work in the scholarship in the *The Literature of the Sages*, and in other works. Let me show you the particular Catch by recounting the assumed historical narrative, in my own words.

Whence the authoritative early rabbinic writings? The "consensus" is that up to the destruction of the Temple state in 70CE, generations of "the sages" were the normative locus for the development and ramifying of teachings and legal dicta which constituted the lived cultural, cultic and legal framework for pre-destruction Judea and Galilee. These teachings and dicta interpreted, complemented and supplemented the official con-stitution of the Pentateuch. Thus "Oral Torah" was largely articulated and justified as interpretive glosses and extrapolations of biblical passages (see also Weiss-Halivni, 1986).

The social upheaval, conflicts, and rapid change engendered by the dissolution of the Maccabean dynasty and the entrenchment of Roman hegemony resulted in the development of numerous types of protest movements. Within that array, the Pharisees remained the most closely aligned with, and the principle preservers of, the teachings of the "sages." Indeed for the most part "the sages" and the "pharisaic sages" are synonymous. But social upheaval and change during the last century and a half of the Second Commonwealth increased internal differentiation and factionalism among the (pharisaic) "sages" themselves. "Schools" developed around specific "sages'" "Oral Torah." As a consequence, teachings increasingly had to bear attributions to the master or school with which it was associated. The crisis of the destruction of the Second Temple forced the issue of maintaining some unifying institution which would encompass the various "sages" and "schools" and which would collect, organize and preserve the "Oral Torah" of the various "sages." That institution was the council/academy of sages (sanhedrin) under the leadership of Yohanan ben Zakkai in the immediate post-destruction era in Yavneh, thereafter led by the rabbinic "nasi" (the "prince" or Patriarch). That process was brought to fulfilment under Rabbi Judah the Nasi (Judah ben Simeon ben Gamaliel) at the end of the second century in the form of the Mishnah, the topically-organized collection ordering and committing to writing the "Oral Torah." Judah's Mishnah was based especially on the earlier "mishnahs" of Rabbi Aqiva and of his student Rabbi Meir. Their "mishnahs" provided the normative touchstones in dealing with contradictory views.

To serve his purpose, Rabbi Judah abandoned for the most part articulating teachings as interpretive glosses of biblical passages. But this long established form for rabbinic teachings is either preserved or revived in post-mishnaic collections (see Weiss-Halivni, 1986), in particular in the halakic midrashim and to some degree in Tosefta (a collection of some of Judah's raw or rejected materials, as well as interpretive glosses and expansions of his Mishnah).

Whatever nuanced version of the above one chooses from whatever modern scholar's work, in the main what one has is a scholarly refinement of rabbinic literature's account of its own literary history.[3] This account, distilled and refined, becomes the description of the early rabbinic and proto-rabbinic social formations, in terms of which the literary history and character of the early rabbinic documents are explained, and in which framework their meaning is elucidated.

To achieve this scholarly refinement, one must emphasize individual rabbinic documents' similarities and de-emphasize their differences, allowing one to

---

3.   As processed by the 10th-century document *Iggeret Rav Sherira Gaon*. See essays in volume edited by Jacob Neusner (1971b).

view the entire corpus as a largely self-consistent whole. But the preceding historical narrative conveniently recommends such a reading of the corpus since,
according to that narrative, individual documents largely recover or reconstruct
the same corpus of proto- and early rabbinic teachings. With such a view of the
antecedents and context of early rabbinic literature, it makes sense to view the
entire literature as a largely self-consistent whole. Around we have gone again.

Just this kind of unrecognized circularity permits such statements as the
following by an otherwise rigorous historian, Shaye J.D. Cohen:

> Linked by their common education, vocabulary, values, and "culture," the
> rabbis clearly constitute a unified group. Rabbinic literature is a
> remarkably homogeneous corpus. If by some magic we could take a
> second-century Palestinian rabbi and deposit him in a fifth-century
> Babylonian academy, he would certainly need to make several adjustments
> (not the least because Babylonian Aramaic and Palestinian Aramaic are
> different dialects), but would soon feel at home. Because of these facts
> rabbinic texts have usually been studied as if they constitute a seamless
> whole, as if all the works together constitute "the" Oral Torah. Because of
> these facts, through this book I have referred to "the rabbis" and "the rab-
> binic period" (1987: 214-15).

Cohen qualifies this in the very next paragraph, but provides only that: several
important qualifications.

With respect to these types of studies,[4] a number of scholars of the last
two-and-a-half decades have been engaged in the scholarly pursuit of Gotcha. I
cannot here review the rounds of Gotcha played.[5] What is remarkable are the
results: an historical reconstruction lacking almost any resolution or acuity. To
illustrate this, consider scholarly works that aim to draw reasonable consensus
from scholarly debate.

Among the most cautiously crafted, recent works of this kind is Lester
Grabbe's *Judaism from Cyrus to Hadrian*. This in the final analysis is what he
thinks we know of the origins and early development of Rabbinism (Grabbe,
1992: 2: 615-16).

> [A] . . . new power structure and a new form of Judaism [that is, the rabbis
> and Rabbinism] began shortly after the destruction [of the Second Temple]
> that was a synthesis of various forms, factions, and sects of pre-70
> Judaism. Although descriptions of Second Temple Judaism have been
> dominated by discussions of various sects, this emphasis is wrong. Most
> Judaism of the time [just preceding the destruction] fell within certain

---

4.   Much of the corpus of Jacob Neusner published between 1970 and his publication of
      Judaism, the Evidence of the Mishnah (1981) bears upon this issue as a critique of antece-
      dent and contemporary scholarship.
5.   An excellent account of those "rounds" up to the end of the first half of the 1980s may be
      found in Anthony J. Saldarini (1986: 437-77).

parameters and shared broad common ground. But the cult-centeredness and other characteristics of Judaism then meant there was no "orthodoxy" as such.

About the Pharisees, one of the sects or factions that were part of his rabbinic synthesis, he proffers that

> much has been written with so little evidence. . . . *If* the pre-70 strata [of the Mishnah] can be associated with the Pharisees, this *would* give us some idea of their beliefs. If so, the description of "table fellowship" sect seems accurate, as far as it goes (although they could have believed other things omitted from the Mishnah) [my emphasis].

After disavowing that the Pharisees can be understood to have "dominated the society and religion of first-century Judaism," Grabbe concludes that "the Pharisees were an important component of pre-70 Judaism and probably of the Judaism [that is, Rabbinism] that developed afterward." Yet, in his view, "the Judaism after 70 was a synthesis, a new creation, an entity that had not existed before and is thus not to be identified with any Second Temple group." Of the elements that went into this synthesis, "one of the more important. . . was the old Pharisaic legal traditions. But this Judaism also included other traditions and interests, especially priestly and scribal ones. At Yavneh, rabbinic Judaism was born." Soon after, Grabbe continues:

> What is clear is that the period from 70 to 135–the Yavneh period in rabbinic literature- was a watershed in the history of Judaism. The Judaism [that is, Rabbinism] arising after 135 was new and different in many essential ways from that before 70. However much the temple and cult formed the basis of theoretical discussion in the emerging rabbinic Judaism, the Jewish temple state had ceased forever.

It is evident from the above that the rounds of Gotcha which Grabbe weighs in the body of his work have produced conclusions so general, on the one hand, and so rife with self-contradictory propositions, on the other, as to be virtually devoid of content.

What is the new Judaism forged by the second-century rabbis? We do not know, for Mishnah, Grabbe admits, does not tell us, because it dwells on a defunct Temple cult, not on a new Rabbinism that allegedly already existed by the time Mishnah was produced. What were the Judaisms of the groups of which (a still unknown) Rabbinism is a synthesis? We do not know that either, only their bearers, mainly, Pharisees, priests, and scribes. What do we know about these latter? Almost nothing, although *if* Mishnah contains pre-mishnaic traditions from the Pharisees, *then we would* know something of this allegedly important precursor of early Rabbinism. The subjunctive is telling. We have come full circle.[6] And

---

6. Grabbe's synthetic conclusions are in general extremely cautious. Therefore, it is telling

is it merely fortuitous that these three late Second Temple "groups" (if that is indeed what all three are) are the Judaic adversaries of the Gospels? I suspect their importation into the picture of rabbinic origins from the New Testament. Since in both New Testament and early rabbinic literature, these groups' allegedly distinctive Judaisms lack any serious definition in both scholarly milieu, their use in the historical reconstruction of rabbinic origins carries no explanatory or elucidating power.

I.iii. Perspectives and Approaches that have contributed to this Book's Method and focus: Neusner's study of Mishnah as an integral document

Jacob Neusner must be largely credited with having blown the whistle on many of the problematic aspects of works that in fact prefigure the more recent works just discussed. He has been lauded by some, argued against or ignored by others. Few, even among those who favour his approach, have adopted or adapted his methods and perspectives. The aforementioned works by David Weiss-Halivni, Shmuel Safrai, and Avraham Goldberg, all written in the late 1980s, give little or no indication that Jacob Neusner's *Judaism, the Evidence of the Mishnah*, much debated when it appeared in 1981, exists.

Neusner pioneered the application of form and redaction criticism to Mishnah and other early rabbinic documents (Neusner, 1971, 1973, 1976-79, 1981).[7] Equally significant is his call to suspend the use of discrete materials culled from a variety of rabbinic documents in historical reconstructions of ancient Judaism and Jewish society until we have ascertained the nature and agendas of each of these texts. Rather, each, to be taken individually in its own right. With respect to each, the plan of the whole (if there should prove to be such a plan) must be examined and an assessment made of how the agenda of the whole has affected individual items contained therein. Thus, Neusner saw individual documents as formed by an "authorship" producing an ouevre shaping all within it; this conflicted with a view that perceived individual texts as largely repositories of some common but growing pool of pre-existent traditions. On this point, the head-on collision between Jacob Neusner and his detractors occurred with respect to materials attributed to, or talking about, named rabbinic masters. It is evident from works such as those by Shmuel Safrai and Avraham Goldberg that pseudonymity, whether partial or outright, on the part of the "editors" of early rabbinic documents was *a priori* unthinkable, and that level of emotion which accompanied this *a*

---

that the scholarship with which he works seems to impel him to this tautological syllogism, which may be summarized as follows: If Mishnah's earliest legal strata are pharisaic, then the Mishnah's table fellowship cult is pharisaic; and if the aforementioned table fellowship cult is pharisaic, and if the earliest strata of mishnaic law is largely phraisaic, then the early rabbinic table fellowship cult derives from the heavy pharisaic component present at the birth of Rabbinism.

7. His work continued in the same vein on other Orders of the Mishnah over the end of the 1970s and the first years of the 1980s. Over the 1980s he applied his methods to the Palestinian Talmud, the Babylonian Talmud, the earlier aggadic midrashim, and the halakic midrashim.

priori stance made it impossible for some to react to Jacob Neusner with any less emotion.[8]

In attempting to study Mishnah as a coherent document with its own integrity, Jacob Neusner analyzed both the literary formulation and the conceptual and legal content of Mishnah tractates. In both content and form he identified the work of an author (in his terminology an authorship). Neusner argues that Mishnah tractates and their major subdivisions *emerge* from carefully defined particular problematics systematically dealt with in relation to a delimited set of principles and general conceptual frames (such as the role of human intention).

Neusner's interest in the literary forms of mishnaic pericopes pre-dates his methodological shift to analyzing Mishnah as a document in its own right. The sum total of two decades of discussion of the subject and the data amassed in support of his conclusions are well summarized in a 1987 volume entitled *Oral Tradition in Judaism: The Case of the Mishnah* (Neusner, 1987a) and stem from two earlier eras in his work. In his *The Rabbinic Traditions about the Pharisees before AD 70* (1971), Professor Neusner identified and coined the term "mishnaic dispute form" to describe the literary pattern evinced by many of the materials attributed in Mishnah and Tosefta to the Houses of Hillel and Shammai. (With this observation his form analyses of rabbinic traditions began.) Not only are "opinions" attributed to named authorities (here the House of Hillel and the House of Shammai) by means of one of a limited number of attributional formulae (e.g., "The House of Hillel say"), but also opinions attributed to the disputants show evidence of precise word-balance, parallelism, chiasm, and mnemonic devices generally. A typical (completely contrived) example would be:

> [Concerning] the sanctification [blessing of the sabbath said over the wine]–
> The House of Shammai say: They wash [their hands], and sanctify [the Sabbath day]
> The House of Hillel say: They sanctify [the Sabbath day], and [then] they wash [their hands before breaking the bread].

In this fictitious, but entirely plausible, example only three words, two verbs, and the conjunction "and" suffice to express the legal views attributed to the disputants. The three words simply appear in reverse order in the two opinions. In many instances opinions would be reduced in Mishnah to two paired verbs of opposite lexical meaning: declares clean, declares unclean, declares fit, declares unfit, etc. These literary tendencies to ellipsis or great economy of expression, balance, pairing, and the like Neunser subsequently came to view as characteristic

---

8.   At a meeting of the Society of Biblical Literature in the latter half of the 1980s my own literary analyses of rabbinic texts was once challenged with the entirely rhetorical, and quite vehemently posed question, "But don't you know that the Talmud is an historical document?" By this my detractor meant summarily to dismiss me as ignorant of a fact evidently clear to him (and anyone else, he supposed) and clearly undermining of my approach. When I responded that I did not know what the questioner meant in stating that the Talmud was an historical document I was perhaps being overly mischievous and provocative.

of the "apodises" *within Mishnah's smallest intelligible literary units.* These observations belie the claim that anyone's opinions have been preserved *ipsissima verba.* Rather, in Neusner's view, at some point in the formulation of the mishnaic "tradition" views were (re)formulated in accordance with these conventions of expression.

Toward the latter part of the 1970s in the context of his comprehensive study, *A History of the Mishnaic Law of Purities* (1976-79), Neusner turned his attention to the literary forms of the mishnaic "protasis" and to unattributed materials generally. He argued that the most common mishnaic form was the declarative sentence (followed by disputes, lists, and several infrequently used forms). More important, Mishnah's declarative sentences could be shown to evince one of five syntactical patterns: the "simple declarative sentence"; the declarative sentence with "duplicated subject"; the declarative sentence exhibiting "mild apocopation"; the declarative sentence exhibiting "extreme apocopation"; two sentences with "balanced" "contrastive" predicates. A (contrived) example of extreme apocopation with balanced constrastive predicates will suffice to indicate what Neusner attempted to categorize:

> He who buys an earthen bowl, and rain falls within, and a mouse walks across the interior–[the bowl] is clean.
> [But if] he poured milk within–[the bowl] is unclean.

Moreover, disputes could be reformulated, for the sake of analysis, into two grammatically whole declarative sentences evincing one or another of these aforementioned patterns. In addition to various syntactically structured declarative sentences, Neusner noted Mishnah's use of lists, such as, 'n items are x: a (and) b (and) c (and) d (and) e. . . ,' or 'a (and) b (and) c (and) d (and) e are x.'

Of crucial importance, however, is Neusner's documentation of a tendency in Mishnah to sustain the use of one of the four syntactical patterns until Mishnah had completed dealing within a given topic. Another one of the four patterns would dominate for the next topic. Neusner concluded on these grounds that the persons who produced Mishnah used the syntactical arrangement of declarative sentences to mark thematic divisions and signal changes in theme. All subsequent discussions by Neusner of Mishnah's modes of expression and of Mishnah's formulation for the purposes of memorization and oral transmission are based upon these two sets of observations made at the beginning and in the latter part of the 1970s. To my knowledge no one has successfully challenged these observations, although many have challenged his interpretation of them and still others have ignored his findings altogether. This book's approach builds upon Neusner's methods and his findings, but takes matters in a slightly different direction, precisely because of my ongoing interest in the social meaning of texts deemed authoritative within a community, here the emergent rabbinic guild. Permit me, then, to present my approach in some greater detail.

I.iv. A plurality of theoretical and methodological constructs

In light of the foregoing–the problems made evident in terminological boobytraps and in circularities, as well as that which Jacob Neusner has already demonstrated of the nature of Mishnah–what requisites must be met by this or any other work undertaking the study of Mishnah and of the origins of the rabbinic guild? How does this work propose to meet those requisites, and what is the status of this book's findings in relation to other works on Mishnah? First and foremost, what is required in the study of the emergence and origins of the early rabbinic guild (and its literature) are some (even heuristic) theoretical and methodological constructs that are not abstract distillations of what rabbinic literature says about itself, its own history, and the history and social formations of those whom the literature claims as its progenitors. Until this pre-requisite is met two problematic states of affairs will persist. (1) There is a high probability of formulating theoretical and methodological constructs applicable to one and only one set of evidence, that from which and for which it was developed in the first place. Here, I submit, one is (mis)using the term theory for something else. (2) There remains an equally high probability of claiming as scholarly conclusions Rabbinism's own myths. In either instance, the construct is weak, because something does not explain or elucidate itself.

It follows, in addition, that an historical reconstruction of early rabbinic social formations will be aided not by one but by many initially disconnected and parallel, theoretical, and methodological paths; the result of each, subjected to several rounds of peer criticism, will lead to probative, *but necessarily partial*, historical reconstructions. In parallel, synthesizing scholars, like Grabbe, will try to integrate these results as they emerge, and this with necessarily *relative* success.

From where will these orienting theoretical constructs come? Not from tailor-made, non-portable constructs that are largely purified distillations of what the evidence to be analyzed says about itself. The constructs must have applicability to, or represent generalizations from, other data, even if just beyond the immediate social and historical horizon of our own.

Why will multiple theoretical and methodological constructs generate partial reconstructions and differently oriented interpretations? Appropriately constructed theoretical frameworks can do nothing other than this, precisely *because* they must accord with the criterion of not being tailor-made for the specific batch of evidence. Jonathan Z. Smith remarked that all theoretical constructs are "creative distortions."[9] They distort, in the very least, by highlighting certain aspects of the evidence while downplaying others. In any analysis and reconstruction some things will come into sharp focus at the expense of blurring elsewhere. Let me turn now to the specific approach adopted in this book, namely, considering Mishnah as a "socially legitimated rhetoric" and subjecting Mishnah to a "socio-rhetorical" analysis, in order to explain what such an approach reveals to us and how it does so.

---

9.   In conversation with me some eight years ago.

I.iv.1. What is revealed by a socio-rhetorical approach, why and how? For over five years, my research on Mishnah and on other early rabbinic texts (see Lightstone, 1994) has focused on the rhetorical character of early rabbinic documents in relation to the social institutions of the early rabbinic guild which legitimated and were legitimated by their revered works.[10] The focus on understanding these texts as evincing a particular rhetorical character provides a distinctive type of theoretical and methodological leverage on two long-problematic issues: the problem of building a social description of the early guild and the question of the social meaning of earliest rabbinic literature. What then do I specifically mean by socio-rhetorical analysis, and how precisely does socio-rhetorical analysis provide this leverage on questions of social meaning and institutions in earliest rabbinism?

To consider the character of mishnaic language as rhetoric is, first, to understand that language as legitimate in terms of some group's social norms for "speaking" authoritatively and persuasively from within and to a specific social milieu.[11] Moreover, understanding the mishnaic data as the expression of some author intending to say with recognized elegance and persuasiveness something coherent to someone overcomes the methodological tendency *ab initio* to break the text into small (presumably pre-existent) parts. The latter point is clear without substantial elaboration; the former is more complex and goes to the heart of this book.

To understand the text as rhetoric allows us to re-establish the link between text and social context on completely different grounds than those adopted by scholars like Shmuel Safrai or Isaiah Gafni (referred to earlier). This is so because "talking" in a certain stylized, patterned manner is never in and of itself self-evidently or "naturally" cogent or appropriate. Rather, it attains an air of self-evidence and cogency within a certain social context. In that social context the speaker's patterns of speech (apart from the specific content):
- accord with accepted (implicit or explicit) rules;
- are recognized as having *prima facie* authority and cogency; and
- may, in addition, be further experienced as "satisfying" and "appropriate" because those patterns replicate the "shape" of other patterned realms of the socially constructed world of the listener.

The first point is straightforward. With respect to the second, what an author assumes is a cogent mode of expression, of patterning of language, tells us about the definitions of persuasiveness and, hence, of institutionalized social definitions of authority and authoritativeness in the author's historical and social context.

---

10.   The next section reproduces, with some revisions, parts of: Jack N. Lightstone, "Tosefta's (Dis)simulation of Mishnah's Rhetoric," paper presented at the Society of Biblical Literature, Philadelphia, November, 1995; Jack N. Lightstone, "The Rhetoric of Mishnah and the Emergence of Rabbinic Social Institutions at the End of the Second Century," paper presented at the Society of Biblical Literature, Chicago, November, 1994; and Lightstone, 1997.

11.   I am indebted both for the term "socio-rhetorical" and for much of the conceptual framework that I intend to convey by the term's use to the work of Vernon K. Robbins and Burton Mack (see Mack and Robbins, 1989; Mack, 1990; Robbins, 1984).

The third point is more complex, and concerns not only rhetoric per se, but the broader, more complex issue of the cogency of a group's shared perceptions about their socially constructed, ordered universe. Groups perceive order in their lives together and in the "topography" that they "inhabit," because they share for realm after realm of that universe (cosmic, territorial, social, cultic, etc.) a set of mappings that they have painted onto each successive realm. To be sure, the cogency of some of those mappings has, in a number of instances, to do with empirical observations about one or another realm, for example, the observed movements of planets. But appealing to a community's empirical experience does not take one very far in accounting for their shared perceptions and mappings of their world, or, more important, for the cogency, that sense of self-evident truth or appropriateness, that these mappings have for members of the community. That sense of cogency, of self-evidence, is socially and affectively, not personally and empirically, grounded. It has to do, on the one hand, with the sharing of these mappings with others. On the other hand, that cogency is the result of members of the group finding the same basic patterns replicated in one humanly ordered realm after another in the group's universe. When fundamentally similar patterning is mapped onto the cosmos, the cult, the social strata of society, to name just several, the individual mappings mutually reinforce one another, rendering each affectively satisfying and self-evident" in light of the others.

The patterning of language in speech or in text can be one such patterned realm of a set comprising a shared, cogent, humanly-constructed universe. That is to say, an author's patterning of language can be experienced as affectively satisfying because it replicates other basic patterning of the social and cultural world of the audience. When that is the case, patterned language encodes and implicitly communicates information about larger socially constructed patterns of the hearer's and speaker's community. Since what is communicated is implicit and non-discursive, we may not discover explicit data about that social and cultural world in patterns of language. However, with data about that social world in hand, we may explore how that world and authoritative patterns of language reflect and reinforce one another in creating a cogent, self-evident universe of shared perceptions of the world. Of course, the rhetorical patterns of any one author may be entirely eccentric, revolutionary or countercultural within his or her social milieu. But Mishnah was promulgated and, from what we can tell, almost immediately accepted as authoritative, as canonical, within one particular social setting, a guild or association of rabbinic sages in the Land of Israel at the beginning of the third century CE. Therefore, within the theoretical frame just outlined, we can explore the mutually reinforcing relationship between Mishnah, with its particular use of language, on the one hand and, on the other, the ways early rabbis mapped out the configuration and boundaries of their guild association in the larger social and cultural context of that era and place. Such an exploration makes Mishnah data of a very different kind for the social history of "Formative Judaism" than the uses made of Mishnah in the works of those social and cultural historians of Ancient Judaism critiqued at the outset of this discussion.

I.iv.2. Some specific social aspects of rhetoric in the Greco-Roman world – The foregoing is, then, the broad methodological and theoretical frame in which I address questions regarding the social meaning and social context. However, to appreciate better the utility of a socio-rhetorical analysis of Mishnah to the social and cultural historian of Ancient Judaism, it is worthwhile to review some basic, specific aspects of rhetoric and its use in the Greco-Roman world.[12]

Rhetoric, in the classical sense of the word, is the art of creatively using appropriate language to persuade in public spheres such as the court, the council, the academy and other such fora of debate and decision in Antiquity and Late Antiquity. The rhetor, then, creatively uses established devices, techniques of expression and of argument to make a particular point. The appropriateness and effectiveness of the modes of expression and argument are a function of social context and situation–that is, who is speaking to whom, about what, and where. What is artful, appropriate, and convincing in a judicial defence might be immediately perceived as tendentious, overstated and, therefore, unconvincing in the school or in the legislative council. Or modes of expression adopted in a public meeting by an aristocrat of senatorial rank might be perceived as pretentious and, therefore, ineffective if uttered by a freedman or equestrian. Thus, rhetoric always points to a social context which defines what is convincing in the mouth of whom. To engage in appropriate rhetoric is to recall, refer to, participate in, and, therefore, to reinforce the social definitions governing such a context.

By extension, rhetoric is an apt descriptor of written texts which recall and reflect, either in fact or in an imaginative act, one or another of these public fora. Thus Cicero's *Pro Flaccum* may be seen as a reconstructed, embellished, and refined literary version of his oral defence of Flaccus in the setting of the Roman Senate's judicial proceedings against the latter. In a different vein, Arrianus, Epictetus's disciple, claims to have preserved in the *Discourses of Epictetus* a faithful rendition of the master's lessons to students in Epictetus's second-century Stoic school in Rome. The claim that the written text provides an accurate rendition of Epictetus's lectures is in all probability not only inaccurate but a rhetorical device in its own right, for that claim is intended to persuade the reader of the authority and authenticity of *Arrianus's* written work by attributing its content (*ipsissima verba*) to Epictetus and by harping back to a classical forum for persuasive speech and argument, the Greco-Roman school.

I.iv.3. The socio-rhetorical study of the Mishnah – Because the issues discussed in two previous subsections are so central to the remainder of this book, permit me to rehearse and synthesize their relevance to the study of Mishnah.

Rhetoric is not only a stylized way of communicating with others. It must, in addition, be recognized as authoritative or persuasive within a social context

---

12.   The remainder of this section repeats, with minor revisions and additions, my unpublished paper, "The Rhetoric of the Mishnah: A Preliminary Glance," presented at the annual conference of the Canadian Society of Biblical Studies, Calgary, 7 June 1994. See also Mack, 1990, and references therein.

which deems that rhetorical style, and therefore the contents it conveys, as normal, appropriate, and particularly legitimate. Hence rhetorical styles reflect, embody, and inform social institutions, and especially social definitions of power and authority within those institutions. Patently this should be so not only in the larger context of the Greco-Roman world, whence the term rhetoric, but it should hold as well for Judaic communities in the Eastern Mediterranean and Middle East. Indeed, in most human communities one would expect that the appropriateness and effectiveness of the modes of expression and argument are a function of social context and situation–that is, who is speaking to whom, about what, and where. Therefore, the existence of a legitimated, authoritative rhetoric bespeaks socially legitimated and supported institutions and social formations. As both a product and a buttress of these institutions and social formations, a text's rhetoric and its social context can be mutually elucidating, when a text's rhetoric is analyzed in relation to a clearly spelled out theoretical and methodological approach.

In the foregoing conceptual framework, I have sought to understand the normative social definitions of authority and authoritative speech implicitly encoded in the rhetorical features of "canonical," early rabbinic documents such as the Babylonian Talmud (Lightstone, 1994) and, in this volume, the Mishnah, the earliest-dated, authoritative rabbinic work.

From both the theoretical and methodological perspectives such studies are enhanced by at least some comparative analysis of the rhetorical features of other, principally rabbinic, documents. Why? Authoritative modes of communication stand not only in a contemporary social setting, in a system of synchronic relationships; they exist as well in an historical context, in a diachronic setting. The significance and meaning of socially sanctioned patterns partly resides and is discovered in the contrasts and continuities with what was and what subsequently becomes authoritative in the life of the group in question. For in any social setting, especially in traditional societies, the past makes an authoritative claim on the present. Hence, in studying the social meaning of Mishnah's rhetorical traits, it is valuable to ask such questions as: What happens to Mishnaic rhetoric and its implicitly communicated definitions of social authority in the aftermath of Mishnah's promulgation and acceptance as the authoritative document par excellence and as the principal object of study in the early third-century rabbinic guild? To what degree have Mishnah's rhetorical features perpetuated or departed from those of antecedent, especially authoritative, Judaic literature?

I.iv.4. The question of a mishnaic "rhetoric" – To persons familiar with Mishnah, the term "rhetoric," if understood as classical Greco-Roman literary forms, might seem at first glance an inappropriate term to apply to this first document of earliest Rabbinism. By extension, the "rhetorical analysis" of Mishnah will seem a peculiar choice of endeavour.[13] In turning to rabbinic documents, here Mishnah,

---

13.   In light of the place of rhetoric in the Greco-Roman world, why would it be either appropopriate or peculiar to talk about the "rhetoric of Mishnah"? Many modern scholars have proposed or identified comparable public or semi-public fora for Mishnah and for its antecedent sources: the "schools" of Rabbi Aqiva and of Rabbi Meir as the origins of

we should, however, be prepared to recognize modes of expression that may or may not resemble what is *classically* categorized as rhetoric. The purpose of Vernon K. Robbins's appendix to this volume is, at least heuristically, to demonstrate that the structuring of the content of a Mishnah "chapter" can be (re)described in terms of the formal rhetorical categories of Hermogenes' *nasmata*. But that does not mean that the social meaning of Mishnah's rhetoric is best mined by trying to understand its rhetorical features as an instance of *Progymnasmata*-like rhetoric, as one might indeed claim for James 2:1-13 (also analyzed by Vernon Robbins in the appendix). As happened with biblical form and redaction criticism, whose meaning and object necessarily changed when Neusner adapted these methods to the analysis of rabbinic texts, the term "rhetoric" and the exercise of rhetorical analysis, when applied to mishnaic evidence, may come to mean and to describe strategies of persuasive expression differing significantly from the rhetoric of ancient Greco-Roman literature. We must be prepared to operate with a rather wide, more inclusive notion of what rhetorical patterns may be. For example, with Mishnah we would be wise not to associate too quickly rhetorical patterning and modes of persuasion with explicit discursive, analogical or metaphorical argument. Establishing what is rhetorical analysis with respect to Mishnah is, therefore, in the doing, and cannot be otherwise.

What this book shows is that Mishnah does evince a rhetoric *of its own* in a far more profound sense than being a literary repository for, and faithful com-

several proto-Mishnahs; the Patriarchal Courts/Councils of the Rabbi Simeon ben Gamaliel II and of Rabbi Judah (ben Simeon) the Prince, in which settings the collection, preservation, and compilation of these traditions into "our" Mishnah took place. For those who hold such views, and I do not count myself among them, the Mishnah preserves the language, agenda, and organization of the materials as formulated by Aqiva and Meir in their "schools." If we understand rhetoric to involve in part choosing subject matter, modes of expression, and the arrangements of these materials in a fashion particularly "appropriate" to their context, then Mishnah on this view might be said appropriately to preserve the authoritative legal rhetoric of early rabbinic masters and their schools.

Even if one assents to this literary history of the Mishnah text, it seems odd to refer to Mishnah's language as rhetoric simply because Mishnah preserves the legal language and agenda of authoritative rabbinic masters and their schools. Generally Mishnah does not explicitly engage in the art of persuasion, if we mean by that term the mustering of arguments and evidence understood by the authors to be convincing in the eyes of the intended readership within a given forum. If one accepts, which I do not, the aforementioned account of Mishnah's second-century sources and antecedents, Mishnah, at first glance, generally persuades its intended readership of the authority of its legal views only by episodic appeal to its authoritative origins (by means of the attribution of some materials to named, primarily second-century rabbinic "authorities") and by the unstated, implicit claim (explicitly made in the 10th century by Sherira) that these authorities' views have been accurately transmitted and preserved first by their students and second by the processes of compilation which produced the "final" Mishnah text (ca. 200CE). As situationally appropriate as faithful preservation, transmission, and subsequent compilation of earlier legal rulings may be for early Rabbinism- and again I do not believe that this accurately describes either what Mishnah is or how it came to be- such a process in and of itself is hardly grounds for speaking of Mishnah's rhetorical character.

pilation of, antecedent, authoritative legal traditions. Mishnah evinces a rhetoric of its own in two important ways, literary and social. First, quite apart from matters of social meaning and the social formation of the earliest rabbinic movement, the book will demonstrate that Mishnah *expresses its subject matter in accordance with rules governing modes of expression.* These rules are pervasive and constitutive of the language of the document in two ways. First, the *same rules seem to govern modes of expression throughout the document,* with several exceptions, in numerous Mishnah tractates spanning all six of Mishnah's major divisions ("Order"). Second, when tractates and their constituent thematic subdivisions ("chapters") can be shown to evince rhetorical patterning, we shall see that *an overwhelming proportion of the language of the text bears the marks of the application of these stylistic rules.*

If the analysis of this book is convincing and if its findings are confirmed by further studies of Mishnah's modes of expression, then not only will I have shown the language of Mishnah to be governed by rules of composition and of expression in a far more extensive manner than is implied by "a rhetoric of faithful preservation of authoritative tradition," but I will also have cast considerable doubt upon such notions of the character and origins of Mishnah altogether. Therefore, we shall have to reconsider issues of social context and social definitions in terms of which the language of Mishnah is "appropriate," cogent or persuasive, for the context of pre-mishnaic masters, disciples, and their (alleged) "schools" can no longer be seen as a sufficient institutional locus for those modes of expression, even if they became the purveyors of it. Herein lies the second sense in which Mishnah's language is "rhetoric," namely, in the social dimension, in exploring the social definitions inherent in, and in seeking the context of the appropriateness and cogency of Mishnah's use of language

II
Early rabbinic rhetoric as priestly-scribal bureaucratic virtuosity

Taken together,[14] my analyses of the use of language in Mishnah indicate that Mishnah's authors rely most heavily on three techniques: (1) morphological repetition, which itself provides a kind of alliteration and assonance; (2) the repetition of similar or identical words and phrases, or of paired opposites, which provide a kind of rhyme, rhythm, and metre, and at times a kind of mechanistic permutative quality to the text; (3) the linking of items with the above-mentioned qualities by means of several repeated, stock, conjunctive formulae ("and," "which/that," "except," and perhaps "says") which give the text not only a list-like quality but a litany-like one. The techniques in themselves seem more appropriate

---

14.   This section largely reproduces, with revisions, parts of my unpublished paper, "The Rhetoric of Mishnah and the Emergence of Rabbinic Social Institutions at the End of the Second Century," presented to the Society of Biblical Literature, Chicago, November, 1994.

to classical poetry, or, for that matter, to choral lyrical texts, than to classical legal documents. By way of illustration only, I provide in Part 2 of the Appendix two pericopes of Mishnah rendered in chart form in order to highlight the use of the aforementioned techniques. Together these pericopes complete the topically and rhetorically defined Mishnah "chapter" beginning at m. Gittin 1:1 and ending at 2:2; Part 1 of the Appendix provides a translation of m. Gittin 1:1-2:2.

I cannot in this limited context document and discuss the mixed and multiple usages of these techniques in rhetorically establishing a mishnaic "chapter." These techniques, as I have demonstrated elsewhere, help define a "chapter's" shank by morphological repetition combined with the reappearance of some dominant phrases as a kind of "aural" theme. In addition, the same techniques serve to link other units to the shank.[15] Nevertheless, the two pericopes charted in the Appendix strongly convey characteristic aural, rhetorical features of Mishnah. To demonstrate something of what Mishnah typically sounds like, I will abstract from that chart the use of just one of the three types of rhetorical devices noted above and to isolate the individual "voices" thereby created.

is required to say:
in my presence it was written;
in my presence it was signed.
cannot say:
in my presence it was written;
in my presence it was signed.
said:
in my presence it was written;
not in my presence it was signed.
said: in my presence it was signed;
not in my presence it was written.

in its entirety,
in part;
in part,
in its entirety

one, one;
two, one;
one, two

day, day;
night, night;
night, day;
day, night

15.   Dov Zlotnick (1988: 72-106) seems to have perceived the presence of some of these features in briefly referring to parts of Mishnah which have a poetic quality.

What does one "hear" and to what ends? Here I must move beyond my limited illustration of, the "aural" quality that is typical of Mishnah. About 20 chapters of Mishnah from some 10 tractates representing all six of Mishnah's divisions have been similarly charted and analyzed.[16] Across almost all, this lyrical or musical rhetoric bears in significant measure[17] the burden of defining, *even of spinning out*, substantive thematic structures and substructures in a mishnaic chapter; "musical" phrases recur and are "inverted" in permutative ways, while an overall "theme" periodically reasserts itself to define the whole thematic "movement." These lyric-like recursions and iterations thereby serve to establish a unit's beginning and end, and they appear at various junctures in between to recall the opening and anticipate the closing of the unit. The same techniques function to mark off and unify subunits with their respective subthemes and to link subunits to sentences which carry those "aural" markers that establish the whole.

As a result of the pervasive application of this rhetoric, Mishnah's authors will have largely effaced the language of any antecedent sources they had at hand. In addition, these rhetorical conventions (re)fashion cases and rulings, even to the point of generating (sometimes unproblematic) cases for the purposes of "completing" or "rounding out" a tightly patterned rhetorical sequence. What assertions, then, are implicitly communicated in that rhetoric?

Jacob Neusner (1977, 1981, 1989b) maintains–and I concur–that the major subdivisions of mishnaic tractates, their "chapters," are "whole" and "complete" in that their content emerges from a generative problematic systematically explored to the point of logical and topical closure. In addition, he characterized Mishnah's enterprise as *Listenwissenschaft*, the "paratactic" (William Scott Green's term [Green, 1983]) presentation of arrays of cases and their ordering and classification with respect to whether one rule or another applies. Through this exercise an ordered, fictive, and ideal world is defined, in which (in the text) the Jerusalem Temple yet stands, and Temple-based judiciary and legislative institutions still operate. Here too I concur.

However, in light of my rhetorical analyses, I would also qualify these claims in important ways. I overstate matters in baldly asserting that Mishnah defines an ideal ordered "world" through the production of comprehensive classificatory lists and related rulings. First, and most obvious, much of that ideal world is left undefined. Whole tractates, about such matters as circumcision, burial, mourning, business, and economics, to name just a few, are absent. Second, why do tractates end where they do, some with over 30 chapters, others

---

16. Some of these have been done by me. Others have been done by my graduate research assistants, Maria Mamfredis and Kelly Menchick. Their work has not only permitted expanding the evidentiary base for my conclusions but also furnished some significant degree of intersubjective validation of the methodology.

17. By this I mean to say that this rhetorical "virtuosity" is a sustained feature of Mishnah as evidenced by the analysis of these 20 chapters. However, sustained as they are, these techniques are not equally or uniformly present throughout. Indeed, such would be the case with respect to the use of any formal rhetorical features in any body of literature.

with only four? Both the tractate on Sabbath, one of the longer, and the tractate on court decrees (m. Horayot), one of the shorter, are incomplete in the sense that one may readily define relevant problems or topics from which whole additional chapters for either tractate may be spun out. Third, it is something of an exaggeration to assert that the deliberations of a "chapter" of a Mishnah tractate bring to closure and completion the generative topic at hand. Tosefta demonstrates how easily one may extend and augment a Mishnah "chapter's" topical program. Whence, then, the distinctive *impression* of closure, comprehensiveness, and wholeness of Mishnah "chapters"?

I suggest that the strong *impression* of closure, comprehensiveness, and wholeness in Mishnah derives in large measure from its rhetoric. The order, patterning, coherence and unity evident in Mishnah's permutative, baroque-like, lyrical rhetoric equals or exceeds "completeness" of the ideal "world" defined in Mishnah's laws. These laws are necessarily non-comprehensive and illustrative, and are amenable to completion and supplementation. It is, then, in Mishnah's lyrical rhetoric that the authors have communicated (implicitly) their aspirations toward complete, well-patterned "wholes" and convey to the reader/auditor their conviction that the purpose of Mishnah law is to strive toward, or exemplify the process of, defining that whole by means of legal classification.

What social definitions of authority and authoritativeness are modelled in the lyrical, permutative, list-like concatenation of cases and rulings, in which the inner logic remains ever implicit and in which "lyrical" completeness is sometimes in itself sufficient, implicit justification for including a case in a list? And what immediate realm in social formation may have been served by rhetorically depicting such expertise or virtuosity as "normal," "appropriate," and "authoritative?"

The question is so framed as to imply an answer: the ability to compose and spin out such lists in such a lyrical fashion in and of itself seems to have become a principal *hallmark* and *mode* of authoritativeness constituting the "mastery" of the "mishnaic" rabbi (literally, "my master"). As a corollary, I further suggest that by their very appearance in such a lyrical, permutative list, both the rules for specified cases and the legal-classificatory "system" which these rules comprise gain an air of self-evident appropriateness. That is to say, the rhetorical form bespeaks the authority of the list-maker-lyricist "master" and lends authority to individual items in the list, to the list as a whole, and to the emerging legal system contained in a series of topically related lists. However, the system or world partially mapped out in such lyrical, permutative list-making is an imagined, utopian, ideal one, in which a Temple and its related institutions still stands and occupies the centre 130 or so years after the historical Temple state's demise.

Thus, the Mishnah rhetorically reinforces and reflects a portrayal of elite, authoritative virtuosity which may be characterized as a mastery of guardianship of the old social and cultic order stewarded by priests and their scribal guild.[18]

---

18.   On Temples and their staff as guardians of world-ordering/classifying legal traditions, see Lightstone (1994: 247-81) and Jonathan Z. Smith (1978: 172-89).

Rabbis, then, portray themselves as similar to, or as heirs of, the priestly-scribal administration of the now defunct Temple state. That mode of virtuosity is represented directly in the substantive agenda of Mishnah, in which unit-circumstances of a Temple-centred world are classified with respect to whether one rule or another applies. In addition, that mastery of guardianship of a divine, allegedly complete and bounded social and cultic world order is paralleled by a distinctive rhetorical style. In that rhetoric, subject domains in the text (its substantive "chapters") are defined, structured, marked off, and bounded by successive, encompassing, layered levels of repetition of morphological forms and of units of sound; subtopics gain an air of completeness and closure via systematic permutation of phrases and words. In all, the lyrical rhetoric is itself an homology of the Temple-centred world assumed and partially defined in Mishnah's substance.

What immediate rabbinic institutions in social formation at the end of the second century may have been served by rhetorically depicting such expertise or virtuosity as "normal," "appropriate," and "authoritative?"

Later in this volume I adduce and analyze evidence culled from early rabbinic sources in support of a particular portrayal of the institutionalization of the rabbinic "guild" over the course of the second century and the onset of the third. I suggest that "in the beginning" the chief institutionalized form of rabbinic authority was the individual sage, surrounded by his disciples, whom the master would in time ordain as full sages. Each would then replicate the circle of his master. Subsequently, nearer the end of the second century, two other institutions arise. One is the rabbinic court, a term early rabbinic sources often use to refer to a Council of the Sages with legislative, training, and judiciary functions, as opposed to a court of law. The late second- or early third-century rabbinic court may or may not have been a standing institution, and the nature and extent of its powers are uncertain. The rabbinic court claims descent from an idealized national council which the early rabbinic sources call the Great Sanhedrin or Great Court of the Temple and which early rabbinic documents portray as operating from ancient times and as a constituent element of any future redemptive restoration of the Temple state.[19] But evidence does not indicate that this rabbinic College/Council of Sages operated as a national council or independent of the other emerging institution. This other institution is the dynastic Patriarchate, probably established, and certainly deemed legitimate, by the Romans (Goodblatt, 1994: 131-231).

I propose that the production toward the end of the second or beginning of the third century of Mishnah, with its particular rhetorical traits, is integrally tied to the institutionalization in the Galilee of a more unified rabbinic movement whose principal institutions were the ruling Patriarchate and an associated Council or College of Sages (sometimes referred to as the Sanhedrin, at other times called the Court or the Patriarch's Court). Since these institutions supplanted the antecedent state of affairs, in which Rabbinism consisted of autonomous circles of

---

19.   On the evidence for a national council in Judean/Palestinian government, see David Goodblatt (1994: 131-231).

masters and disciples, the normative character and authority of the master-disciple circles had to be both overcome and transferred to the newly formed organizational arrangements. And a balance of power between the Patriarchate and the College of Sages had to be defined. Mishnah, which came to be attributed to Judah the Patriarch's personal editorial activity, preserves the identity of the earlier rabbinic sages, each of whom allegedly constituted the centre of a renowned circle of master and disciples. At the same time their individuality (beyond their names) is considerably effaced and subsumed within a new united literary whole, imposing its peculiar lyrical rhetorical style on everything and everyone. The individual and the individual's inherent authority are preserved only in the new whole, soon to become the chief object of study of would-be sages, just as the College of Sages subsumed the circles of individual masters.

In addition, Mishnah, in its lyrical, clockwork rhetoric, modelling what I have called a priestly-scribal virtuosity of comprehensively mapping "the world," implicitly lays claim to priestly-scribal authority for the College of Sages under Patriarchal leadership. I stress that this transpires not only at the level of the legal substance of Mishnah, which defines aspects of an ideal Temple-centred state, but also by means of implicitly communicated, non-discursive "knowledge" of "how things really are" given in Mishnah's pervasive rhetorical traits, which model the requisite "mastery" of the guild.

II.i. Whence this virtuosity? The question of the origins of the rabbinic guild

Let us now anticipate my conclusions regarding rabbinic origins.[20] Whence the rabbis? I can propose a response from my particular theoretical and methodological viewpoint if I restate the question as: Whence in late first- or second-century Roman Judea and/or Galilee the virtuosity or expertise modelled in Mishnah's pervasive rhetoric traits? Who, in all likelihood, would possess this expertise so as to be able to train others in its intricacies? Expertise of this type would have resided historically in some group, class or profession operating in some institutionalized social setting, where that expertise is "bought and paid for."

To summarize the conclusions argued in chapter 5, I suggest that the most likely institutional point of origin for such things would be somewhere within the Temple-state's administration itself, before its demise in 70CE. I shall suggest that those persons who are at the largely veiled origins of Rabbinism are "refugees" from the Temple-state's national bureaucracy and administration who, having lost their institutional base, first tried to preserve and pass on their professional guild expertise. Moreover, the very production and promulgation of Mishnah, the first "canonical," rabbinic document, suggests finally managing to create or to find a new institutional home at the end of the second century, the Patriarch's administration of Galilean (and Southern Syrian) Jewry, for the exercise and perpetuation of that guild expertise. No wonder that with time and with a new

20.   This section largely reproduces, with revisions and additions, sections of my paper entitled "Mishnah's Imag(in)ed Temple and the Social Formation of the Early Rabbinic Guild," presented to the Canadian Society for the Study of Religion, Montreal, June 1995.

institutional setting, the implicit claim to be Temple-priestly administrators would seem increasingly less germane, and Mishnah's rhetoric less cogent and socially significant.

III
Outline of the book

The remainder of this volume comprises three major parts. The first, chapter 2, undertakes to uncover the characteristic rhetorical features of much of the Mishnah. It does so by performing a close rhetorical analysis of an exemplary mishnaic "chapter," m. Gittin 1:1-2:2. Proceeding to generalize and draw conclusions from so-called "typical" or "representative" passages potentially poses methodological difficulties, as the choice of what will stand as representative can beg the question of what is, if anything, representative. In defence of proceeding in this manner, permit me to make several points. First, I do not claim for an instant that the passage in question aptly represents all of the Mishnah. (Whole Mishnah tractates immediately spring to mind which seem rhetorically quite different from m. Gittin 1:1-2:2; m. Eduyyot and m. Avot are obvious counterpoints.) Second, m. Gittin 1:1-2:2 represents only five percent of the passages, culled from a number of the Mishnah's tractates and principal divisions, analyzed in similar fashion by me and my graduate research assistants, Dr. Maria Mamfredis and Ms. Kelly Menchick. However, even the entirety of what we have so analyzed cannot be said to stand for all of the Mishnah. Third, and more to the point, I am making more circumspect claims than would appear to be the case at first glance: (a) m. Gittin 1:1-2:2 and the other mishnaic "chapters" analyzed but not presented in this volume are not aberrations in Mishnah, and, consequently, (b) our findings and the conclusions we draw from them are useful, even if not final, definitive or complete. The results and the conclusions drawn are, I maintain, valid for some significant subsection of the mishnaic evidence, at the very least. For that reason they provide a basis for subsequent study, refinement, supplementation, and discussion undertaken by others and by me.

The second major part of this volume, chapters 3 and 4, undertakes to compare the rhetorical features of the Mishnah passages identified in chapter 2's analysis of m. Gittin 1:1-2:2 and the rhetorical characteristics of passages of other principally rabbinic texts, similarly analyzed. Chapter 3 compares the rhetorical features of Mishnah and the Tosefta (meaning "The Supplement"), a document written as early as 50 years after the promulgation of the Mishnah. The Tosefta's literary kinship to the Mishnah is such that some modern scholars have viewed the Tosefta or its constituent passages as having served as a source for Mishnah's authors. (I hasten to add that I do not share this view, and chapter 3's analyses of Tosefta bear out my stance. Chapter 4 conducts a similar comparison with Semakhot ("On Funerary Rites and Mourning"), a somewhat later text which on first appearances seems to try to replicate Mishnah's literary features.

There are several reasons for pursuing these comparative analyses. First, I have argued that formal rhetorical features inform and reflect social definitions of authority because the rhetoric itself bespeaks socially recognized authoritativeness within a defined social context. If, therefore, formal rhetorical patterning of language in the Mishnah means something in itself about social definitions of authoritativeness apart from the Mishnah's idiomatic content, then it should be possible to communicate different, perhaps competing or revised, social meanings by modifying a given rhetoric in a coherent and consistent direction. Where we have examples of texts closely "related to" yet rhetorically different from the Mishnah, we are in a position to test the cogency of what we have claimed to uncover about mishnaic rhetoric.

To underscore this point about the value of comparison, permit me an analogy from language. Imagine that you are the first to claim to have uncovered the character and function of English syntax, arguing that "man bites dog" and "dog bites man," similar as they are in vocabulary, say something significantly different. We would lend cogency to this claim by comparing English speakers' use of many sentences with similar vocabulary yet different word order. In this manner, we would uncover the significance of the word order, apart from the vocabulary. We would rightly conclude that English, which is not a highly inflected language, depends significantly upon syntax to convey meaning. By contrast, in a highly inflected language, which is less dependent upon word order for meaning, close comparison of variations of word order would not reveal *sistent and systemic variation*, the hallmarks of meaning and significance.

Comparing Mishnah and "kindred" texts is something like comparing English sentences with similar vocabulary but different word order. Mishnah, the first document produced by the early rabbinic guild, was soon followed by other rabbinic texts dealing with the same, complementary or supplementary subject matter. Yet these texts either subtly or significantly depart from Mishnah's rhetorical patterning in favour of their own equally pervasive patterning of language. Mishnah's rhetorical features and its particular meaning will stand out in relief against the backdrop of the literary characteristics of these other texts. A second reason for engaging in these comparisons has already been noted: within a traditional religious society, the past makes an authoritative claim on the present. Cultural change occurs less often through massive rejection of the old in favour of the radically new than by modification of the old in a clear but consistent direction, often with the accompanying claim of complete continuity with a previous authoritative form. As mentioned, the Mishnah became *the* authoritative document within the rabbinic guild after its promulgation. Yet within 50 to 100 years rabbinic documents, sometimes subtly, ultimately significantly, shift away from mishnaic rhetoric. And all the while the guild continues to revere and (one might suppose) to study the Mishnah as the rabbinic document par excellence. To make a comparative study of these shifts is to shed light on the tensions and transformations at the level of social formation and social definitions in the early rabbinic guild. In sum, we can view the social definitions reflected and legitimated by mishnaic rhetoric against a dynamic context of social change within the rabbinic movement in the Galilee from the late second century CE through the several subsequent centuries.

In the concluding section of this book, chapter 5, I will explicitly draw the lines from rhetorical to social and historical analysis. It is in this final chapter that I concentrate specifically upon the social meaning and consequences of mishnaic rhetoric. I shall ask what definitions of social authority are reflected and upheld by that rhetoric and what specific historical and social contexts and institutions were the theatres for the exercise of these modes of social authority. Here socio-rhetorical analysis must be complemented by socio-historical analysis and reconstruction so that the results of each shed light on the other. In this final section, I shall consider the question of the origins of the rabbinic movement and offer some proposals taken in light of this book's socio-rhetorical analyses. I can think of no question whose answer has eluded me more over the course of more than 25 years as a student of the early rabbinic movement and its literature. The (albeit speculative) conclusion I have reached on this matter directly follows from having adopted a socio-rhetorical approach to the rabbinic movement's earliest literary work.

2

Mishnaic Rhetoric

I
The study of Mishnah's rhetoric:
Toward a new methodology

Building upon Neusner's observations about Mishnah's literary traits, the work in the current chapter leads me to identify three principal classes of stylistic devices extensively used to construct Mishnah's characteristic rhetorical patterning:

1. concatenating and joining formulae;
2. repetition and controlled variation of word, especially verb morphology;
3. repetition based upon phonological and/or semantic homologies.

Let me briefly explain each. First, Mishnah appears to call upon a surprisingly limited stock of joining terminology. Among the most frequently used are "and," "which," "except" and "say(s)." Second, (as noted by Neusner in the context of analyzing the mishnaic protasis), Mishnah will repeat not a word or phrase but a morphological form, such as a particular verb tense, as some sort of literary marker. Since morphological or grammatical inflection in Hebrew is effected by standard prefixes and suffixes, the repetition of morphological form effects obvious, pronounced assonance, alliteration, and/or rhyme. Third, Mishnah evinces not only deliberate repetition of morphological form, but also, and especially, of precise words and phrases. I dub this phenomenon homophonic-homosemantic markers, since in reading the text of Mishnah the "mind's ear" repeatedly hears the same "sound bytes," to borrow a contemporary media neologism. I count, as well, among the latter the use of a word or phrase followed by its exact semantic opposite, such as clean followed by unclean, or fit followed by unfit. The remainder of this essay attempts to demonstrate in preliminary fashion how Mishnah uses these principal types of stylistic devices by documenting and analyzing their appearance in a "chapter" of a Mishnah-tractate.

Let me anticipate this chapter's conclusions, in order to better direct and attune the reader's ear in advance to characteristics of the passages presented below. What this preliminary analysis will suggest is that the mishnaic editors' use of literary and stylistic devices is far more extensive and encompassing than Mishnah students have previously maintained. For example, the complex use of multiple levels of homophonic-homosemantic markers far exceeds in extent, complexity and, I will argue, in function, the tendency, already documented by Neusner, to balance carefully the apodoses within a mishnaic pericope. I maintain that balanced apodoses within mishnaic passages is in fact the tip of a much larger rhetorical iceberg affecting the formulation of Mishnah's language in both protases and apodoses, and both within and across pericopes constituting a "chapter" of a Mishnah tractate. Indeed, at times homophony extends even across these larger subdivisions of tractates (although the limitations of this paper's preliminary demonstration will not permit me here to document the latter claim). If these extensive encompassing literary and stylistic phenomena represent the "demands" or the "requisites" of something being recognized as "authentically mishnaic," then we are not dealing here with merely editorial reworking of antecedent materials to create a more unified whole (which, according to Neusner, may be memorized for promulgation). Rather, what Mishnah's literary and stylistic requisites represent is an entirely comprehensive mode of discourse, a kind of "discourse universe" all its own. It is as if one could speak of talking Mishnah, the way one speaks of talking French or English, or perhaps, more accurately, the way an ancient could be said to be talking in perfect, unbroken diatribe, with full knowledge that in the appropriate social context to talk in such a way immediately carries the mark of authenticity and authority.

II
Applying the method:
A rhetorical "scoring" of m. Gittin 1:1-2:2

With these anticipated conclusions already in mind, the remainder of this chapter presents and analyzes rhetorical traits of the first large subdivision of Mishnah Tractate Gittin. M. Gittin 1:1-2:2 appears below in a graph-like or chart-like manner. The text has not only been segmented, but also "scored," much as different voices' or instruments' notes appear in parallel lines of music across a choral or symphonic score. Here, however, the various voices are different types of stylistic or rhetorical markers and devices, and the parallel lines of our "score" run vertically down the page. Those "voices" in vertical columns from left to right are: (1) conjunctive-concatenating formulae; (2) logical-argumentational operators; (3) a "catch-all" column for other formulaic terms not accounted for in the first two columns; (4) morphological markers; (5-7) *three* columns dedicated to three levels of homophonic-homosemantic (and antisemantic) markers; (8) a last column containing simply what is left after the other voices have had their say.

Some few explanatory words about the choice of voices and their number are in order. The dedication of three columns to homophonic-homosemantic markers represents the complexity of their use; as noted, these markers operate at several levels simultaneously through the mishnaic subdivision. In order readily to observe this, more than one column was necessary. Using three, as opposed to two or four, is a pragmatic decision only; three seemed to suffice to be able to see or hear the number of levels at which these markers operate in this mishnaic passage. As we shall see, linguistic terms which help constitute argument, which our "score" places in the second column from the left, hardly appear in our sample Mishnah passage. One may well wonder, therefore, what terms I had thought would occupy column two, and given that I have hardly found them, why I have bothered to reserve a column for such formulae. The type of logical or argumentational terminology I had in mind is represented in the following schema of an argument: "if" with respect to case a, "which" has characteristic b+, the law is x, "then" with respect to case a', "which" has characteristic b "only," "all the more so should" the law be x. "If," "then," "which," "only," and "all the more so should" are stock linguistic terms that both mark and help constitute one variation of the (so-called) "standard" rabbinic argument *a fortiori*. These and other standard logical argumentational terms are found more frequently in Tosefta, the halakic midrashim, and the two Talmuds. Hence, representing their relatively infrequent appearance in Mishnah seems important in coming to grips with the character, meaning, and context of Mishnah's particular rhetoric. Below is a segmented translation of m. Gittin 1:1-2:2, followed by a rhetorically "scored" presentation of same.

1:1.
a.   One who brings a writ from a Mediterranean province–
b.   it is required that he should say: In my presence it was written and in my presence it was signed [by the witnesses].
c.   R. Gamaliel says: Also one who brings [a writ] from Rekem and from Heger [must be able to so declare].
d.   R. Eliezer says: Even [one who brings a writ] from Kefar Luddim to Lud [must be able to so declare].
e.   And sages say: It is not required that he should say: In my presence it was written, and in my presence it was signed [by the witnesses]– except him who brings [a writ] from a Mediterranean province and him who takes [a writ to a Mediterranean province].
f.   And one who brings [a writ] from province to province in the Mediterranean provinces–
g.   it is required that he should say: In my presence it was written and in my presence it was signed [by the witnesses].
h.   R. Simeon b. Gamaliel says: Even from district to district [within a single Mediterranean province must make such a declaration].

1:2.
a.   Rabbi Judah says: [One must make the declaration if taking a writ]:
b.   from Rekem to the East, and Rekem is like the East;
c.   from Ashqalon to the South, and Ashqalon is like the South;
d.   from Akko to the North, and Akko is like the North.
e.   R. Meir says: Akko is like the Land of Israel with respect to writs.

1:3.
a.   One who brings a writ within the Land of Israel–
b.   it is not required that he should say: In my presence it was written and in my presence it was signed [by the witnesses].
c.   If there are challengers to it[s validity], it[s validity] shall stand upon [the authentication of] it[s witnesses'] signatures.
d.   One who brings a writ from a Mediterranean province,
e.   and cannot say: In my presence it was written, and in my presence it was signed [by witnesses]—
f.   if there are upon it [the signatures of] witnesses, it[s validity] shall stand upon [the authentication of] it[s witnesses'] signatures.

1:4.
a.   One [and] the same are writs [of divorce] of women and manumission papers of slaves;
b.   they equated [them] with regard to one who takes [them to a Mediterranean province]

and with regard to one who brings [them from a Mediterranean province].

c.   And this is one of the ways [only] that they equated writs [of divorce] of women with manumission papers of slaves.

1:5.

a.   Any writ [of divorce] that has upon it [the signature of] a Samaritan witness

b.   is unfit,

c.   except for writs [of divorce] of women and manumission papers of slaves.

d.   It once happened that they brought before R. Gamaliel in Kefar Otnai a writ [of divorce] of a woman,

e.   and its witnesses were Samaritan witnesses,

f.   and he declared [it] fit.

g.   Any bonds issuing from [court] bureaus of the gentiles—

h.   even though their signatories are gentiles—

i.   are fit,

j.   except for writs [of divorce] of women and manumission papers of slaves.

k.   R. Simeon says: Also these are fit.

l.   They specified [that the latter were unfit] only when they were done in a nonprofessional tribunal.

1:6.

a.   One who says: Give this writ [of divorce] to my wife and this manumission bond to my slave—

b.   if he desired to retract with respect to both of them, he may retract, the words of R. Meir.

c.   But sages say: With respect to writs [of divorce] of women, [he may retract]; however not with respect to manumission papers of slaves,

d.   because they benefit one when not in his [or her] presence, but they obligate him [or her] only in his [or her] presence;

e.   since if he should desire not to feed his slave, he is allowed, but not to feed his wife, he is not allowed.

f.   He said to them: But lo he renders unfit his slave for the [eating of] heave offering [if the owner is a priest], just as he renders unfit his wife.

g.   They said to him: Because he is his property [and she is not].

h.   One who says: Give this writ [of divorce] to my wife and this manumission bond to my slave,

i.   and he died—

j.   they may not give [either] after [the person's] death.

k.   [One who says:] Give a maneh to such-and-such person,

l.   and he died—

m.   they may give [the maneh] after [the person's] death.

2:1

a.   One who brings a writ from a Mediterranean province,

b.   and one said: In my presence it was written, however not in my presence was it signed [by the witnesses];

c.   in my presence it was signed [by the witnesses], however not in my presence was it written;

d.   in my presence it was written in its entirety, and in my presence it was signed in part;

e.   in my presence it was written in part, and in my presence it was signed

	in its entirety—
f.	[the writ] is unfit.
g.	One says:In my presence it was written, and one [i.e., another] says: In my presence it was signed—
h.	[the writ] is unfit.
i.	Two [bring writ and] say: In our presence it was written, and one says:In my presence it was signed—
j.	[the writ] is unfit.
k.	And R. Judah declares fit.
l.	One says: In my presence it was written, and two [i.e., both] say: In our presence it was signed—
m.	[the writ] is fit.

2:2

a.	It [the writ] was written in the daytime and was signed in the daytime,
b.	[or was written]in the night time and was signed in the night time,
c.	[or was written] in the night time and was signed in the day time—
d.	[the writ] is fit.
e.	[The writ was written] in the daytime and was signed in the night time—
f.	[the writ] is unfit.
g.	R. Simeon declares [such a writ] fit,
h.	for R. Simeon used to say: All writs that were written in the daytime and were signed in the night time
i.	are unfit,
j.	except for writs [of divorce] of women.

[m. Git. 1:1-2:2, trans. my own]

I turn now to the rhetorical scoring of the same "chapter" of Mishnah Tractate Gittin.

Chart 2.1: Rhetorical "scoring" of m. Gittin 1:1-2:2

Column 1 = Conjunctive/Coordinating formulae (CC)
Column 2 = Logical/Analogical formulae (LA)
Column 3 = Other Formulae (OF)
Column 4 = Morphological markers (M)
Column 5 = Homophonic-Homosemantic/antisemantic markers, level 1 (HH1)
Column 6 = Homophonic-Homosemantic/antisemantic markers, level 2 (HH2)
Column 7 = Homophonic-Homosemantic/antisemantic markers, level 3 (HH3)
Column 8 = Other Content (OC)

CC	LA	OF	M	HH1	HH2	HH3	OC
1:1							
			A. One who ($ה$ + 3rd sg. pres. part)				
				brings a writ			
					from ($מ$) a Mediterranean province		
							B. it is required

CC	LA	OF	M	HH1	HH2	HH3	OC
that (שׁ)						he should say: In my presence it was written	
and						in my presence it was signed [by the witnesses].	
							C. R. Gamaliel
says: Also (אף)			one who (ה + 3rd sg. pres. part) brings [a writ]	from			
							Rekem
and				from			
							Heger [must be able to so declare].
							D. R. Eliezer
says: Even (אפילו)			[one who] [brings] [a writ]	from (מ)			
							Kefar Luddim
					to		
							Lud [i.e., Lydda, must be able to so declare].
E. And							sages
say:						it is not required	
that						he should say: In my presence it was written,	
and						in my presence it was signed [by the witnesses]–	
except (אלא)			him who (ה + 3rd sg. pres. part.) brings [a writ]	from a Mediterranean province			
F. and							

CC	LA	OF	M	HH1	HH2	HH3	OC
			him who				
			(ה + 3rd sg. pres. part.)				
			takes				
			[a writ]				
				[to]			
				[a Mediterranean]			
				[province.]			
G. And							
			he who				
			(ה + 3rd sg. pres. part.)				
			brings				
							[a writ]
				from			
				province			
				to			
				province			
				in the Mediterranean			
				provinces (emended to pl.)–			
					H. it is required		
that							
					he should say:		
					in my presence it was written		
and							
					in my presence it was signed [by the witnesses.]		
							I. R. Simeon b. Gamaliel
says:							
Even (אפילו)							
				from			
				district			
				to			
				district			
							[within a single Mediterranean province must make such a declaration].
1:2							
							A.1. Rabbi Judah
says:							
							[one must make the declaration if taking a writ:]
				from			
				Rekem			
				to			
				the East,			
and							

CC	LA	OF	M	HH1	HH2	HH3	OC
					Rekem is		
					like		
					the East;		
					A.2. from		
					Ashqalon		
					to		
					the South,		
and							
					Ashqalon is		
					like		
					the South;		
					A.3. from		
					Akko		
					to		
					the North,		
and							
					Akko is		
					like		
					the North.		
							B. R. Meir
says:							
					Akko is		
					like		
					the Land of Israel with respect		
					to		
							writs [and not North of the frontier].
1:3							
			A. One who				
			(ה + 3rd sg. pres. part.)				
			brings				
							a writ
				within			
				the Land of Israel–			
					B. it is not required		
that							
			he should				
						say:	
						In my presence it was written	
and							
						in my presence it was signed [by the witnesses].	
C. If							
					there are		
							challengers
					to it[s validity],		
			(3rd sg. imperf.)				
					D. it[s validity] shall stand upon		

CC   LA   OF   M   HH1 HH2 HH3   OC
                                                                    [the authentication
                                                                    of]
                                            it[s witnesses']
                                            signatures.

                            E. One who
                            (ה + 3rd sg. pres. part.)
                                        brings
                                        a writ
                                                from
                                                a Mediterranean
                                                province,

F. and
                                                        cannot say:
                                                        In my presence it was written,

and
                                                        in my presence it was signed [by
                                                        witnesses]–

G. if
                                            there are
                                            upon it
                                            [the signatures of]
                                            witnesses,
                                            H. it[s validity]
                            (3rd sg. imperf.)
                                            shall stand
                                            upon
                                                            [the authentication
                                                            of]
                                            it[s witnesses']
                                            signatures.

1:4

[and]
                                                            A. One

                                                    the same (lit. one)
                                                            are
                                        writs
                                        [of divorce]
                                        of women

and
                                        manumission papers
                                        of slaves–

                            B. they (3rd pl. perf.)
                                        equated
                                                            [them]
                                                with regard to
                            one who
                            (ה + 3rd sg. pres. part.)
                                        takes
                                                            [them to a Mediter-
                                                            ranean province]

CC	LA	OF	M	HH1	HH2	HH3	OC
and				with regard to			
			one who				
			(ה + 3rd sg. pres. part.)				
			brings				
							[them from a Mediterranean province].
C. And							
							this is
					one		
							of the ways [only]
that							
			they (3rd sg. perf.)				
				equated			
				writs			
				[of divorce]			
				of women			
					with		
				manumission papers			
				of slaves.			

1:5
A. Any (כל)

CC	LA	OF	M	HH1	HH2	HH3	OC
				writ			
				[of divorce]			
that							
				has			
				upon it			
							[the signature of]
				a Samaritan			
				witness			
				is unfit,			

B. except for (חוץ מ)

CC	LA	OF	M	HH1	HH2	HH3	OC
				writs			
				[of divorce]			
				of women			
and							
				manumission papers			
				of slaves.			

C. It once happened (מעשה ש)
that

CC	LA	OF	M	HH1	HH2	HH3	OC
			they (3rd pl. perf.)				
				brought			
							before R. Gamaliel
					in (lit. to)		
							Kefar Otnai
				a writ			
				[of divorce]			
				of a woman,			
D. and							
					its witnesses		

CC	LA	OF	M	HH1	HH2	HH3	OC
							were
					Samaritan witnesses,		
E. and							
							he declared [it]
					fit (comp. unfit).		
F. Any							
				bonds			
			(ה + 3rd. pl. part.)				
							issuing from [court] bureaus of the
					gentiles–		
G. even though (אַף עַל פִּי שֶ)							
					their signatories are gentiles–		
					H. are fit,		
I. except for							
				writs [of divorce] of women			
and							
				manumission papers of slaves.			
							J. R. Simeon
says: Also (אַף)							
							these
					are fit.		
							K. They specified [that the latter were unfit]
only (אֶלָא)							
							at such time
that							
							they were done in a non-professional tribunal.
1:6							
			A. One who (ה + 3rd sg. pres. part.)				
				says: Give (sg. imp.) this writ [of divorce]			
		to					
				my wife			
and							
				this manumission bond			
		to					

CC	LA	OF	M	HH1	HH2	HH3	OC
				my slave–			
B. if						he desired	
						to retract	
						with respect to (ב)	
							both of them,
						C. he may retract,	
the words of							
							R. Meir.
D. But							
							sages
say:							
						with respect to	
				writs			
				[of divorce]			
				of women,			
						[he may retract];	
E. however (אבל)							
						not	
						with respect to	
				manumission papers			
				of slaves,			
	F. because (לפי שׁ)						
			they (3rd. pl. part.)				
						benefit one	
when (שׁ)							
						not	
						in his [or her] presence,	
G. but (ו)							
			they (3rd pl. part.)				
						obligate him [or her]	
only							
						in his [or her] presence;	
	H. since if						
			he should (3rd sg. imperf.)				
						desire	
						not	
						to feed	
				his slave,			
						he is allowed,	
I. but							
						not	
						to feed	
				his wife,			
						he is	
						not	
						allowed.	
J. He said to them:							
But lo (והרי)							
			he (3rd sg. part.)				
						renders unfit	

CC	LA	OF	M	HH1	HH2	HH3	OC
				his slave			
							from the [eating of] heave offering [if the owner is a priest],
	K. just as						
			he (3rd sg. part.)				
					renders unfit		
				his wife.			
L. They said to him:							
	Because						
							he is
				his			
							property [and she is not].
			M. One who (ה + 3rd sg. pres. part)				
			says:				
			Give (pl. imp.)				
			this				
			writ [of divorce]				
			to				
			my wife				
and							
			this				
			manumission				
			bond				
			to				
			my slave,				
and							
					he died–		
			N. they may (3rd pl. imperf.)				
			not				
			give (3rd pl. imperf.)				
						[either]	
					after [the person's] death.		
			O. Give				
						a maneh	
			to				
						such-and-such person,	
P. and							
					he died–		
			Q. They may (3rd pl. imperf.)				
			give				
						[the maneh]	
					after [the person's] death.		

CC	LA	OF	M	HH1	HH2	HH3	OC
2:1							
			A. One who (ה + 3rd sg. pres. part.) brings a writ	from a Mediterranean province,			
B. and					one said: In my presence it was written,		
C. however (אבל)					not: In my presence it was signed [by the witnesses];		
					D. In my presence it was signed [by the witnesses],		
E. however					not: In my presence it was written;		
					F. In my presence it was written in its entirety (כלו),		
G. and					in my presence it was signed in part (חציו);		
					H. in my presence it was written in part,		
I. and)					in my presence it was signed in its entirety—		
			J. [the writ] is unfit (3rd sg. pass. part.).				
		(3rd sg. part.)	K. One				
					says: In my presence it was written,		
L. and		(3rd sg. part.)		One [i.e., another]			
					says: In my presence it was signed—		
			M. [the writ] is unfit (3rd sg. pass. part.).				
		[bring	N. Two				

CC	LA	OF	M	HH1	HH2	HH3	OC
				a writ and]			
			(3rd pl. part.)				
						say:	
						In our presence it was written,	
O. and							
					One		
			(3rd sg. part.)				
						says:	
						In my presence it was signed–	

P. [the writ]
    is unfit (3rd sg. pass. part.).

Q. And

                                      R. Judah

(3rd sg. part.)

    declares fit.

R. One

(3rd sg. part.)

    says:
    In my presence it was written,

S. and

    two (i.e., both)

(3rd pl. part.)

    say:
    In our presence it was signed–

T. [the writ]
    is fit (3rd sg. pass. part.).

2:2

    A. It [the writ]

(3rd sg. pass. perf.)

    was written
    in the daytime

B. and

(3rd sg. pass. perf.)

    was signed
    in the daytime,

C. [or]

    [was written]
    in the nighttime

D. and

(3rd sg. pass. perf.)

    was signed
    in the nighttime,

E. [or]

    [was written]
    in the night time

F. and

(3rd sg. pass. perf.)

CC	LA	OF	M	HH1	HH2	HH3	OC
					was signed in the daytime–		
		G. [the writ]		is fit (3rd sg. pass. part.).			
		H. [The writ]		in the daytime	[was written]		
I. and			(3rd sg. pass. perf.)		was signed in the nighttime–		
		J. [the writ]		is unfit (3rd sg. pass. part.);			
			(3rd sg. part.)		declares fit,		K. R. Simeon
L. for							R. Simeon
used to say: All				writs			
that			(3rd pl. pass. perf.)	were written in the daytime			
M. and			(3rd pl. pass. perf.)		were signed in the night time		
						N. are unfit (3rd pl. pass part.)	
O. except for							

writs [of divorce] of women.
[trans. and charting my own]

In order to isolate and analyze the stylistic and rhetorical features documented in our "scored" chart of m. Git. 1:1-2:2, I begin with linguistic markers which help set off and unify the largest literary unit(s). I subsequently examine markers which serve to define smaller, constituent passages. The "scored" presentation of m. Git. 2:1-2 together with m. Git. 1:1-6 anticipates what we shall find: rhetorical indicators mark 1:1 through 2:2 as the first "chapter" of the Mishnah tractate, with m. Git. 2:2 being drawn in the wake of 2:1 as the formal closing excursus. A precise set of linguistic markers define and tie together the whole. One such marker is morphological, the use of

    (1)   *the heh-emphaticus with a verb in the 3rd singular present participial form.*

The others are the following homophonic, homosemantic or antisemantic markers:

(2/2') *brings(/takes);*

(3) *writ;*

(4/4') *from(/to);*

(5) *a Mediterranean province(s);*

(6) *(is required to) say(/said);*

(7) *in my presence it was written;*

(8) *in my presence it was signed (both 3rd. sing. pass. imperf. niph'al).*

The repetition of a "critical mass" of these seven markers at frequent junctures in the "chapter" helps to establish the larger unit's rhetorical coherence and unity. At this most encompassing level, markers 7 and 8 seem especially important. Later we shall see that individual items from among the list of 8 also provide integrating markers for constituent subunits of the chapter. However, for the moment, I direct our attention to the rhetorical, stylistic strategies helping to unify and integrate the "chapter" as a whole. To make more visible the markers serving the latter function let us filter out everything else. The next "scored" chart (2) does just this; the relevant rhetorical markers appear in boldface. The subsequent chart (3) documents graphically the appearance and distribution of the 8 unifying markers appearing in boldface in Chart 2's truncated rhetorical "score."

Chart 2.2: Rhetorical markers serving to define the "chapter"

Column 1 = Conjunctive/Coordinating formulae (CC)
Column 2 = Logical/Analogical formulae (LA)
Column 3 = Other Formulae (OF)
Column 4 = Morphological markers (M)
Column 5 = Homophonic-Homosemantic/antisemantic markers, level 1 (HH1)
Column 6 = Homophonic-Homosemantic/antisemantic markers, level 2 (HH2)
Column 7 = Homophonic-Homosemantic/antisemantic markers, level 3 (HH3)
Column 8 = Other Content (OC)

CC	LA	OF	M	HH1	HH2	HH3	OC
1:1							
			A. One who				
			(ה + 3rd sg. pres. part)				
			brings				
			a writ				
				from (מ)			
				a Mediterranean			
				province–			
					B. it is required		
that							
				he should say:			
				·In my presence it was written			
and							
				in my presence it was signed [by the witnesses].			
						C. ...	
C. Also							

CC	LA	OF	M	HH1	HH2	HH3	OC
			one who (ה + 3rd sg. pres. part) **brings** [a writ]	**from**			
E. But							sages
say:						it is not required	
that						**he should say:** **In my presence it was written,**	
and						**in my presence it was signed** [by the witnesses]–	
except				**him who** (ה + 3rd sg. pres. part.) **brings** [a writ] **from a Mediterranean province**			
F. and				**him who** (ה + 3rd sg. pres. part.) **takes** [a writ] [to] [a Mediterranean] [province.]			
G. And				**he who** (ה + 3rd sg. pres. part.) **brings** [a writ] **from** province **to** province in **the Mediterranean provinces** (emended to pl.)–			
						H. it is required	
that						**he should say:** **in my presence it was written**	
and						**in my presence it was signed** [by the witnesses.]	

CC	LA	OF	M	HH1	HH2	HH3	OC
							I. ...
1:3							
			A. One who				
			(ה + 3rd sg. pres. part.)				
			brings				
			a writ				
				within			
				the Land of Israel–			
						B. it is not required	
that							
			he should				
						say:	
						In my presence it was written	
and							
						in my presence it was signed [by the witnesses].	
C. If...							
			E. One who				
			(ה + 3rd sg. pres. part.)				
			brings				
			a writ				
				from (מ)			
				a Mediterranean			
				province,			
F. and							
						cannot **say:**	
						In my presence it was written,	
and							
						in my presence it was signed [by witnesses]–	
G. if ...							
2:1							
			A. One who				
			(ה + 3rd sg. pres. part.)				
			brings				
			a writ				
				from			
				a Mediterranean			
				province,			
B. and							
						one **said:**	
						In my presence it was written,	
C. however							
						. not:	
						In my presence it was signed [by the witnesses];	
						D. In my presence it was signed [by the witnesses],	
E. however							
						not:	

CC	LA	OF	M	HH1	HH2	HH3	OC
						In my presence it was written;	
						F. **In my presence it was written**	
					in its entirety,		
G. and							
						in my presence it was signed	
					in part;		
						H. **In my presence it was written**	
					in part,		
I. and							
						in my presence it was signed	
					in its entirety—		
				J. [the writ]			
					is unfit (3rd sg. pass. part.).		
						K. One	
			(3rd sg. part.)				
						says:	
						In my presence it was written,	
L. and							
						One [i.e., another]	
			(3rd sg. part.)				
						says:	
						In my presence it was signed—	
				M. [the writ]			
					is unfit (3rd sg. pass. part.).		
						N. Two	
				[bring a writ and]			
			(3rd pl. part.)				
						say:	
						In our presence it was written,	
O. and							
						One	
			(3rd sg. part.)				
						says:	
						In my presence it was signed—	
				P. [the writ]			
					is unfit (3rd sg. pass. part.).		
Q. But							
							R. Judah
			(3rd sg. part.)				
					declares fit.		
						R. One	
			(3rd sg. part.)				
						says:	

CC   LA   OF   M   HH1   HH2   HH3   OC

In my presence it was written,

S. and

two (i.e., both)

(3rd pl. part.)

say:

In our presence it was signed—

T. [the writ]

is fit (3rd sg. pass. part.).

Chart 2.3: Distribution of rhetorical markers 1 through 7 in chart 2.2

Section		Marker nos.	1	2/2'	3	4/4'	5	6	7	8
1:1,	A-B		X	X	X	X	X	X	X	X
	C		X	X		X				
	E							X	X	X
			X	X		X	X			
	F		X	X						
	G		X	X		X/X'	X	X	X	X
1:3,	A		X	X	X			X	X	X
	E		X	X	X	X	X	X	X	X
2:1,	A-C		X	X	X	X	X	X	X	X
	D									X
									X	
	E								X	X
	H								X	X
	K-L							X	X	
								X		X
	N-O							X	X	
								X		X
	R-S							X	X	
								X		X

The graphical representation in Chart 3 dramatically demonstrates how rhetorical markers set off the larger mishnaic subdivision, or "chapter," by what can only be designated repetition of words and phrases at frequent junctures. Specifically, the rhetorical markers helping define the whole dominate at 1:1, 1:3, and 2:1, roughly at the beginning, middle, and end of the "chapter." The absence of "a writ" (marker 3) at several places (at 1:1,C,E,F,G and at 2:1,D on) is of no particular concern. "A writ" is clearly understood at all of these sections, and its specification in all relevant instances would itself be contrary to good mishnaic rhetorical style, which offsets obvious (and, from the semantic point of view, unnecessary) repetitiousness with substantive lacunae. Indeed, the laconic character of Mishnah language allows other phrases to be repeated rhythmically and to be heard without interruption or hesitation. A stunning example of this is in fact 2:1,K-S which, using our marker numbers, sets the rhythm, 6,7,6,8/6,7,6,8/6,7,6,8 (i.e., the thrice-repeated sequence, "says," "in my presence it was written, "say," "in my presence it was signed"). The inclusion in 2:1,K-S of a substantial selection of markers 1 through 5 would mask entirely this elegant rhythm.

Considering, then, 1:1, 1:3, and 2:1 to function *rhetorically* as the core of the larger subdivision, let us examine an illustrative example of (1) how other pericopes of the chapter are stylistically unified with this core and (2) by what means rhetorical unity and coherence are effected with individual pericopes. The stylistic, rhetorical relationship of 2:2, the concluding excursus, first, to 2:1 and, second, to 1:5 provides one apt example of how a smaller unit of Mishnah rhetorically adheres to the shank of the "chapter." First, and most obvious, fragments of what I previously referred to as marker 7 ("in my presence it was written") and marker 8 ("in my presence it was signed") provide the verbs and the morphology (3rd sg. pass. perf.) for all the protases of 2:2. The fragments "was written" and "was signed" are really "diminished" tones of markers 7 and 8, and in subsequent graphical representations (chart 5) I will therefore refer to them as:

(7-) *was written;*

(8-) *as signed.*

Furthermore, the passive participial forms of the verb כשר (fit) and its semantic opposite פסול (unfit) are used throughout 2:1 and 2:2, after having been introduced at 1:5. I add to the growing list of markers:

(9/9') *is fit/is unfit.*

With respect to this last marker, note too that the opening and concluding phrases of the "saying" attributed to R. Simeon at 2:2,L ("all [כל] writs that [ש]...except for writs of divorce of women") recalls 1:5A-B, F-I ("any [כל] writ that [ש]... except writs of divorce of women and manumission papers of slaves").

Thus far I have dealt with the rhetorical ties binding 2:2 to 2:1 and to the "chapter's" shank generally. What provides rhetorical unity and coherence within a small unit like 2:2 or 2:1? Obviously, markers 7-, 8-, and 9 may do double duty, both integrating 2:2 and 2:1 and effecting unity within the final excursus at 2:2 and within 2:1. In addition, the antisemantic pair:

(10/10') *in the daytime/in the nighttime*

operates internally within 2:2 only. Within 2:1 two rhetorical devices, both homophonic/antisemantic, function to bind the unit together:

(11/11') *in its entirety/in part (in 2:1,F-J);*

(12/12') *One/Two (in 2:1,K-T).*

The homophonic quality of alternating the terms "in its entirety (כלו)" and "in part (חציו)" is enhanced by a morphological feature shared by both terms, the use in both instances of the third person singular pronominal suffix. This makes the antisemantic word pair constituting marker 11 rhyme.

Chart 4 gives a "scored" representation of 2:1 and 2:2, and of parallel sections at 1:5. Inter-pericopaic rhetorical markers (7-, 8-, and 9/9') again appear in boldface type. Intra-pericopaic rhetorical unifiers (marker 10/10', 11/11', and 12/12') are in italics. Chart 5, like chart 3, graphically represents the distribution in 2:1 and 2:2 of rhetorical markers 8- through 12/12'.

Chart 2.4: "Scored" rhetorical rendition of m. Git. 2:1 and 2:2, and parallel language at 1:5, highlighting inter- and intra-pericopaic unifying rhetorical devices

CC	LA	OF	M	HH1	HH2	HH3	OC
1:5							
A. Any (כל)							
	that						
				writ [of divorce]			
					has upon it		
							[the signature of]
					a Samaritan witness	**is unfit,**	
	B. except for (חרץ מ)						
				writs [of divorce] of women			
	and						
				manumission papers of slaves.			
	F. **Any**						
				bonds			
			(ה + 3rd pl. part.)				
							issuing from [court] bureaus of the
					gentiles –		
	G. even though						
					their signatories are gentiles –		
					H. **are fit,**		
	I. except for						
				writs [of divorce] of women			
	and						
				manumission papers of slaves.			
2:1							
			A. One who (ה + 3rd sg. pres. part.)				
				brings a writ			
					from a Mediterranean province,		
	B. and						
						one said:	

CC	LA	OF	M	HH1	HH2	HH3	OC
							In my presence **it was written**,
C. however						not: In my presence **it was signed** [by the witnesses];	
						D. In my presence **it was signed** [by the witnesses],	
E. however						not: In my presence **it was written**;	
						F. In my presence **it was written** *in its entirety* (כלו),	
G. and						in my presence **it was signed** *in part* (מקצתו);	
						H. In my presence **it was written** *in part*,	
I. and						in my presence **it was signed** *in its entirety*—	
					J. [the writ]	**is unfit (3rd sg. pass. part.)**.	
			(3rd sg. part.)		K. *One*	says: In my presence **it was written**,	
L. and			(3rd sg. part.)		*One* [i.e., another]	says: In my presence **it was signed**—	
					M. [the writ]	**is unfit (3rd sg. pass. part.)**.	
			(3rd pl. part.)	[bring a writ and]	N. *Two*	say: In our presence **it was written**,	
O. and			(3rd sg. part.)		*One*	says: In my presence **it was signed**—	
					P. [the writ]		

CC	LA	OF	M	HH1	HH2	HH3	OC
					is unfit (3rd sg. pass. part.).		
Q. But (ו)							
							R. Judah
			(3rd sg. part.)				
					declares **fit**.		
					R. *One*		
			(3rd sg. part.)				
S. and							
						says:	
						In my presence **it was written**,	
					two (i.e., both)		
			(3rd pl. part.)				
						say:	
						In our presence **it was signed**—	
				T. [the writ]			
					is fit (3rd sg. pass. part.).		
2:2							
				A. **It** [the writ]			
			(3rd sg. pass. perf.)				
						was written	
							in the daytime
B. and							
			(3rd sg. pass. perf.)				
						was signed	
							in the daytime,
C. [or]							
						[was written]	
							in the nighttime
D. and							
			(3rd sg. pass. perf.)				
						was signed	
							in the nighttime,
E. [or]							
						[was written]	
							in the nighttime
F. and							
			(3rd sg. pass. perf.)				
						was signed	
							in the daytime–
				G. [the writ]			
					is fit (3rd sg. pass. part.).		
				H. [The writ]			
						[was written]	
							in the daytime
I. and							
			(3rd sg. pass. perf.)				
						was signed	

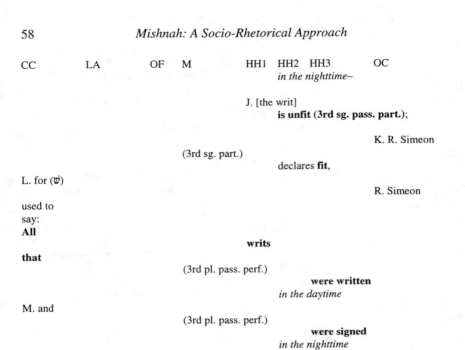

CC   LA   OF   M   HH1   HH2   HH3   OC

in the nighttime–

J. [the writ]

is unfit (3rd sg. pass. part.);

K. R. Simeon

(3rd sg. part.)

declares **fit**,

L. for (ﬡ)

R. Simeon

used to say: **All**

writs

that

(3rd pl. pass. perf.)

were written
in the daytime

M. and

(3rd pl. pass. perf.)

were signed
in the nighttime

N. **are unfit (3rd pl. pass. part.)**

O. **except for**

writs [of divorce] of women.

Chart 2.5: Distribution of rhetorical markers 7-, 8-, and 9/9'-12/12' in m. Gittin 2:1-2

	Section	Marker 12/12' One/ Two	7- written	8- signed	11/11' all/ part	10/10' day/ night	9/9' fit/ unfit
2:1,	B-C		X	X			
	D-E			X			
			X				
	F-G		X		X		
				X	X'		
	H-I		X		X'		
				X	X		
	J						X'
2:1,	K-L	X	X				
		X		X			
	M						X'
	N-O	X'	X				
		X		X			
	P						X'
	Q						X

R-S	X	X			
	X'		X		
T					X
2:2, A-B		X		X	
			X	X	
C-D				X'	
			X	X'	
E-F				X'	
			X	X	
G					X
H-I				X	
			X	X'	
J					X'
K					X
L-M		X		X	
			X	X'	
N					X

Chart 4 provides stark visual evidence of the patterning of markers that, first, unify 2:1 and 2:2 and, second, define subsections of the whole. With respect to the first, "[it] was written" and "[it] was signed," and "fit" and "unfit" appear with cadenced regularity throughout 2:1 and 2:2. The subunits of 2:1-2 stand out in the chart because of the appearance of tight vertical blocks or "pillars" of homophonic and antisemantic usage:

> 2:1, F-J is rhetorically identifiable by the use of "in its entirety" (marker 11) and "in part" (marker 11') in the pattern, all-part/part-all;
>
> 2:1, K-T by "one" (marker 12) and "two" (marker 12'), giving us the pattern, one-one/two-one/one-two;
>
> 2:2, B-J by "in the daytime" (marker 10) and "in the nighttime" (marker 10'), exhibiting the arrangement, day-day/night-night/night-day/day-night (2:2,L-N simply repeats the final pair for "Simeon's" differing ruling).

As already documented and discussed, other marker patterns define 2:1 as part of the "chapter's" shank, and terms and phrases of Simeon's "saying" repeats the terms and phrases which characterize subunits at 1:5, as does the use of "fit" and "unfit" throughout 2:1-2. In sum, the use of rhetorical devices, and especially of homophonic, homosemantic, and antisemantic patterning defines the larger literary division (or "chapters") by creating a rhetorical shank, to which other units are bound by these same devices. Finally, these devices mark off the smallest integral subunits of the whole. Note that at no time during the analysis have we needed to consider the legal content of the "chapter" in order either to identify the boundaries of the whole or of its constituent parts, or to assess their level of integration and unity.

III
Socio-cultural meaning and significance:
An argument toward interim conclusions

III.i. Mishnaic rhetoric: preliminary methodological and conceptual issues, and initial proposals

Further analysis of this and other mishnaic "chapters," by me and by others,[1] will serve to verify whether the rhetorical phenomena that we have identified above operate in much of Mishnah. But if that should be the case, if this passage and my analysis of it should prove not to be eccentric for Mishnah, what significance might one impart to these findings? As an obviously heuristic exercise, permit me provisionally and briefly to address this question on the basis of the evidence in hand.

First, as a methodological point, ascribing meaning and significance to the rhetorical phenomena identified implies that Mishnah's authors could have otherwise gone about their task. That is to say, we must be satisfied that there are alternative modes in which the tractate's authors could have cast the substance of m. Gittin 1:1-2:2. This requisite is central precisely because I will seek to attribute meaning and significance to particular recurrent, ordered and structured *ways of saying things*, quite apart from precisely *what is being said*. Like all communicative action, meaning is (implicitly) imparted because the actors could have acted in accordance with some other pattern, but did not. Thus in linguistic patterning, the sequence, dog bites person, tiger eats child, bear gnashes hunter, can be said implicitly to communicate by repeated structural relationships the "assertion" that animals prey on humans. That assertion is implicitly communicated because one could have produced the series, person bites dog, child eats tiger, hunter gnashes bear, and thereby have implicitly conveyed the opposite. Of course, one may adopt a rhetorical mode which, relatively speaking, eschews implicit communication in favour of explicit discursive expression of idiomatic content. This book, for example, adopts such a rhetorical mode. However, the phrase "relatively speaking" in the previous sentence is not gratuitous; this book too adheres to a rhetorical form, with recognizable patterns, and stock phrases and terminology. These patterns and terminology implicitly communicate "assertions" about how I wish to be taken, namely, as a competent academic within a certain professional milieu. Hence any piece of writing or of speech may, I submit, be located somewhere on a rhetorical continuum. Toward one end of that continuum explicit discursive expression is dominant. At the other end, implicit non-discursive communication prevails. The extreme ends of the continuum are fictions, since no mode of speech or of writing is likely to be wholly one or the other. From the evidence adduced above about Mishnah, in which extreme literary patterning is evident, I locate mishnaic rhetoric well to one side of the continuum's centre among modes of expression that are heavily laden with implicit meanings.

---

1.   As already noted, graduate students, Dr. Maria Mamfredis and Kelly Menchick and I have analyzed some 20 chapters of Mishnah in this manner; m. Gittin 1:1-2:2 is not atypical when seen in light of the content of these other mishnaic chapters.

This being said, it is evident that Mishnah's authors had many other culturally and/or religiously sanctioned models for expressing Mishnah's content. For example, one such model will have been the rhetorical style of legal sections of the Pentateuch. Therefore, to have chosen the mode of rhetoric in evidence in our Mishnah passage is significant, in the sense of implicitly communicative. (Indeed, I believe that a study of the rhetorical models in evidence for ancient and Late Antique Judaism will only further highlight the distinctiveness as well as the deliberate character of the mishnaic authors' choice of rhetoric.) What meaning and significance may be ascribed to the mishnaic rhetorical patterns at hand I shall return to later, after venturing several more interim conclusions based on our evidence.

My second point is an interim, text-historical conclusion, again of methodological import to ascribing significance to Mishnah's rhetoric. I draw the reader's (or listener's) attention to the fact that I have slipped into talking about Mishnah's "authors," as opposed to using the more commonly accepted terms, "editors" and "redactors." I propose that the type of rhetorical phenomena documented earlier overwhelmingly supports the hypothesis that most of the language of the "chapter" has come from the same hand(s) that put the "chapter" together. Indeed, only the language of what is located in the extreme righthand column of our scored charting of m. Gittin 1:1-2:2 has not been largely determined by the chapter's rhetorical "machine." That remainder appears, moreover, relatively insignificant as a proportion of the chapter's language. In short, while it is reasonable that some significant proportion of Mishnah's law rests upon earlier rulings and traditions, the language of Mishnah's sources is irretrievably gone. Moreover, the degree of reformulation of these supposed antecedent sources is such that one must consider whether the content, too, of these sources has been significantly modified in being recast so as to be integrated into the mishnaic context as typically mishnaic content, that is, with the appropriate level of homophony and homo- or antisemantics.[2]

My third interim point is a related text-historical conclusion of methodological consequence to matters of the meaning and significance of mish-

---

2. Neusner (1981) gives an account of his adaptation of H.A. Wolfson's "hypothetical deductive method" to piece together a "history" of Mishnah's purity law. Applying this method Neusner attempted to describe 'mishnaic' purity law's several stages of development from before 70CE to 200CE. It is undeniable that Neusner's method produced consistent and coherent results. However, Neusner's method is designed to stratify mishnaic law by relatively broad legal themes and subjects. It cannot establish that the particular formulation of a given case treated in Mishnah predates the work of Mishnah's authors. Our provisional findings suggest that the opposite is the case for much of Mishnah. This has serious repercussions in talking about the "history" of mishnaic law, for it implies that Mishnah's editors have (re)fashioned the details of the cases to which rulings are attached. Moreover, the precise character of the rulings are also formulated in accordance with the rhetorical requisites of the final document. So we must seriously ask ourselves whether *in their details* mishnaic law predates Mishnah? I suspect not, and I suggest that only the legal themes or problem areas defined by earlier late first- and second-century rabbis may have informed Mishnah's authors.

naic rhetoric. On the basis of the evidence adduced I further propose that a proportion of Mishnah's legal cases has been generated by the stylistic rules that have
governed the authors' enterprise. For example, I argued in connection with the
data in charts 3 and 4 that mishnaic rhetoric defines and creates unity within subunits by tightly patterned homophonic/antisemantic sequences like: day-day/night-
night/night-day/day-night in 2:2. One effect of adhering to this rhetorical requisite
is that it generates cases merely by the permutation of homophonic/antisemantic
markers. Mishnah's editors must then provide rulings for these rhetorically created cases, whether or not the cases thereby generated are even problematic or
cogent. Who needs to be told that a writ of divorce both written and signed during
the daytime on the self-same day is a valid writ? Surely the case appears only
because of the demands of good mishnaic rhetorical style. Indeed, the redactors of
the Babylonian Talmud tacitly admit that this is the case; with respect to such
junctures in Mishnah where permutated lists of cases appear, the Babylonian Talmud asks, Why do I [need] all these [cases to be ruled upon] (see, e.g., b. Bekorot
2a)?

Taken together our interim, preliminary claims about the evidence at hand
add up to the following: Mishnah's authors adopt a deliberate, distinctive rhetorical style, the demands of which not only largely efface the language of any antecedent sources but also (re)fashion cases and rulings, even to the point of generating
(sometimes unproblematic) cases for the purposes of "completing" or "rounding
out" a tightly patterned rhetorical sequence. I submit that, to a significant degree,
precise content in Mishnah is the handmaiden of Mishnah's rhetorical style and
patterning. What assertions, then, are implicitly communicated in that rhetoric?

As an entry to addressing this question, I would recall two aspects of Mishnah. First, J. Neusner has claimed–and I have concurred–that the major subdivisions of mishnaic tractates, their "chapters," are "whole" and "complete" in that
their content emerges from a generative problematic systematically explored to
the point of logical and topical closure. Second, Neusner called Mishnah's enterprise *Listenwissenschaft*, the "paratactic" (to use W.S. Green's term) presentation
of arrays of cases and their ordering and classification with respect to whether one
rule or another applies. Through this exercise an ordered, fictive, and ideal world
is defined, in which the Jerusalem Temple yet stands, and Temple-based judiciary
and legislative institutions still operate under the charge of the traditional priestly
classes and their scribal bureaucracy. Here, too, I concur, and, in support of this
point, my own rhetorical studies of Mishnah demonstrate that the dominant stock
terminology of Mishnah is "conjunctive" as opposed to "logico-argumentative."
That is to say, Mishnah's stock terminological operators, as we have seen, rather
meagre in variety, serve almost exclusively to join discrete items together. This is
dramatically demonstrated in scored chartings of Mishnah passages by the relative
paucity of materials in column 2 and the frequent appearance of terms in column
1.

To a certain extent it is, however, a serious overstatement to assert that
Mishnah defines an ideal ordered "world" through the production of com-
prehensive lists of classified objects or circumstances which comprise that world.
How so? First, and most obvious, much of that ideal world is left undefined.

Whole tractates, about such matters as circumcision, burial, mourning, business, and economics, to name just a few, are absent. Second, Why do tractates end where they do, some with over 30 chapters, others with only four? Both the tractate on Sabbath, one of the longest, and the tractate on court decrees (i.e., m. Horayot), one of the shortest, are incomplete in the sense that one may readily define relevant problems or topics from which whole additional chapters for either tractate may be spun out. Third, it is somewhat of an exaggeration to assert that the deliberations of a "chapter" of a Mishnah tractate bring to closure and completion the generative topic at hand. For one, Tosefta demonstrates how easily one may extend and augment any Mishnah "chapter's" topical program. Whence, then, the distinctive *impression* of closure, comprehensiveness, and wholeness of Mishnah "chapters?"

I suggest that the strong impression of closure, comprehensiveness, and wholeness in Mishnah derives in large measure from its rhetoric. That rhetoric, we have seen, relies most heavily on three techniques: (1) morphological repetition, which itself provides a kind of alliteration and assonance; (2) the repetition of similar or identical words and phrases, or of paired opposites, which provide a kind of rhyme, rhythm, and metre, and at times a kind of mechanistic permutative quality to the text; (3) the linking of items with the above-mentioned qualities by means of several, repeated, stock, conjunctive formulae ("and," "which/that," "except," and perhaps "says") which give the text not only a list-like quality but a litany-like one. The techniques in themselves seem more appropriate to classical poetry, or, for that matter, to choral lyrical texts, than to classical legal documents.

The use in Mishnah of these rhetorical patterns extends beyond providing poetic or lyrical effects. The first and second techniques also define larger thematic units: (1) they serve to establish a unit's beginning and end; and (2) they appear at various junctures in between to recall the opening and anticipate the closing of the unit. These same techniques function to mark off and unify subunits with their respective subthemes and to link subunits to sentences which carry those markers that establish the whole.

I can illustrate the use of these rhetorical mechanisms by means of an overly simplified schema of a contrived Mishnah "chapter." In that schema the letter "M" represents a morphological marker and the letters "b," "c," "d/d'," and "e" each stand for homophonic and/or antisemantic markers. I suggest that the rhetorical pattern of a "characteristic" short Mishnah "chapter" might schematically look like:

> pericope 1. M and b and c;
> pericope 2. [(c, d) and (c, not d')] | [(not c, d') and (not c, d)];
> perciope 3. M and b and c;
> pericope 4. [M, b, e] | [M, e, b];
> pericope 5. M and b and c.

The "whole" is established by rhetorical markers present at "pericopes" 1, 3, and 5. "Pericopes" 2 and 4 each display their own internal unifying patterning but are rhetorically linked to 1,3, and 5.

The schema of our fictive Mishnah chapter aptly demonstrates what I earlier proposed: the combined effect is not so much poetic as lyrical or musical in a baroque-like manner; "musical" phrases recur and are "inverted" in permutative ways, while an overall "theme" periodically reasserts itself to define the whole "movement." All this transpires at a level above and beyond, or, at times, imposing itself upon and affecting, Mishnah's content. In a very real sense, the order, patterning, coherence, and unity evident in Mishnah at the rhetorical level equal or exceed that of the ideal "world" defined in Mishnah's laws, which are necessarily non-comprehensive and illustrative, and are amenable to completion and supplementation. It is, then, in Mishnah's lyrical rhetoric that the authors have communicated (implicitly) their aspirations toward complete, well-patterned "wholes" and convey to the reader/auditor their conviction that the purpose of Mishnah-law is to strive toward, or exemplify the process of, defining that whole by means of legal classification. Having perceived that implicitly communicated message, scholars of Mishnah have appropriately sought that expected comprehensive wholeness in Mishnah's legal content.

Recalling our initial discussion of theoretical and conceptual issues, two sets of questions remain. The first concerns rhetoric as an "artifact" of, or model for, authority and authoritativeness within a social setting for which it was recognized as "appropriate." In what social context and in accordance with what accepted social models of authority might Mishnah's rhetoric have been perceived as "normal," cogent, and *prima facie* persuasive?[3] And, in a related vein, what modes of authority and authoritativeness does Mishnah model for those who accepted the document as "canonical?" The second set of queries concerns our theoretical model that humanly created "universes" have for their participants an air of self-evidence because in humanly ordered realm after realm basic patterns recur. The experience of this recurrence or "homology of patterning" psycho-emotionally reinforces shared perceptions of that "universe." In this vein we may inquire whether the type of rhetorical patterning found in Mishnah replicated in some basic manner the "shape" of other aspects of the humanly created universe inhabited by rabbis at the end of the second century and the beginning of the third.

Addressing these questions, particularly the latter, requires some reconstruction, on evidentiary grounds other than the rhetoric itself, of the institutional provenaces of late second- and early third-century Palestinian Rabbinism. Such a task, and an assessment within that context of Mishnah's particular rhetoric, constitute my current, ongoing research. What I offer in the remainder of this chapter must, therefore, be understood to be a preliminary statement only.

III.ii. Mishnaic rhetoric and early rabbis as priestly-scribes

We have found in Mishnah the repeated use of (1) concatenating conjunctive terminology; (2) morphological repetition, especially of verb forms and participial nouns (like, "One who brings," המביא); and (3) several hierarchically organized, encompassing or bounded levels of homophony, homosemantics, and

---

3.   When the question is phrased in this manner, its seems probable, even evident, that J. Neusner's thesis that Mishnah's literary features facilitate promulgation through memorization and oral transmission, while in itself correct, is an incomplete response.

antisemantics. Moreover, the last-named rhetorical device in particular is (4) used in a poetic and lyrical fashion characterized not only by simple repetition but also by systematic inversion and permutation; these techniques (5) impart unity, coherence, boundaries, and a sense of completeness and closure to rhetorical-topical "chapters" and subsections of "chapters." Thus the language of Mishnah, so often said to be terse and laconic to the point of near unintelligibility without substantial interpolation, is also repetitive, permutative almost to the point of redundancy and substantive triviality, where self-evident rulings about clearly unproblematic circumstances may appear simply to complete the permutative rhetorical process.

What is not to be found in mishnaic rhetoric? Most obvious is the lack of persuasion through what I or, in my view, ancient Greek and Latin rhetoricians would recognize as argument. Let me elaborate upon and nuance this last claim, since it is the reason I have invited Vernon K. Robbins to attempt to (re-)describe the structure of m. Gittin 1:1-2:2 in terms of the rhetorical 'canons' of the *Rhetorica ad Herennium* and Hermogenes' *Progymnasmata*. Robbins argues that the organization of the elements constituting this Mishnah chapter can be characterized as instances of these canons of rhetorical elaboration. The fact that Robbins can do this does not mean that mishnaic rhetoric is simply or primarily an instance of the deliberate application of these canons; it does not mean that classical rhetorical elaboration is what mishnaic rhetoric 'is about' with respect to the social significance of Mishnah's pervasive rhetorical features. Robbins's analysis does demonstrate that the 'fit' of such classical greco-roman rhetorical canons upon a mishnaic "chapter" can be achieved. But, to my mind, Robbins's work equally highlights that the fit is a rather 'loose' or 'highly general' one. Being a mishnaic master seems quite different from, or askew of, being a rhetor, despite the similarities adduced by Robbins, even when one makes allowances for the fact that Mishnah stands within a particular Judaic authoritative tradition of the Greco-Roman society and culture. At best, then, being a mishnaic master seems such a highly particular or specific mode of being a Greco-Roman rhetor that it is in such specificities that the social meaning of Mishnah's rhetorical features will best be sought.[4]

What else does Mishnah seem not to be or do? There is little explicit attempt to justify either why a case is cogent or why the ruling is appropriate. There is little or no explicit appeal to the authority of antecedent authoritative texts or bodies of tradition. (The attribution of "disputing" opinions to named

---

4.   My own conclusion is that the similarities adduced by Robbins in the appendix are a result of the fact that those who produced Mishnah understood good organization. Moreover, many of the classical Greco-Roman canons of rhetorical elaboration are themselves induced from observation of what counted as well organized attempts at persuasion in Greco-Roman literature and social venues with which the framers of these canons were familiar. At this rather basic level, it should little surprise one that what counts as good organization in the latter should also be present in the former. After all the authors of Mishnah and Greco-Roman rhetoricians were both part of eastern Mediterranean society in the late Roman period.

authorities is arguably no substitute for such justification, as virtually all authorities "cited" in Mishnah are "johnny-come-latelys" at the time of Mishnah's authorship; they are essentially "mishnaic" masters.) Nor does one generally find contrary positions or counter-arguments raised in order to be surmounted. There is virtually no appeal to analogy, or use of simile or metaphor. We find little or no invoking of ancient, longstanding practice or historical origins. Finally, Mishnah's authors do not even present a discursive, coherent account of any one subarea of mishnaic law, like Maimonides' code, in which account a certain degree of justification and persuasion derives expressly from the systematic, almost essay-like, didactic quality in spelling out and explication of a legal topic area.[5] Mishnah's rhetoric is anything but didactic and only remotely discursive; that is why the student of Mishnah is so challenged in understanding the implicit rationale and unifying reasoning that governs the spinning out of cases and their attendant rulings in a given topic area. That the general absence in Mishnah of these modes of argument or persuasion is significant and meaningful is indicated, in part, by the very fact that at episodic junctures in Mishnah one discovers virtually all of these types of argument and justification.

We are left then to consider what form of authority and authoritativeness is reflected and/or modelled in the lyrical, permutative, list-like concatenation of cases and rulings, in which the inner logic remains ever implicit and in which "lyrical" completeness is sometimes in itself sufficient, implicit justification for including a case in a list.

The question, admittedly, is so framed as to imply an answer: I propose that the ability to compose and spin out such lists in such a lyrical fashion was in and of itself a principal *hallmark* and *mode* of authoritativeness constituting the "mastery" of the "mishnaic" rabbi (literally "my master"). As a corollary I further suggest that by their very appearance in such a lyrical, permutative list, both the rules for specified cases and the "system"[6] which these rules comprise gain an air of self-evident appropriateness. That is to say, the rhetorical form bespeaks the authority of the list-maker-lyricist "master" and lends authority to individual items in the list, to the list as a whole, and to the emerging legal system contained in a series of topically related lists.

To further characterize the mode of social authority modelled in Mishnah's rhetorical character, let us turn to some pervasive traits of the substance, as opposed to the rhetorical patterns, of Mishnah.

Mishnah, as noted, presents organized, "coherent," and "complete" (in the rhetorical and lyrical sense) lists of cases.[7] But each case must then be ruled upon.

---

5. Compare, for example, m.Gittin 1:1-2:2 (analyzed in this essay) to chapter 1 of Maimonides' Mishneh Torah, Hilkot Gittin. The Constitutions of Justinian have this same essay-like or treatise-like, almost didactic quality.
6. That mishnaic rulings constitute a mishnaic legal "system," that is, within large areas of law a coherently ordered realm emerges from and, therefore, informs the rulings, has been argued by J. Neusner in a number of works. See, e.g., Neusner, 1981 and, more recently, Neusner, 1989b.
7. This and the five subsequent paragraphs repeat, with substantial revision and expansion, the argument of a section of Lightstone, 1995.

And by so doing, Mishnah's list-maker in effect proceeds to classify each case with respect to whether one rule or another applies. Where do these cases "come from" and what is the total effect of their classification with respect to whether the rule is one way or another?

We have already either shown or intimated that cases tend to arise for classification for one of several reasons: rhetorically, they may result from the systematic permutation of circumstances (such as, a+b/a-b/-a+b/-a-b, where "a" and "b" may be circumstances which may be present or absent);[8] a case may arise because it serves to develop and systematically treat a topic (see Neusner, 1981; 1989b); a case may arise because an underlying, general principle, like the role of human intention, is indirectly put forward and explored by generating a series of cases in which intention is the operative variable that determines the ruling (see Neusner, 1981; 1989b). In all of these instances, one may say that the cases or situations Mishnah classifies by its rulings are "ideal" or "imaginary." That is not to say they cannot arise or have never arisen in historical "reality." Rather, I mean to say only that, that is not why cases tend to arise or be included in Mishnah.[9] There is another, more concrete way in which Mishnah's classified legal system concerns an imaginary or ideal world. Mishnah's laws assume the operation of the entire Temple system of cult, judiciary and legislature, and administration. Much of Mishnah's laws directly concern that Temple system. True, a number of legal subject areas treated by Mishnah may apply (as well) outside of, or apart from, the Temple. But in Mishnah, as a whole, the overarching Temple cult and government is the assumed larger context. Insofar as that Temple system had ceased to exist between one-and-a-quarter and one-and-a-half centuries before Mishnah's authorship, Mishnah's Temple system is an "ideal" reconstruction of the original.[10]

Mishnah, then, focuses on an enduring underlying classification of the "objects" of its "ideal" or "imaginary" world (both physical and social). For Mishnah, it would appear, that ideal world and its inherent order constitute the enduringly real. That is the world worth classifying in lyrical, ordered lists. That is the world the mastery of which makes one a master. To be an expert in Mishnah, that is, to study and know its lists, to comprehend its underlying classificatory system, and to understand the principles which inform that system, is to be a living, breathing

8.   In this regard, compare chapters 1, 2, and 8 of Mishnah Bekorot, which spin out three sets of parallel cases by means of the identical permutation of circumstances. In other words, the subject matter of the shank of three chapters (out of a total of nine) are *generated* by the same permutative exercise.

9.   Again, I think that such a conclusion follows from the combined results of our analyses of the rhetorical patterning of Mishnah "chapters" and the results of Neusner's analysis of the legal content of Mishnah (see Neusner, 1981; 1989b).

10. None of the above is meant to say that all of Mishnah's portrayal of the Temple-centred world is necessarily fictive. Just as Mishnah is not primarily an act of remembering that historical world, a systematic attempt at forgetting, either. Rather, the focus of Mishnah's framers is elsewhere and better captured by the terms "ideal," "imaginative," "hypothetical," or "theoretical," than by the words "remembering," "forgetting," "historical," or "fictive." For an entirely different perspective on Mishnah's content and historical realities to which it may relate, see Maccoby, 1986; Gafni, 1987.

text of Mishnah's mapping of reality. Virtuosity and authority derive from knowing how the world really is. Insofar as the study and comprehension of Mishnah played a significant part in becoming a rabbi, a "master," in the Land of Israel in the early third century, then the rabbi claimed "mastery" because the rabbi is the comprehensive repository of knowledge about and the underlying principles of "the world order" as expressed by Mishnah's lists.

In the Near East during Classical, Greco-Roman, and Late Antiquity, temples and their officials–priests, scribes (and sometimes prophets)–were the repositories and guardians of such knowledge. Thus in Egypt the "sacred books" resided in temples under the aegis of its "priests, scribes and prophets" (see Fishbane, 1985:21-37; J.Z. Smith, 1978; Breasted, 1962, 1964; Harris, 1971). II Kings portrays Josiah's reform as having been sparked by finding "the Torah of Moses" in a repository in the Jerusalem Temple. And Mishnah itself supposes that an official copy of the Torah resides in the Temple (Mishnah Kelim 15:6). When in Sassanid Persia the Zend-Avesta was first committed to writing, a limited number of copies were deposited in several major temples in different districts of the Empire. In these temples the official versions could be consulted to resolve all doubt about "how things really are." This transpired even as Zoroastrian tradition and "literature" endured on a day-to-day basis in its oral form among the priests of local Zoroastrian shrines (see Boyce 1986:132-44). Indeed, it is remarkable and highly instructive that with respect to basic rhetorical features Late Sassanid Zoroastrian literature provides such close comparisons to Mishnah and its particular *Listenwissenschaft*. The *Bundahis* (ca. sixth or seventh century CE), like much of the earlier Zend-Avestan literature of which the *Bundahis* is a partial epitome, is overwhelmingly preoccupied with classification and list-making. In Zoroastrian ritual or legal texts from the end of the Sassanid era, the likeness to Mishnah's use of language emerges more starkly still. Anyone who has analyzed the literary form of Mishnah and who has dealt with the content of its Division of Purities will feel herself or himself in familiar territory in reading the *Shayast La-Shayast*. In all, the *Shayast La-Shayast* exhibits the preoccupation with classificatory list-making evident in the Bundahis, but translated into a legal framework.[11] In the case of the *Bundahis* and the *Shayast La-Shayast*, however, actual cultic centres continue to function even after the Muslim conquest. These fire temples provide the context for the preservation and application of these documents (Boyce 1986:132-44). Indeed, in both the Sassanid and Muslim periods literary activity remained the principal prerogative of the priestly class and associated temple personnel.

In light of the above, it is noteworthy that the "world" constructed by Mishnah's lists is one in which the Temple and its related institutions of cult, national governance, administration, and judiciary (destroyed over a century earlier) con-

---

11.   While I have been struck by the similarity of the *Bundahis* and the *Shayast La-Shayast* to Mishnah at the level of general rhetorical characteristics, I note that J. Neusner has remarked upon the formal similarity between another post-mishnaic rabbinic document, Sifra, and the Pahlavi *Nirangestan* (Neusner, 1987a:102).

stitute the centre (see Neusner, 1981). With the perspective provided by Zoroastrian texts dating from around the Muslim conquest of Persia, one may better appreciate that with the demise of the Jerusalem cult, rabbis presented themselves through Mishnah as priest-like or priestly-scribe-like and, therefore, as the direct inheritors of priestly knowledge and priestly authority. Clearly establishing that claim and implicitly asserting in Mishnah that the "world" has not fundamentally changed with the destruction of the Jerusalem cult (see Neusner, 1981) appears for nascent Rabbinism a first important order of business. Indeed, perhaps that is precisely why Mishnah is not generally couched as a reminiscence or even reconstruction of that "world," but as an attempt at construction, development, and extension of it. The Temple world in some sense exists still; and so does priestly-scribe-like authority. Therefore, as priestly-scribe-like "masters" they do not lay claim to the authority merely to preserve but also to create and define that ordered, coherent Temple-centred universe, a claim which can only be acted upon and realized in the abstract and in an ideal "realm." The ordered, coherent, permutative, lyrically balanced, and bounded character of mishnaic rhetorical patterns is the counterpart in rhetoric of the implicit claims to the priestly-scribal authority to define in Mishnah's legal classificatory system an ordered, ever-more coherent, encompassing ideal world. The order and coherence of the lyrical rhetorical patterning in itself lends a sense of order and completeness to the "world" as given in Mishnah's legal content, which can, in fact, only ever be a partial, proximate, and incomplete rendering.

Mishnah, then, chooses to describe in hierarchical lists and related rules this "classical" Temple-centred world and thereby implies that its model enduringly holds. It does this rather than focus upon the institutions which by 200CE must already have emerged to replace that Temple and its administration. This fact represents clearly the kind of authority to which Mishnah's editors wished to lay claim. The rabbis and their disciples who produced and received the Mishnah, were a kind of priest, even while patently they were not. Perhaps it would be more appropriate to say that they thereby portrayed themselves as the direct successors of the Jerusalem priests, possessing their knowledge of "the world" and exercising the attendant authority of the now defunct priesthood. Among the skills which one would expect such a priest-like guild to value would be those related to (1) accurate retention and transmission of relevant data; and, more importantly, (2) extension and development of knowledge to its fullest extent. Indeed (the probably post-mishnaic)[12] Mishnah Tractate Avot, perhaps the first apology for

---

12. The scholarly consensus on the dating of Avot is treated by J. Neusner (1987a:152). For myself, I find remarkable the apparent lack of interest among scholars concerning the dating of Avot. For example, neither A. Goldberg (1987a:211-62) nor M.B. Lerner (1987:263-82) pronounce on the issue. Why should the matter attract so little attention? I suspect that if one is of the view that sayings attributed in Avot to particular rabbinic masters stem in some significant sense from them, then the issue of the dating of these sayings' "collection" in a document diminishes in importance. But surely this is to put matters backwards, since the literary characteristics and dating of the document must greatly affect one's assessment of the meaning and reliability of the attributions to earlier masters.

the authority of early rabbinic traditions and masters, expresses the importance of at least the former as a key rabbinic intellectual virtue.

III.iii. Mishnaic rhetoric and the organization and institutionalization of the early rabbinic movement

Thus the Mishnah rhetorically reinforces and reflects a portrayal of elite, authoritative virtuosity which may be characterized as a mastery of guardianship of the old priestly-scribally stewarded social and cultic order. That mode of virtuosity is directly represented in the substantive agenda of Mishnah, in which unit-circumstances of a Temple-centred world are classified with respect to whether one rule or another applies (Neusner, 1981; 1989b). In addition, that mastery of guardianship of a divine, allegedly complete, and bounded social and cultic world order is paralleled by a rhetorical style of an almost lyrical nature. In that rhetoric subject domains in the text (its substantive "chapters") are defined, structured, marked off, and bounded by successive, encompassing levels of repetition of morphological forms and of "sound bytes," and subtopics gain an air of completeness and closure via systematic permutation of phrases and words. In all, the lyrical rhetoric is itself an homology of the Temple-centred world assumed and partially defined in Mishnah's substance.

Why might such a model of the "real" world, whether communicated explicitly in Mishnah's substantive agenda or represented implicitly in Mishnah's lyrical rhetoric, be experienced as particularly cogent, and self-evidently appropriate, by late second- or early third-century rabbis? Or to put matters otherwise, what aspects of these rabbis' organized lives together might be implicitly, homologically reflected and reinforced in the rhetoric of their first authoritative *oeuvre*? Surely, as we have argued, that "lived" organized world is not the Temple state or even a memory of the lived experience of the order of that Temple state. That order does not exist except in the intellectual pursuits that define the early circles of rabbinic masters and disciples. The hypothesis suggested by the evidence seems clear. If there is a lived order with a similarly bounded, closed topography reflected in Mishnah, we should look toward the institutionalized life of the rabbinic circle(s) of master(s) and disciples as the (re)new(ed) Temple and priesthood. Here are neither itinerant, charismatic missionaries of a new cult that transcends ethnic and national boundaries, like the emergent, Roman church universal, nor local Holy Men who provide the focus of loyalty for a distinct sub-community in a larger society. For the circle of masters and disciples *is* society, *is* Israel, as it should be according to the Pentateuchal constitution of Yahweh's Temple state. And like the realm outside the Temple state, the social territory outside the group is the undifferentiated, chaotic realm of polluted things.

To explore this hypothesis of the reciprocal, reinforcing, homological relationship between the literary and rhetorical traits of Mishnah and social mappings or transformations of the organized rabbinic movement at the end of the second century and the beginning of the third, I must recall my earlier warning concerning the severe limitations imposed by the evidence. What, then, may one say with either requisite caution or qualifiers? On the one hand, one may note with confidence that named persons, in particular, named rabbinic figures from the several generations preceding Mishnah's redactors, figure so importantly at the turn of the third century that attributions to them must be preserved, and, on the other, that they must be neutralized or homogenized within some overarching, unified system and pervasive rhetoric, that effaces all personal traits. These persons matter a great deal, at the same time as their mattering at all is a situation to be overcome. That appears to me to be one meaning communicated by Mishnah's literary and formal characteristics. In few words, we see a turning point from individual item to overarching system and encompassing, lyrical rhetoric, just as Mishnah takes each item of its (ideal) world and integrates it into an all-inclusive taxonomy communicated in a pervasive rhetoric.

In these aspects, Mishnah may offer a precise homology for the social and political transformation of the rabbinic movement occurring from approximately 165CE to 220CE. Of this transformation we have only the vaguest echoes. Indeed, given the problematic nature of even that evidence which exists, any attempts to describe the events in question must not be mistaken by the reader as anything more than speculation. Let me tie these threads of evidence together.

A number of students of Mishnah have noted a veiled conflict invading some mishnaic and (especially) toseftan legal pericopae, between the rabbinate and the patriarchate. In a number of instances, that conflict is expressed openly, as in the story of the deposition of Gamaliel II (see Goldenberg, 1977). Tosefta, which has many more narrative passages than Mishnah and which dates perhaps as early as several decades after Mishnah's redaction, registers several such sources, as well as a depiction of rabbinic organization at the turn of the second century in which the rabbinic movement found its unified institutionalization in a "college" of rabbis, of which the patriarch was the president. The latter is portrayed at times as "first among equals" and at times as simply "first" outright. The college is depicted as having both legal and judicial authority, as well as an instructional mandate.

Two observations *ab initio* lead me to suspect that all of these sentiments, conflicts, and institutional forms are anachronistically assigned to the end of the first century and the beginning of the second. First, the passages from which these impressions are culled cannot with certainty be dated earlier than AD200 or so. Second, stories from third- to sixth-century sources depict the relationship between Judah the Patriarch (died ca. 220) and the rabbinate as particularly stormy at times. Third, only in stories from third- to sixth-century sources about the "administration" of Judah the Patriarch, do we have claims put forward by rabbinic literature regarding Roman authorities working with, and therefore tacitly recognizing the authority of, the rabbinic college led by its Patriarch, initially Judah. (It matters not whether that recognition by Rome was indeed the case.) In sum, the evidence, meagre (and, in some cases, late) as it is, may derive from some important organizational transformation of Rabbinism at the end of the second and beginning of the third centuries. This transformation appears to have taken place in the time, and probably under the auspices, of Judah, whose authority so to transform rabbinism may have been in serious doubt among the rabbis.

With this set of working hypotheses in hand, some of the redactional Tendenzen in evidence in the earlier mishnaic and toseftan sources may be rendered more intelligible. A representative analysis will suffice to sensitize one to the editorial artifacts both of the transformation referred to, and its retrojection to an earlier period in the development of rabbinism.

Mishnah Sanhedrin 2:1ff and the correlative pericopes at Tosefta Sanhedrin 8:1, both of which in their current versions stem from late second and early third centuries, provide an apt example of the phenomenon described. The two pericopes document successive stages in the projection upon the earliest rabbinism of a unified, institutionalized rabbinic body. The passages are all the more interesting because that projection operates at the implicit level; a set of assumptions appears to have informed the editorial processes that gave the pericopes their final forms. Mishnah Sanhedrin 4:3-4a purports to provide a description of the Great or the Lesser Sanhedrin in pre-70 Palestine. As is the case with much of Mishnah's pericopes dealing with the world of the Temple cult and Temple-based government, m. Sanh. 4:3-4a would be more safely regarded as an ideal reconstruction. Already in the Mishnah text, however, the description of the Great Sanhedrin is rabbinized.

A.1   The Sanhedrin was [arranged] as a semi-circle [the size of half of] a threshing floor,
A.2.   so that they [the members] may see one another.
B.   And two scribes of the judges stand before them, and write the laudatory evidence and the condemning evidence.
C.1.   Rabbi Judah says, three [scribes]:
C.1.1. one writes the laudatory evidence,
C.1.2. and one writes the condemning evidence,
C.1.3. and the third writes the laudatory evidence and the condemning evidence.
D.   And three rows of the disciples of the sages sit before them.
E.   Each and every one [of the disciples] knows his place [in the seating order].

[Mishnah Sanhedrin 4:3-4a]

The pericope is currently cast as a narrative. In reality, the form is typically mishnaic; its narrative elements remain superficial. The mere substitution at A.1 of a participle for the verb "to be" in the perfect tense transforms the whole into language and form typical of the greater part of Mishnah at its general, penultimate level of redaction. Thus A is an anonymous law, followed by a mishnaic dispute at B-C dependent upon A for intelligibility. D proffers another anonymous law, similarly dependent upon A. I stress the superficiality of the narrative characteristics for obvious reasons. The whole from a stylistic standpoint is part and parcel of Mishnah's general literary framework (and no doubt purpose), and, therefore, prima facie cannot be separated from the late second-century context of Mishnah's penultimate redactors.

As to the pericope's substance, D is most enlightening for our purpose. For until D we have only Mishnah's ideal formulation of a non or pre-rabbinic Israelite legislative and judicial body. No rabbinic title or office appears in A-C. The terms, "scribes of the judges" in B has no rabbinic ring to it. D, however, rabbinizes the whole, by introducing the disciples of the sages, a standard rabbinic title. D, then, would have us view the members of the Sanhedrin as sages, that is, rabbis. By implication, the permanent presence of the disciples of the sages also turns the idealized institution of A into an institution of learning (or of training) as well as a judiciary or legislative body, as is established by the context. Here then in a pericope of late second-century formulation is evidence that rabbinism had begun to see an authoritative council constituted of rabbis and rabbis-in-training as a principle institution of Israel in which were merged legislative, judicial, and educational mandates. This view of matters they projected backward into the period before 70CE.

Viewing Mishnah Sanhedrin in this light makes the glosses provided by the editors of Tosefta all the more understandable. For they take still further the *Tendenzen* of the Mishnah's editor. In the passage which follows, direct citations of the Mishnah appear in boldface.

A.1   **The Sanhedrin was [arranged] as a semi-circle [the size of half of] a threshing floor,**

A.2.   so that they [the members] may see one another.

B.1.   The nasi sits in the middle [position on the circumference],

B.2.   and [the] elders sit to his right and to his left.

C.   Said Rabbi Eleazar b. Rabbi Sadoq, "When Rabban Gamaliel sat at Yavneh, [my] father sat to his right and [the] elders to his left.

D.1.   And why did one aged-man sit to his right?

D.2.   because of the honour due an aged-man.

E.1.   **Three rows of the disciples of the sages sit before them,**

E.2.   the greatest in the first, the second ranked in the second, and the third ranked in the third.

> [Tosefta Sanhedrin 8:1; see also parallel, Yerushalmi Sanhedrin 1:4]

The (apparent) gloss at C of the Mishnah citation (at A) functions to make explicit the rabbinic constitution of the Sanhedrin. In addition, in its present context C represents the organization of the sages at Yavneh in the decades following the events of 70CE as in continuity with the institutions of governance before the destruction. The sages, now clearly under the presidency of the rabbinic *nasi* (Gamaliel II) are portrayed as functioning at Yavneh in the same manner and capacity as their predecessors of the earlier period.

It is, however, only by appending C to A and B that the toseftan editors achieve this effect. C, however, does not depend in literary terms on A-B. C in no significant manner reflects the language of A. Only the reference to elders finds a counterpart in B–hardly enough to show literary dependency, as opposed to editorial refinement. D glosses and does depend upon C; "elder" at D must mean "more aged" and does not designate an office, as is the case in B. In all, C (with or without the further explanatory gloss of D) is intelligible on its own. As such there is no reason to suppose that it originally glossed either our Mishnah passage, that it refers to the Sanhedrin, rabbinized or not, or that it relates to any other formal, institutionalized council or academy. C, viewed as a tradition independent of the current context, merely offers an attributed narrative as precedent for a simple protocol, custom or etiquette (made explicit at D), which dictates that the place of honour in a seating arrangement belongs to the older person. It is, then, via the editorial processes of early third-century rabbinic circles that an early rabbinic sanhedrin/academy ruled by a rabbi-patriarch appears before us.

The toseftan and mishnaic passages just analyzed provide just two examples of how late second- or early third-century editors shape or reshape their materials in a manner that implies or assumes the prior existence of an institution which the texts upon closer analysis belie. As one peruses, however, still later sources dealing with rabbinic organization in the late first and second centuries, the explicit portrayals of a sanhedrin/academy led by the *nasi* become commonplace, as we noted.

I cannot attempt here an exhaustive treatment either of the subject or of the primary sources. (A good study of the evolution of early Palestinian rabbinic institutions is waiting for an author.) Our analysis of two interdependent pericopae suffices to lend credence to the notion that rabbinism was not organized about a central sanhedrin/academy under patriarchal rule before the latter decades of the second century. Moreover, that redactors of the late second and early third centuries reshape materials in a manner that projects such an institution back onto an earlier period suggests that such an institution accords with their contemporary state of affairs. In this regard, one may note with interest the language of such passages in Tosefta as Shevi'it 4:17 (ed. Zuckermandel p. 67, line 5): "Rabbi [Judah the Patriarch] and his court (בית דינו) permitted ... [it]."

The end of the second century, therefore, marks a major transformation in the organizational structure of rabbinism. (From what, we have yet to say.) The editing and promulgation of Mishnah as rabbinism's official document coincides with that structural evolution or revolution.

What now of that which went before? We turn now to that state of affairs that obtained earlier in the second century and, probably, at the close of the first. Again the literary and rhetorical characteristics of Mishnah implicitly communicate much.

We have already adduced a number of Mishnah's literary and substantive traits in support of our argument. Specifically, we have referred to the laconic, truncated, and highly formalized nature of Mishnah's language. Attributed and unattributed materials appear to be couched in the same pervasive forms and formularies. So the individual, and to all appearances the individual's view, is preserved, but in name only. For not only the style but the substance of attributed materials has been recast by redactors to fit the larger context. In terms of Mishnah's substance, we have already mentioned that Mishnah, via its laconic, truncated, list-like rulings, constructs an ideal world, organized as concentric, bounded realms around a central Temple cult and Temple-based government. Items of that world, especially problematic ones, are considered for the purposes of exploring, defining, and maintaining the taxonomy upon which that ideal construction depends (Lightstone, 1988; Neusner, 1983b). At this point, we must recall some characteristics of Mishnah in service of our argument.

As intimated earlier, much of Mishnah, indeed almost all of the fifth order and much of the sixth, systematically develops Pentateuchal law (see Neusner, 1983b). In light of this state of affairs, so assiduously to avoid citing or acknowledging scripture can only be deliberate and significant. Since in language and modes of analysis Mishnah exhibits a closed, self-contained character, I attribute the lack of references to scripture to the same avoidance. Namely, here too Mishnah would retain its boundedness and closure, requiring reference to nothing outside of itself, even to scripture.

So Mishnah's feigned independence from scripture, viewed in larger structural terms, appears readily intelligible, particularly so when one considers that those same circles responsible for Mishnah, and its portrayal of an ideal, circumscribed, Temple-centred universe fixed the canon of Hebrew Scriptures. Both fixed and closed wholes, Mishnah and scripture structurally mirror each other; each lends weight and credibility to the perceptions of a world implicitly and explicitly conveyed by the other.

I argued above (see also Lightstone, 1988) that shared perceptions of reality, whether communicated explicitly or implicitly in word, ritual, and literature, retain their saliency and verisimilitude because of their relationship to social experience. Social institutions are thereby made to "feel" particularly well suited to "the way things really are" in the world. The early rabbis in imagining the contours of sacred space mirror in scriptural canon and in Mishnah their social institutions and experience, to the limited degree that they may be described, of the first seven decades of the second century CE.

First, the earliest rabbinic groups would have had no established, traditional norms for defining rabbinic roles, institutions, or authority. Second, the immediate social context of early rabbinism appears limited to the close circle of master and disciples. This view of matters is consistent with the pervasive impetus to preserve the names, and putative traditions, of different masters with apparently diverse views. Mishnah Avot, perhaps the latest stratum of Mishnah, preserves along with the notion of the chain of tradition, an exceedingly strong ethos of discipleship, in which individual masters were "served" by and taught a limited number of closely associated disciples. The notion of "service to the master" appears in a number of passages in Tosefta. Of particular interest, and fame, is the Toseftan passage which provides an account of the origin of disputes. According to the Toseftan text the divergence of views among the early rabbis represents the detrition of Torah and the process of its transmission. Tosefta offers the failure of "disciples to serve their masters" as the explanation. Both the notion of service to the master, and the depiction of a fractious rabbinate and diversity of tradition in late first- and second- century rabbinism, as well as the negative valence assigned to that diversity are consonant with the hypothesis that earliest rabbinism was chiefly organized as small circles of masters and their disciples, and that by the end of the second century a movement toward supplanting that earlier state of affairs with some other had begun. Third, of the larger social environment, we know that the wars of 70CE and especially 135CE brought about significant dissolution of the fabric of Judean society, sparking migration of much of the Jewish populace. Thus the circle of master and disciples will have provided an island of order in this sea of chaos. Here in this insular structure, the early rabbis adumbrated in the realm of the mind a Temple state that, in their view, had once stood in the earthly Jerusalem. The latter effected in the realm of the mind that which the rabbinic circles must achieve with respect to the chaos about them.

Thus far, then, the earliest, albeit implicitly communicated testimony to the organization of earliest rabbinism in second-century Palestine. Again, Palestinian evidence from some time in the third to the fifth centuries gains in significance when considered in light of Mishnah and Tosefta. A telling example is Yerushalmi Sanhedrin 1:3.

A.	Said Rabbi [Judah the Patriarch (*nasi*)]:
B.	In the beginning each and every one used to ordain (or: designate, ממנה) their disciples.
C.1.	For instance, Rabban Yohanan b. Zakkai ordained Rabbi [E]liezer and Rabbi Joshua.
C.2.	And Rabbi Joshua, Rabbi Aqiva.
C.3.	And Rabbi Aqiva, Rabbi Meir and Rabbi Simeon.
D.	When Rabbi Meir sat [as a sage] first [i.e., before Simeon], Rabbi Simeon was despondent.
E.	Said to him Rabbi Aqiva: By your life! I and your creator recognize your strength[s].
F.1.	[The sages] reversed [their view] and bestowed honour on this house [i.e., that of the Patriarch].
F.2.	They said: A court which ordained without the foreknowledge of the *nasi*– the ordination is no ordination;
F.3.	and the nasi who ordained without the foreknowledge of the court—the ordination is an ordination.
G.1.	[Subsequently the sages] reversed [their view again] and decreed
G.2.	that a court ordains only with the foreknowledge of the *nasi*,
G.3.	and that the nasi ordains only with the foreknowledge of the court.

[Talmud Yerushalmi Sanhedrin 1:3]

The pericope comprises three principal parts. (A-B)+(F-G) appears to be the tradition attributed to Judah the Patriarch. The reference at F.1 to "this house," that is the Patriarchal dynasty, clearly means to convey the notion that Judah is still the source. Moreover, since F.1. seems integral to the language and formal traits of F-G, as shown by the parallel formulation at G.1. mitigates against concluding that F.1. is editorial joining language. Into this pre-existent unit, then, C+(D-E) has been interpolated. "For instance" at C is typically used as joining language by the Yerushalmi's redactors. Why the list (C) should have been interjected seems obvious. In its current context it serves to illustrate the point of A. But D-E offers nothing in the current context. Indeed the little excursus about Meir and Simeon takes us far afield from the intent of the pericope as a whole. In all probability D-E migrated to its current location because it already glossed C when the latter circulated independently. Why is all this literary analysis relevant to our interests?

Viewed, independently of its current context, C+(D-E) deals, like Mishnah Avot, with the chain of tradition–Yohanan to Joshua to Aqiva to Meir. Eliezer and Simeon, while ordained, do not constitute the main conduits of authoritative rabbinic tradition.

With the preoccupation of C+(D-E) removed from the field of vision, the point of the pericope as a whole becomes transparent. At issue are the changes in rabbinic organization, over what time frame we cannot say, and the tensions which arose and were addressed in the course of these developments. That these issues are dealt with indirectly via the matter of the authority to ordain makes the testimony to the changes in the institutions of rabbinic authority all the more valuable. In the beginning, according to this source, the chief institutionalized form of rabbinic authority was the individual sage, surrounded by his disciples, whom he would in time ordain as full sages. Each would then replicate the circle of his master. Subsequently, two other institutions arise. One is the rabbinic court, a term early rabbinic sources often use to refer to a council of the sages with legislative, training and judicial functions, as opposed to a court of law. The other institution is the dynastic Patriarchate. These two jockeyed for control, finally reaching a *modus vivendi*.

I would not give this later source as much credence as I do were it not the case that we find indirectly, yet explicitly, referred to institutional forms and developments implicit in much of Mishnah's pervasive literary characteristics. We return with this observation to the issue which generated this chapter, the relationship of the redaction of an authoritative text and social transformation. Goody's studies of other cultures and communities suggest that the redaction of canonical texts facilitate the development of institutions geared to preserving and studying these texts and dedicated to producing and promoting the privileged status and authority of a class of scholars. In these latter developments, Goody maintains, religious scholars and their institutions emerge within a society as a defined and differentiated realm (Goody, 1986). While all this may be seen to apply to late second-century Rabbinism and to Mishnah, our evidence permits us to move beyond these general propositions to more specific claims. We may see much of the inner workings of this process as regards the role Mishnah may have played in facilitating the social and organizational developments within Rabbinism of this period.

From the analysis of the foregoing section I proffer as a preliminary conclusion that the production of Mishnah, with its particular rhetorical traits, is integrally tied to the institutionalization in Palestine of a more unified rabbinism whose principal social forms were the ruling Patriarchate and the College of Sages (sometimes referred to as the Sanhedrin, at other times called the Court or the Patriarch's Court). This state of affairs probably supplanted, over the final decades of the second century, the antecedent state of affairs in which Rabbinism consisted of autonomous circles of masters and disciples. The normative character and authority of the latter had to be both overcome and transferred to the newer state of affairs. And a balance of power between the Patriarchate and the united College of Sages had to be defined. Mishnah, which came to be attributed to Judah the Patriarch's personal editorial activity, preserves the identity of the earlier rabbinic sages, each of whom constituted the centre of a circle of master and disciples. At the same time their individuality (beyond their names) is considerably effaced and subsumed within a new united literary whole, imposing its peculiar lyrical, rhetorical style on everything and everyone. The individual and the individual's inherent authority are preserved only in the new whole, soon to become the chief object of study of would-be sages. So Mishnah, in its lyrical, clockwork rhetoric, represents, preserves, builds upon, and borrows the authority of the old social form in order to supplant it with another. All this transpires not only at the level of the legal substance of Mishnah, which defines aspects of an ideal Temple-centred state, but also by means of implicitly communicated, non-discursive "knowledge" of "how things really are" given in the pervasive rhetorical traits of Mishnah itself.

3

Tosefta's (Dis)simulation of Mishnah's Rhetoric

I
Comparative advantages

In order to understand the place of this and the next chapter, it is worth returning whence we began. The Introduction stated that our study of Mishnah derives from a focus on the "rhetorical" character of early rabbinic texts in relation to the social institutions of the early rabbinic guild which legitimated and were legitimated by the rhetorical character of their revered, incessantly studied documents. Understanding these texts as evincing a particular rhetorical character gives us theoretical and methodological leverage on the problem of the social "meaning" of an "authoritative" text. This is so because "rhetoric" is not just a privately stylized way of communicating with others. To "work," a rhetorical style must be recognized by a community, guild or group as authoritative or persuasive. Within a social context which deems that rhetorical style to be normal and particularly legitimate, both the substance of what is thereby conveyed and the person(s) conveying that substance will *prima facie* have the "ring of authority." Rhetorical styles, therefore, reflect, embody, and inform social institutions and social roles, especially those of power and authority; the "appropriateness" and effectiveness of the modes of expression and argument are a function of social context and situation–that is, who is speaking to whom, about what, and where. What is artful, appropriate, and convincing in a judicial defence might be immediately perceived as tendentious, overstated, and, therefore, unconvincing in the school or in the legislative council.[1] "Official" texts, consequently evince and model authoritative social definitions of roles and modes of communicating appropriate to those roles within a particular social sphere.

That is where we began this book on core aspects of Mishnah's rhetorical style. And in the previous chapter attempted to characterize salient features of Mishnah's rhetoric as a means of getting at the early rabbinic movement's social definitions of authoritative roles and skills–the professional skills that made one a rabbi and a member of a particular "class" or "professional" group called "the rabbis" or "the sages." The current chapter undertakes a comparison of Tosefta's rhetorical features with those already described for Mishnah. (Chapter 4 does the same with yet another early rabbinic text, Maseket Semahot.) Why is such a comparative exercise important to further the objectives of this book on the social meaning of Mishnah's rhetoric? Again, let me review some remarks made in the Introduction.

1.　　See above, pp. 19-23, and esp. n.13 and n.14.

As demonstrated in my work on the rhetoric of the Babylonian Talmud (Lightstone, 1994:49-75, 173-245), authoritative modes of communication, including both rhetoric and social institutions and roles stand not only in a contemporary social setting, in a system of synchronic relationships, but also in an historical context, too, in a diachronic setting. Hence the social significance and meaning of rhetorical patterns partly resides in comparison, that is, in the contrasts, continuities, and discontinuities, with what was and what subsequently becomes authoritative in the life of the group in question. For in any social setting the past "makes an authoritative claim" on the present, especially in "traditional" societies. So in studying the social meaning of Mishnah's rhetorical traits, I have found it valuable to ask, What happens to Mishnaic rhetoric and its implicitly communicated definitions of social authority in the aftermath of Mishnah's promulgation and acceptance as the authoritative document par excellence and as the principal object of study in early third-century rabbinic guilds? Do subsequent documents of the early rabbinic corpus try to replicate, modulate, and/or modify Mishnah's rhetoric and so offer us an echo of the history of the social role or professional group we might call "the mishnaic rabbis"? It is easy to point to rabbinic documents that largely displace or overturn Mishnah's rhetorical traits. But until the promulgation of the Babylonian Talmud in the sixth or early seventh century, none of these documents succeeded in supplanting Mishnah as the core authoritative document the study and mastery of which made one a rabbinic master. For our purposes the contra-mishnaic rhetoric of texts will not help us place in relief Mishnah's rhetoric and its social meaning as much as texts which both imitate and fail to imitate (or modify) dominant rhetorical traits of Mishnah.

The rhetorical traits of Tosefta, the most Mishnah-like, post-mishnaic document of the early rabbinic guild, provide an apt entry into such comparisons. Engaging in a socio-rhetorical analysis of Tosefta against the backdrop of Mishnah addresses the issue of how the social definitions of the role of the "rabbi" implicitly modelled in Mishnah's rhetorical traits were both accepted and remodeled over the course of the third century in the early rabbinic guild of the Galilee.

In order meaningfully to compare Tosefta and Mishnah's rhetorical traits, I apply to Tosefta the very same method designed to bring into relief Mishnah's rhetorical character. Remember, that method was designed for and derives from the exercise of classifying recurrent rhetorical patterns and stock formulae and formularies of Mishnah, and no other document. And that is precisely why I will try to apply that method to Tosefta–precisely to see how well or how poorly the method serves to capture any stylized rhetoric evinced by Tosefta. To see how well or poorly that method works with Tosefta is to glimpse where Tosefta has both simulated and deviated from the rhetoric modelled by Mishnah. That is to say, the results of applying this method to Tosefta is significant, because the extent to which chapter 2's classificatory system applies to Tosefta is an important measure of the relative "rhetorical distance" of Tosefta from Mishnah and, therefore, of the former's implicitly communicated, authoritative model of "being rabbi" from the latter's. For these purposes I will analyze the section of Tosefta (t.

Gittin 1:1-2:2) that correlates with the Mishnah "chapter" examined in the previous chapter.

II
Comparing t. Gittin 1:1-2:2 and m. Gittin 1:1-2:2

In chapter 2, I identified three principal classes of stylistic devices used to construct Mishnah's characteristic rhetorical patterning:
1. concatenating and joining formulae;
2. repetition and controlled variation of word, especially verb, morphology;
3. repetition based upon phonological and/or semantic homologies.

Let me briefly characterize each once again. First, Mishnah appears to call upon a surprisingly limited stock of joining terminology, most frequently, "and," "which," "except," and "say(s)." Second, Mishnah will repeat not a word or phrase but a morphological form, such as a particular verb tense (e.g., המביא, הכותב, המוליך–all masculine, singular present participle prefixed by the *heh-emphaticus*)–as some sort of literary marker (see Neusner, 1977, 1981). As stated in the previous chapter, since morphological or grammatical inflection in Hebrew is effected by standard prefixes and suffixes, the repetition of morphological form produces assonance, alliteration, and/or rhyme. Third, Mishnah uses repetition of precise words and phrases. I dubbed this phenomenon homophonic-homosemantic markers, since in reading the text of Mishnah the ear repeatedly hears the same "sound bytes." I counted, as well, among the latter the use of a word or phrase followed by its exact semantic opposite, such as "unclean" (טמא) followed by "clean" (טהור), or "fit" (כשר) followed by "unfit" (פסול).

Chart 1 below offers a "scored" chart of t. Gittin 1:1-2:2 similar to the previous chapter's scored chart of m. Gittin 1:1-2:2. As before, column 1 groups concatenating devices; column 4 documents morphological verb forms. Columns 5, 6, and 7 reserved for repetition based upon phonological and/or semantic homologies, since multiple "voices" using this last device seem to operate simultaneously in a typical Mishnah "chapter." For other Mishnah chapters, two columns might suffice to bring these voices into view; at other times four might be better. Columns 2 and 3, which are almost devoid of content, require some commentary. Rhetoric is usually conceived to be the art of persuasion through argument. Thus I thought it useful to capture in the score formal logico-argumentative terms and formulae, which figure so prominently in other rabbinic texts, such as the Bavli. (The "bareness" of this column for m. Gittin 1:1-2:2 itself spoke volumes to us.) Column 3 was intended as a "catch-all" for other types of rhetorical formulae; again it is tell-tale that it remains blank. The rightmost column (8) is reserved for substance that does not evince any features that permit it to fall within the other classifications; it is in effect a column for "free-formed" idiomatic language.

Before readers peruse the segmented translation and the chart providing the mishnah-like "scoring" of Tosefta, I should like to make them aware of one significant potential distortion I have knowingly introduced into the exercise. I

have deliberately introduced a bias into the classification of the language of
Tosefta by trying to avoid placing items in the rightmost column. This is the
column reserved for what appears to be language not evincing one or another of
Mishnah's typical rhetorical devices. In other words, I have biased the scored
chart in favour of representing Tosefta as more "Mishnah-like" rather than less.
By so doing, I make the burden of proof which I must bear heavier, when I argue
for the distinctiveness of Mishnah's rhetoric, on the one hand, and Tosefta's
"drift" away from Mishnah's implicitly communicated "world," on the other.
Nevertheless, what we shall see, I will argue, is both a remarkable rhetorical
similarity between Tosefta and Mishnah and subtle and significant departures.

I turn, then, to the segmented translation of t. Gittin 1:1-2:2, which is
immediately followed by Chart 1, the rhetorical "scoring" of the toseftan passage.
To better appreciate the literary relationship between t. Gittin 1:1-2:2 and m. Gittin 1:1-2:2, in both the segmented translation and "scored" chart, passages of
Tosefta which "cite" our Mishnah "chapter" appear all in capital letters; Tosefta
passages that "cite" other sections of Mishnah or of Tosefta are in upper and
lower case. I should note in this regard that I mark a section of Tosefta as a
"citation" of Mishnah (or some other passage in Tosefta) the first time only that
the cited language appears in these Toseftan passages; thereafter I consider the
same verbatim phrases to be "intra-toseftan" repetition.

1:1

a.   One who brings a writ in a boat is like ONE WHO BRINGS FROM outside the Land.
b.   IT IS REQUIRED THAT HE SHOULD SAY:IN MY PRESENCE IT WAS WRITTEN
        AND IN MY PRESENCE IT WAS SIGNED [=m. 1:1A-B].
c.   [One who brings] from across the Jordan is like ONE WHO BRINGS FROM [INSIDE]
        THE LAND OF ISRAEL,
d.   and IT IS NOT REQUIRED THAT HE SHOULD SAY: IN MY PRESENCE IT WAS
        WRITTEN AND IN MY PRESENCE IT WAS SIGNED [=m. 1:3A-B // t. 1:3A-B].
e.   ONE WHO BRINGS A WRIT FROM A MEDITERRANEAN PROVINCE
f.   [AND] CANNOT SAY: IN MY PRESENCE IT WAS WRITTEN AND IN MY
        PRESENCE IT WAS SIGNED—
g.   if he is able to make it STAND UPON ITS SIGNATURES [=m. 1:3E-G],
h.   [the writ] is fit,
i.   and if not
j.   [the writ]is unfit.
k.   They used to say:
l.   They said: it is required that he should say: In my presence it was written and in my
        presence it was signed not to rule stringently [but] rather to rule leniently in his regards.
m.   One who brings a writ from a Mediterranean province [and] it was not written in his
        presence and it was not signed in his presence—
n.   lo, this one returns it to its place [of original execution], and ONE CONVENES in its
        regard A COURT [= m. 3:6], and one establishes it[s validity] upon [the strength of] its
        signatures, and one brings it [back to where it is to be delivered], and ONE SAYS: AN
        AGENT OF A COURT AM I [m. 3:6].

o.   Inside the Land of Israel an agent appoints [another] agent.
p.   Rabban Simeon ben Gamaliel says: An agent does not appoint [another] agent in the
        case of writs [of divorce].

q. At first they used to say: FROM PROVINCE TO PROVINCE [m. 1:1G]—
r. [it is required in such cases that one say: in my presence it was written
    and in my presence it was signed.
s. [Subsequently] they retracted to say: From neighbourhood to neighbourhood.
t. R. SIMEON B. GAMALIEL SAYS: ALSO FROM DISTRICT TO DISTRICT [m. 1:1I].

1:2
a. A stringency [applies] as regards a [writ of divorce from a] Mediterranean province
    which does not [apply] as regards a [writ of divorce from] the Land of Israel,
b. and [another stringency [apply] as regards a [writ of divorce from] the Land of Israel
    which does not [apply] as regards a [writ of divorce from a] Mediterranean province,
c. [namely] that [as regards] ONE WHO BRINGS [A WRIT] FROM A MEDITERRA-
    NEAN PROVINCE-
d. IT IS REQUIRED THAT HE SHOULD SAY:IN MY PRESENCE IT WAS WRITTEN,
    AND IN MY PRESENCE IT WAS SIGNED [m. 1:1A-B // t. 1:1 Ab-B].
e. Even though (emended as per t. Lieberman) THERE ARE CHALLENGERS TO IT[S
    VALIDITY] [m. 1:3C],
f. it is fit (emended as per t. Lieberman).

1:3
a. [And] ONE WHO BRINGS A WRIT FROM THE LAND OF ISRAEL (emended as
    per t. Lieberman)—
b. IT IS NOT REQUIRED THAT HE SHOULD SAY: IN MY PRESENCE IT WAS
    WRITTEN, AND IN MY PRESENCE IT WAS SIGNED [m. 1:3A-B // t. 1:1C-D).
c. IF there are upon it [the signatures of] witnesses,
d. IT[S VALIDITY] IS ESTABLISHED UPON [THE AUTHENTICATION OF] ITS
    [WITNESSES'] SIGNATURES [m. 1:3D].

e. How have [that is, what means were envisaged when] they said: IT[S VALIDITY]
    SHALL STAND UPON [THE AUTHENTICATION OF] ITS [WITNESSES'] SIGNA-
    TURES [m. 1:3D]?
f. If witnesses said: this is our handwriting,
g. it is fit.
h. [If they said:] This is our handwriting and [i.e., but] we do not recognize either the
    man['s name] or [lit., and] the woman['s name],
i. it is fit.
j. [If they said:] This is not our handwriting, but others testify with respect to them that it
    is their handwriting,
k. or [it is the case] that [a sample of] their handwriting had come forth [i.e., been
    produced in evidence] from another place,
l. it is fit.

m. R. MEIR SAYS: ACCO and its environs are LIKE THE LAND OF ISRAEL AS
    REGARD WRITS [OF DIVORCE] [m. 1:2B],
n. and sages say: Acco and its environs are like [the territory] outside the Land [of Israel]
    as regards writs [of divorce].
o. An incident occurred with respect to [some]one from Kefar Sasi who brought before R.
    Ishmael a writ of divorce.
p. Said to him R. Ishmael: From where [do] you [come]?
q. He said to him: From Kefar Sasi, [within] the environ of the Land [of Israel].
r. He said to him: Even so [as regards] you[rself], IT IS REQUIRED THAT you SAY: IN
    MY PRESENCE IT WAS WRITTEN, AND IN MY PRESENCE IT WAS SIGNED [m.
    1:1B // t. 1:1B], and witnesses are not needed [to authenticate the signatures].
s. After he went forth, said before him R. La'ii (Erfurt: Ila'i): My Master, Kefar Sasi is

	[within] the environ of the Land [of Israel]; [it is] closer to Sephoris than Acco is!

t.   [within] the environ of the Land [of Israel]; [it is] closer to Sephoris than Acco is!
He said to him: Since the incident has gone forth [i.e., already resulted] in a permissive ruling, [then] [the ruling] has gone forth [i.e., should not be retracted].

1:4

a.   R. Judah says: Even though its two witnesses are Kutim [Samaritans],

b.   it is fit.

c.   Said R. Judah [THE FOLLOWING] INCIDENT OCCURRED: THEY BROUGHT BEFORE R. GAMALIEL TO KEFAR OTNAI A WRIT OF DIVORCE, AND ITS WITNESSES WERE KUTIM [i.e., Samaritans],

d.   AND HE DECLARED IT FIT [m. 1:5C-E].

e.   ANY BONDS ISSUING FROM [COURT] BUREAUS OF GENTILES—EVEN THOUGH THEIR SIGNATORIES ARE GENTILES [m. 1:5F-G]—

f.   R. Aqiva declares fit in the case of all of them,

g.   and sages declare [them] unfit in the case of WRITS OF DIVORCE AND in the case of MANUMISSION PAPERS OF SLAVES [m. 1:5I].

h.   Said R. Lazar son of R. Yosah: Thus they said to the elders at Sidon: R. Aqiva and the sages did not dispute concerning bonds issuing from [court] bureaus of gentiles, that even though their signatories are gentiles

i.   [they] are fit.

j.   Concerning what did they dispute?

k.   Concerning [those] THAT WERE DONE IN A NON-PROFESSIONAL TRIBUNAL [m. 1:5Kb]—

l.   that R. Aqiva declares fit in the case of all of them,

m.   and the sages declare [them] unfit in the case of writs of divorce and in the case of manumission papers of slaves.

n.   Rabbi Simeon b. Gamaliel says: Even writs of divorce and manumission papers of slaves are fit in the case of a place [in] which an Israelite does not sign.

1:5

a.   Said R. Lazar: We said to R. MEIR: For what [reason] [do you hold your view]: THEY BENEFIT A slave WHEN NOT IN HIS [OR HER] PRESENCE [m. 1:6F].

b.   HE SAID TO US [m. 1:6Ja]: It is but A LIABILITY [OR OBLIGATION] [m. 1:6G] [imposed] upon him.

c.   For if he was a slave of a priest, [then] it is the case (lit. it is found) [that] one RENDERS him UNFIT FOR (lit. from) [EATING] HEAVE-OFFERING [m. 1:6Jb].

d.   We said to him: And lo, is it not [the case that] IF HE [THE PRIEST] should WISH NOT TO FEED him, and not to support him, the AUTHORITY [m. 1:6Ha,Ib] is his [to decide]?

e.   He said to us: And lo, is it not [the case that] A SLAVE OF A PRIEST THAT FLED AND A WIFE OF A PRIEST THAT REBELLED—LO, THESE [PERSONS] EAT OF HEAVE-OFFERING [t. Ter. 10:8].

f.   But [with respect to] a wife it is not so! Rather they owe her food, and they declare her unfit for (lit., from) [eating] heave-offering.

1:6

a.   ONE WHO SAYS [m. 1:6 A&M]: GIVE THIS MANEH TO SO-AND-SO [m. 1:6O], which I owe to him,

b.   [or] give this maneh to so-and-so, [which is] a collateral deposit, which he has [placed] in my possession (lit., hand),

c.   [or] TAKE [m. 6.1 // t. 4(6):1] this maneh to so-and-so, [which is] a collateral deposit, which he has [placed] in my possession—

d.   IF ONE WISHES TO RETRACT,

e. ONE MAY NOT RETRACT [m. 1:6B].

f. And one is liable for it, until one shall receive what is one's.

1:7

a. [One who says:] Take this maneh to so-and-so,

b. [or] give this maneh to so-and-so—
    if one wishes to retract,

c. one may retract [m. 1:6].

d. [If] one went and found that [the beneficiary] HAD DIED [m. 1:6P],

e. one shall return it to the one who gave [it].

f. If [that person] died [in the interim],

g. one shall return it to his [or her] heirs.

1:8

a. [One who says:] MAKE so-and-so RECEIVE [m. 6:1//t. 4(6):1] this maneh,

b. [or] MAKE so-and-so BENEFIT [t. 4(6):1] from his gift,

c. [or] make so-and-so receive this deed of gift,

d. [or] make so-and-so benefit from this deed of gift—

e. if one wishes to retract,

f. one may not retract [m. 1:6].F.

g. [If] one went and found that [the intended beneficiary] had died,

h. one shall give [it] to his heirs (follows Erfurt and Lieberman in t.).

i. And if after [the intended beneficiary's] death [the intended beneficiary] benefited,

j. one returns [it] to the one who gave [it] (following Erfurt and Lieberman in t.),

k. for they do not benefit one who died AFTER DEATH [m. 1:6Q].

1:9

a. [One who says:] CARRY [t. 4(6):2b] this maneh to so-and-so,

b. [or] BEAR [t. 4(6):2b] this maneh to so-and-so,

c. [or] LET this maneh BE [t. 4(6):2b] for so-and-so by your [own] hands,

d. and [the benefactor] died–

e. if his heirs wished to compel him [to return the money],

f. they may not.

g. And one need not say [i.e., all the more so] as regards one who says: Make him benefit,

h. and as regards one who says: Make him receive.

2:1

a. ONE WHO BRINGS A WRIT FROM A MEDITERRANEAN PROVINCE [m. 2:1A//m. 1:1A//m. 1:3E],

b. and gave it to her, and did not SAY: IN MY PRESENCE IT WAS WRITTEN, AND IN MY PRESENCE IT WAS SIGNED [m. 2:1b-c//m. 1:1b//m. 1:3f]—

c. lo, this one takes it from her, even after three years, returns, and gives it to her,

d. and shall say to her: In my presence it was written and in my presence it was signed.

2:2

a. wife is trusted when she shall say: This writ, which you gave to me, [which] is torn, is unfit (see t. 7:11; t. BB 11:11), [or which] is torn, is fit.

b. [If] there was torn in it a tear of a court,

c. it is unfit.

d. R. Simeon says: One glues [together] the torn [pieces], and gives [it] to her, and SAYS to her: IN MY PRESENCE IT WAS WRITTEN, AND IN MY PRESENCE IT WAS SIGNED [m. 2:1B-C//m. 1:1B//m. 1:3F].

e. ONE SAYS: IN MY PRESENCE IT WAS WRITTEN, AND ONE [i.e., ANOTHER]

SAYS: IN MY PRESENCE IT WAS SIGNED—

f.   [THE WRIT] IS UNFIT.

g.   TWO [BRING A WRIT AND] SAY: IN OUR PRESENCE IT WAS WRITTEN, AND ONE SAYS: IN MY PRESENCE IT WAS SIGNED—

h.   R. JUDAH declares fit [m. 2:1K-O,Q] in this [case].

i.   R. SIMEON says: Even [if] ONE WROTE IT (m.: it was written) TODAY (m.: in the daytime) [m. 2:2A], AND ONE SIGNED IT (m.: it was signed) ON THE MORROW (m.: in the nighttime) [m. 2:2B]—

j.   [THE WRIT] IS FIT [m. 2:2G].

k.   One wrote it in the Land [of Israel], and one signed it outside [the Land of Israel]—

l.   IT IS REQUIRED THAT HE SHOULD SAY: IN MY PRESENCE IT WAS WRITTEN, AND IN MY PRESENCE IT WAS SIGNED [m. 1:1B].

m.   One wrote it outside [the Land of Israel], and one signed it inside the Land [of Israel]—

n.   it is not required that he should say: In my presence it was written and in my presence it was signed.

> [t. Gittin 1:1-2:2, ed. Lieberman; translation by J. Lightstone in collaboration with Dr. Maria Mamfredis]

Let us now turn to the same text in rhetorically "scored" format.

Chart 3.1: Rhetorical "scoring" of t. Gittin 1:1-2:2

Column 1 = Conjunctive/Coordinating formulae
Column 2 = Logical/Analogical formulae (LA)
Column 3 = Other Formulae (OF) = ip 16,16
Column 4 = Morphological markers (M) = ip 20,20
Column 5 = Homophonic-Homosemantic/antisemantic markers, level 1 (HH1)
Column 6 = Homophonic-Homosemantic/antisemantic markers, level 2 (HH2)
Column 7 = Homophonic-Homosemantic/antisemantic markers, level 3 (HH3)
Column 8 = Other Content (OC)

CC	LA	OF	M	HH1	HH2	HH3	OC
1:1							
			A.1. One who (ה)				
			(ה+sg. 3rd pl. active part.)				
			brings				
			A writ				
				in a boat			
A.2.is like (כ)							
			ONE WHO				
				BRINGS			
				FROM			
				outside the Land			
					B.IT IS REQUIRED		
THAT (ש)							
					HE SHOULD SAY:		
					IN MY PRESENCE IT WAS		
					WRITTEN		
AND							
					IN MY PRESENCE IT WAS		
					SIGNED [=m. 1:1A-B]		
			C.1. [One who				
			brings]				

CC	LA	OF	M	HH1	HH2	HH3	OC
					from		
					across the Jordan		

C2. is like (כ)

        ONE WHO

           BRINGS
           FROM
           [INSIDE] THE LAND OF ISRAEL,

and

               D. IT IS NOT REQUIRED

THAT

               HE SHOULD SAY:
               IN MY PRESENCE IT WAS WRITTEN

AND

               IN MY PRESENCE IT WAS SIGNED [=m. 1:3A-B // t. 1:3A-B]

        E. ONE WHO

           BRINGS
           A WRIT
           FROM
           A MEDITERRANEAN
           PROVINCE

f. [AND]

               CANNOT SAY:
               IN MY PRESENCE IT WAS WRITTEN

AND

               IN MY PRESENCE IT WAS SIGNED—

G.1. if

        he (3rd sg. part.)

           is able
           to make it STAND
           UPON
           ITS SIGNATURES [=m. 1:3E-G],
        G.2. [the writ]
        (3rd sg. pass. part.)
           is fit,

H. and (ו missing in Erfurt)
if

           not
        [the writ]
           is unfit (פסול).

I. they use to say (הוי אומ'):

They said (לא אמרו):

               it is required

that (שׁ)

               he should say:
               In my presence it was written

CC	LA	OF	M	HH1	HH2	HH3	OC
and							in my presence it was signed
not (לא)					to rule stringently (להחמיר)		
[but] rather (אלא)					to rule leniently (להקל)		
							in his regards (עליו).
			J. One who				
				brings a writ			
				from a Mediterranean province			
[and]					it was not written in his presence		
and					it was not signed in his presence		
K.1. Lo this (missing in Erfurt)							
			one (3rd sg. active part.)				
				returns			
					it		
							to
					its		
							place [of original execution]
K.2. and							
			ONE				
							CONVENES (lit., makes) in
					its regard (לו)		
					A COURT [= m. 3:6]		
K.3. and							
			one				
				establishes it[s validity] upon [the strength of] its signature			
K.4. and							
			one				
				brings it [back to where it is to be delivered]			
K.5. and							

CC	LA	OF	M ONE	HH1	HH2	HH3	OC
						SAYS:	
							AN AGENT OF A COURT AM I [m. 3:6].
				L. Inside the Land of Israel an agent			
			(3rd sg. act. part.)				
				appoints (lit., makes) [another] agent.			
							M. Rabban Simeon ben Gamaliel
says:							
				an agent does not			
		appoint					
				[another] agent in the case of writs [of divorce].			
N.1. At first they used to say:							
				N.2. FROM PROVINCE TO PROVINCE [m. 1:1G]—	[it is required in such cases that one say: in my presence it was written		
and					in my presence it was signed.		
O.1. [Subsequently] they retracted to say:				O.2. from neighbourhood to neighbourhood			
							P. R. SIMEON B. GAMALIEL
SAYS: ALSO (אף)				FROM DISTRICT TO DISTRICT [m. 1:1I].			

CC	LA	OF	M	HH1 HH2 HH3	OC
1:2					

A stringency
[applies]
as regards a (ב)
[writ of divorce
from a]
Mediterranean province

which

does not [apply]
as regards a (ב)
[writ of divorce
from]
the Land of Israel,

B. and

[another stringency
applies]
as regards a
[writ of divorce
from]
the Land of Israel

which

does not [apply]
as regards a
[writ of divorce
from a]
Mediterranean province;

C. [Namely] that

[as regards]

ONE WHO

BRINGS
[A WRIT]
FROM
A MEDITERRANEAN PROVINCE
IT IS REQUIRED

THAT

HE SHOULD

SAY:
IN MY PRESENCE IT WAS
WRITTEN,

AND

IN MY PRESENCE IT WAS
SIGNED [m. 1:1A-B // t. 1:1 Ab-
B].

D. Even though (אַף עַל פִּי:
emended as per t. Lieberman)

THERE ARE

CHALLENGERS
TO IT[S VALIDITY] (עליו) [m. 1:3C],

(3rd sg. pass. part.)

E it is fit (כשר: emended as per t.
Lieberman).

CC	LA	OF	M	HH1	HH2	HH3	OC
1:3							
A. [And]							
			ONE WHO				
				BRINGS			
				A WRIT			
				FROM			
				THE LAND OF ISRAEL			
				(emended as per t. Lieberman)—			
							B. IT IS NOT REQUIRED
THAT							
			HE SHOULD (3rd sg. imperf.)				
					SAY:		
					IN MY PRESENCE IT WAS WRITTEN,		
					IN MY PRESENCE IT WAS SIGNED [m. 1:3A-B // t. 1:1C-D)		
AND							
C. IF							
				there are upon it [the signatures of] witnesses,			
			D. IT[S] (3rd sg. act. part.)				
					[VALIDITY] IS ESTABLISHED UPON [THE AUTHENTICATION OF] ITS [WITNESSES'] SIGNATURES [m. 1:3D].		
E. How [that is, what means were envisaged when]							
			they (3rd pl. perf.)				
					said:		
				F. IT[S VALIDITY] SHALL STAND UPON [THE AUTHENTICATION OF] ITS [WITNESSES'] SIGNATURES [m. 1:3D]?			
G. If							
			(3rd pl. perf.)	witnesses			
					said		
				this is our handwriting,			
				H. it is fit			
I. [If							
			they				
						said:]	

CC	LA	OF	M	HH1	HH2 HH3	OC
					this is our handwriting	
and [I.e., but]						
					we do not	
			(3rd pl. act. part.)			
					recognize either the man['s name]	
or [lit. And]						
					the woman['s name] J. it is fit.	
K. [If			they		said:]	
					this is not our handwriting	
but (אבל)						
					others	
			(3rd pl. act. part.)			
					testify with respect to (ב) them	
that						
					it (הוא) is their handwriting,	
L. or (או) [its is the case] that						
					[a sample of] their handwriting	
						had
			(3rd sg. act. part.)			
						come forth [i.e., been pro-duced in evidence]
					from another	
						place,
					M. it is fit.	
						N. R. MEIR
SAYS:						
					ACCO	
and						
					its environs are LIKE THE LAND OF ISRAEL AS REGARD (ל) WRITS [OF DIVORCE] [m. 1:2B],	
O. and						
						sages

CC	LA	OF	M	HH1	HH2	HH3	OC
say:							
					Acco		
and							
					its environs are like [the territory] outside the Land [of Israel] as regards (ל)		
				writs [of divorce].			
P. An incident occurred with respect to (מעשׂה ב)							
							[some]one
					from Kefar Sasi		
who (שׁ)							
		(3rd sg. perf.)					
					brought		
						before	
							R. Ishmael
				a writ of divorce (אשׁה).			
Q. Said to him:							
							R. Ishmael
					from		
							where
				[do] you [come]?			
R. He said to him:							
					from Kefar Sasi, [within] the environ of the Land [of Israel].		
S.1. He said to him: Even so (אף)							
							[as regards] you[rself]
				S.2. IT IS REQUIRED THAT you SAY: IN MY PRESENCE IT WAS WRITTEN,			
				IN MY PRESENCE IT WAS SIGNED [m. 1:1B // t. 1:1B],			
AND							
					witnesses		
							are not needed [to authenticate the signatures].
T. and							
U. After (לאחר שׁ)							
			(3rd sg. perf.)	he			
					went forth,		

CC	LA	OF	M	HH1	HH2	HH3	OC
V. said before him							
							R. La'ii (Erfurt: Ila'i): My Master (רבי),
					Kefar Sasi is [within] the environ of the Land [of Israel]--		
							W. closer to Sephoris than Acco is!
X. He said to him: Since (הואיל ו) the incident (מעשה)							
			(3rd sg. perf.)				
					has gone forth [i.e., already resulted]		
in (ב)							
							a permissive ruling (היתר),
	[then]						
							[the ruling]
			(3rd sg. perf.)				
					has gone forth [i.e., should not be retracted].		

1:4

CC	LA	OF	M	HH1	HH2	HH3	OC
							A. R. Judah
says: Even though (אף על פי ש)							
					its two witnesses are Kutim [Samaritans], B. it is fit.		
C. Said							
							R. Judah
[THE FOLLOWING] INCIDENT occurred (מעשה ש ERFURT: ;מעשה ו)							
			THEY (3rd pl. perf.)				
					BROUGHT BEFORE		
							R. GAMALIEL
					TO KEFAR OTNAI A WRIT OF DIVORCE,		
D. AND							
					ITS WITNESSES		

CC	LA	OF	M	HH1	HH2	HH3	OC
			(3rd pl. perf.)				
					WERE KUTIM,		
E. AND							
			HE (3rd pl. perf.)				
					DECLARED IT FIT [m. 1:5C-E].		
F. ANY (כל ה)							
				BONDS (שטרות)			
			(ה + 3rd. pl. part.)				
					ISSUING FROM (ב) [COURT] BUREAUS OF (של) GENTILES—		
G. EVEN THOUGH (אף על פי ש)							
					THEIR SIGNATORIES ARE GENTILES [m. 1:5F-G]—		
							H. R. Aqiva
			(3rd sg. act. part.)				
					declares fit		
in the case of (ב)							
					all of them,		
I. and							
							the sages
					declare [them] unfit		
in the case of							
					WRITS OF DIVORCE		
AND in the case of							
					MANUMISSION PAPERS OF SLAVES [m. 1:5I].		
J. Said							
							R. Lazar son of R. Yosah:
Thus (כך) They said to (אמרו להן ל)							
							the elders at (ב) Sidon:
							K. R. Aqiva and the sages
			(3rd pl. perf.)				
did not dispute concerning (על)							
				bonds (שטרות)			
			(ה + 3rd. pl. part.)				
					issuing from (ב) [court] bureaus of (של)		

CC	LA	OF	M	HH1	HH2	HH3	OC
					gentiles,		
L. that even though (אַף עַל פִּי שׁ)							
					their signatories are gentiles		
			[they] (3rd pl. part.)				
					are fit.		
M. Concerning what							
			(3rd pl. perf.)				
did they dispute?							
N. Concerning [those] THAT							
			(3rd pl. perf. niph'al)				
							W E R E D O N E (נעשׂוּ) I N A N O N - PROFESSIONAL T R I B U N A L (הדיוט) [m. 1:5Kb]—
O. that							
							R. Aqiva
			(3rd sg. past.)				
					declares fit		
in the case of (בּ)							
					all of them,		
P. and							
							the sages
					declare [them] unfit		
in the case of							
					writs of divorce		
and in the case of							
					manumission papers of slaves.		
							Q. Rabbi Simeon b. Gamaliel
says: Even (אַף)							
					writs of divorce		
and							
					manumission papers of slaves		
			(3rd pl. part.)				
					are fit		
in the case of (בּ)							
							a place
[in] which (שׁ)							

CC	LA	OF	M	HH1	HH2	HH3	OC
							an Israelite does not
			(3rd sg. part.)				
					sign.		
1:5 A.1. Said							R. Lazar:
We said to (אמרנו לו ל)							R. MEIR
For what [reason] (מפני מה) [do you hold your view]?							
			A.2. THEY (3rd. pl. part.)				
							BENEFIT A
				slave			
WHEN (ש)							
							NOT IN HIS [OR HER] PRESENCE [m. 1:6F]?
B. HE SAID TO US [m. 1:6Ja]:							
	It is but						
							A LIABILITY [OR OBLI-GATION] [m. 1:6G] [imposed] upon him.
	C. For (ש) if (אם)						
							he was
				a slave of a priest,			
	D. [then] it is the case (lit. it is found, נמצא) [that]						
			one (3rd sg. act. part.+ 3rd sg. masc. suf.]				
							RENDERS him UNFIT FOR (lit. from) [EATING] HEAVE-OFFERING [m. 1:6Jb].
E. We said to him: And							
	lo, is it not (הלא) [the case that] IF (אם)						
							HE [THE PRIEST]
			(3rd sg. imperf.)				
							should WISH NOT TO FEED him,

CC	LA	OF	M	HH1	HH2	HH3	OC
and							not to support him
							F. the AUTHO-RITY
							[m. 1:6Ha,Ib]
							is his [to decide]
							(הרשות בידו)?

G. He said to us:
And

lo, is it not
[the case that]

| | | | | A SLAVE OF A PRIEST | | | |

THAT (שׁ)

(3rd sg. perf.)

FLED

H. AND

A WIFE
OF A PRIEST

THAT

(3rd sg. perf.)

REBELLED—

I. LO, (הרי)

THESE [PERSONS]

(3rd pl. act. part.)

EAT OF
HEAVE-OFFERING
(t. Ter. 10:8).

J. But (אבל)

[with respect to]

a wife

it is not so
(אינו כן)!
K. Rather
(אלא)

(3rd pl. act. part.)

they owe her
food,

L. and

(3rd pl. act. part.)

they declare
her
unfit
for (lit., from)
[eating] heave-offering.

1:6

A. ONE WHO
(ה+3rd sg. part.)
SAYS
[m. 1:6 A&M]:
(3rd sg. imperf.)

CC	LA	OF	M	HH1	HH2	HH3	OC
				GIVE	THIS MANEH TO SO-AND-SO [m. 1:6O],		
B. which (שׁ)							
			(3rd sg. perf.)		I		
					owe to him,		
C. [or]			(3rd sg. imper.)	give			
					this maneh to so-and-so,		
D. [which is] which					a collateral deposit,		
					he has [placed] in my possession (lit. hand),		
E. [or]			(3rd sg. imper.)	TAKE (הולך) [m. 6.1 // t. 4(6):1]	this maneh to so-and-so,		
F. [which is] which					a collateral deposit,		
					he has [placed] in my possession—		
G. IF			ONE (3rd sg. perf.)			WISHES TO RETRACT	
			ONE (3rd sg. imperf.)			MAY NOT RETRACT [M. 1:6B].	
H. And			one (3rd sg. perf.)				is liable for it,
I. until (עד שׁ)			one (3rd sg. imperf.)	shall receive			what is one's.

1:7

CC	LA	OF	M	HH1	HH2	HH3	OC
			A. (3rd sg. imperf.)	Take (הולך)			
			this maneh		to so-and-so,		
B. [or]							

CC	LA	OF	M	HH1	HH2	HH3	OC
			(sg. imp.)				
				give			
					this maneh		
					to so-and-so—		
C. If							
			one (3rd sg. perf.)				
						wishes	
						to retract	
			one (3rd sg. imperf.)				
						may retract (M. 1:6).	
D. [If}							
			one (3rd sg. perf.)				
				went (הלך)			
and							
			(3rd sg. perf.)				
					found		
that							
					[the beneficiary]		
					HAD DIED [m. 1:6P],		
			E. one (3rd sg. imperf.)				
						shall return it	
						(יחזיר)	
					to		
			the one who				
			(3rd sg. perf.)				
				gave [it].			
F. If							
			[that person]				
			(3rd sg. perf.)				
					died		
					[in the interim],		
			G. one (3rd sg. imperf.)				
						shall return it	
					to		
					his [or her] heirs.		

1:8

CC	LA	OF	M	HH1	HH2	HH3	OC
			A. (3rd sg. imper. hifil)				
				MAKE			
					so-and-so		
				RECEIVE			
				[m. 6:1//t. 4(6):1]			
					this maneh,		
B. [or]							
			(3rd sg. imper. hifil)				
				MAKE			
					so-and-so		
				BENEFIT			
				[t. 4(6):1]			
					from (ב)		
					this gift,		

CCC	LA	OF	M	HH1	HH2	HH3	OC
C. [or]							
			(3rd sg. imper. hifil)				
				make			
					so-and-so		
				receive			
					this deed of (שטר)		
					gift,		
D. [or]							
			(3rd sg. imper. hifil)				
				make			
					so-and-so		
				benefit			
					from		
					this deed of		
					gift,		
E. If							
			one (3rd sg. perf.)				
						wishes	
						to retract	
			one (3rd sg. imperf.)				
							may not retract (m. 1:6).
F. [If]							
			one (3rd sg. perf.)				
				went (הלך)			
and							
			(3rd sg. perf.)				
					found		
that							
					[the intended beneficiary] had died,		
			G. one (3rd sg. imperf.)				
				shall			
				give [it]			
					to		
					his heirs		
					(G. follows Erfurt and Lieberman in t.)		
H. And if							
					after [the intended beneficiary's] death [the intended beneficiary]		
			(3rd sg. perf.)				
					benefited,		
			I. one (3rd. sg. imperf.)				
						return [it]	
					to		

CC	LA	OF	M	HH1	HH2	HH3	OC
			the one who (3rd sg. perf.)				
				gave [it] (following Erfurt and Lieberman in t.),			
J. for (ש)							
			they (3rd pl. act. part.)				
					do not		
				benefit			
			one who (ל+3rd sg. perf.)				
				died			
					AFTER DEATH [m. 1:6Q].		
1:9							
			A. (3rd. sg. imper.)				
				CARRY (שא) [t. 4(6):2b]			
					this maneh to so-and-so,		
B. [or]							
			(3rd sg. imper.)				
				BEAR (טול) [t. 4(6):2b]			
					this maneh to so-and-so,		
C. [or]							
			(3rd sg. imperf.)				
				LET			
					this maneh		
				BE [t. 4(6):2b]			
					for (ל) so-and-so		
							D. by your [own] hands,
E. and							
					[the benefactor]		
			(3rd. sg. perf.)				
				died			
F. If							
					his heirs		
			(3rd. pl. perf.)				
				wished			
							to compel him [to return the money],
			G. they (3rd pl. act. part.)				
							may
					not.		
H. And							
			one (3rd sg. act. part.)				
					need not say [i.e., all		

CC	LA	OF	M	HH1	HH2	HH3	OC

as regards (ב)

one who (3rd sg. act. part.)

    says:

(3rd. sg. imper.)

    make

    him

    benefit,

I. and
as regards (ב)

one who (3rd sg. act. part.)

    says:

(3rd. sg. imper.)

    make

    him

    receive.

2:1

    A. ONE WHO (ה+3rd sg. act. part.)
        BRINGS
        A WRIT
        FROM
        A MEDITERRANEAN
        PROVINCE
        [m. 2:1A//m. 1:1A//m. 1:3E],

B. and

(3rd sg. perf.)

    gave

    it

    to her,

C. and

    did not SAY:
    IN MY PRESENCE IT WAS
    WRITTEN,

AND

    IN MY PRESENCE IT WAS
    SIGNED
    [M. 2:1b-c//M. 1:1b//M. 1:3f]—

D. Lo this

one
(3rd sg. act. part)

    takes

    it

    from her,

E. even (אפילו)

    after

    three years,

(3rd sg. imperf.)

    F. returns (יחזור),

G. and

(3rd sg. act. part.)

    gives

    it

CC	LA	OF	M	HH1	HH2	HH3	OC
					to her,		
H. and							
			(3rd sg. imperf.)				
					shall say		
					to her:		
						in my presence it was written	
and							
						in my presence it was signed.	
2:2							
			A. (3rd sg. fm. part. niph'al)				
			a wife				
							is trusted
when (ש)							
			she (3rd sg. fm. imperf.)				
					shall say:		
				This writ,			
which							
			you (3rd sg. perf.)				
				gave			
					to me,		
B. [which]							
			(3rd sg. perf. niph'al)				
					is torn,		
					is unfit		
					(see t. 7:11; t. BB 11:11),		
C. [or which]							
			(3rd sg. perf. nitpaal)				
					is torn,		
					is fit.		
D. [If]							
			(3rd sg. perf. niph'al)				
					there was		
					torn		
					in it		
					a tear		
					of		
					a court,		
					E. it is unfit.		
						F. R. Simeon	
says:							
			One (3rd sg. act. part.)				
						glues [together]	
					the torn [pieces],		
G. and							
			(3rd sg. act. part.)				
				gives			
				[it]			
					to her,		
H. and							
						SAYS	
					to her:		
						IN MY PRESENCE IT WAS WRITTEN,	

CC   LA   OF   M   HH1 HH2 HH3   OC
AND

                                   IN MY PRESENCE IT WAS SIGNED
                                   [m. 2:1B-C//m. 1:1B//m. 1:3F].

                                I. ONE
                  (3rd sg. part.)

                                   SAYS:
J. AND   IN MY PRESENCE IT WAS WRITTEN,

                              ONE [i.e., ANOTHER]
                  (3rd sg. part.)

                                   SAYS:
                                 IN MY PRESENCE IT WAS SIGNED—
                       K. [THE WRIT]
                              IS UNFIT (3rd sg. pass. part.).

                                L. TWO
                               [BRING
                               A WRIT AND]
                  (3rd pl. part.)

                                 SAY:
                                 IN OUR PRESENCE IT WAS WRITTEN,

M. AND

                             ONE
                  (3rd sg. part.)

                                   SAYS:
                                 IN MY PRESENCE IT WAS SIGNED—
                                         N. R. JUDAH
                  (3rd sg. part.)

                        declares fit (מכשיר)
                        [m. 2:1K-O,Q]

                                       in this [case] (בזה).

                                           O. R. SIMEON
says:
Even [if] (אפילו)

                  ONE (3rd sg. perf.+
                  3rd sg. pron. suf.)

                              WROTE IT (m.: it was written)
P. AND   TODAY (m.: in the daytime) [m. 2:2A],

                  ONE (3rd sg. perf.+
                  3rd sg. pron. suf.)

                              SIGNED IT (m.: it was signed)
                              ON THE MORROW (m.: in the night-time) [m. 2:2B]—
                       Q. [THE WRIT]
                            IS FIT (3rd sg. pass. part.;

CC	LA	OF	M	HH1	HH2 HH3	OC
					// M. 2:2 H-K)	
					[m. 2:2G].	
			R. One (3rd sg. perf.+ 3rd sg. pron. suf.)			
						wrote it
					in the Land	
					[of Israel],	
S. and						
			one (3rd sg. perf.+ 3rd sg. pron. suf.)			
						signed it
					outside	
					[the Land of Israel]—	
						T. IT IS REQUIRED
THAT (ψ)						
						HE SHOULD SAY: IN MY PRESENCE IT WAS WRITTEN,
AND						
						IN MY PRESENCE IT WAS SIGNED [m. 1:1B].
			U. One (3rd sg. perf.+ 3rd sg. pron. suf.)			
						wrote it
					outside	
					[the Land of Israel],	
V. and						
			one (3rd sg. perf.+ 3rd sg. pron. suf.)			
						signed it
					inside the Land	
					[of Israel]	
					(of Israel missing in Erfurt)—	
						W. it is not required
that (ψ)						
						he should say: In my presence it was written
and						
						in my presence it was signed.

[t. Gittin 1:1-2:2, ed. Lieberman; trans. and charting by the author, based on preliminary trans. and charting by the author's graduate research student, Dr. Maria Mamfredis]

Before proceeding with our analyses of Tosefta's rhetorical characteristics in comparison with those of Mishnah, it will prove useful to graphically represent Tosefta's substantive relationship especially to Mishnah Gittin 1:1-2:2, as well as to other sections of Mishnah and of Tosefta. As we shall see, Tosefta's rhetorical features, and in particular the degree to which they either imitate or depart from Mishnah's, emerge in rather higher "resolution" when examined in light of what Tosefta seems to achieve substantively as a "companion" document (see Goldberg, 1987b) to Mishnah. Chart 2 documents these substantive relationships for t. Gittin 1:1-2:2. Adapting Neusner's taxonomy of Tosefta's relationship to Mishnah (see Neusner, 1991b, 1986e), Chart 2 classifies toseftan passages as either "explicating," "complementing" or "supplementing" correlative Mishnah passages.[2] By explicating I mean stating in fuller, more complete, and/or explicit terms what, at least in the toseftan author's view, the Mishnah passage means. By complementing, I mean the extension and completion of the subject matter of a Mishnah passage; here Tosefta substantively adds to, but stays within, the subject matter of the correlative Mishnah passage. Supplemental materials add subject matter not in Mishnah; we may assume that the toseftan authors saw the added subject matter as being related to the overall theme of the Mishnah "chapter" *ad locum*, that is, issues that Mishnah might have raised in this thematic context, but did not. What we shall see later in our analyses is that complementing Mishnah and especially explicating it has a profound and significant effect on the rhetorical characteristics of Tosefta.

Chart 3.2: Relationship of t. Gittin 1:1-2:2
to Mishnah and Tosefta

() = explicates; [] = complements; { } = supplements

Tosefta	relates to our m., t.	cites our m.	cites other m., t.	relates to other m., t.
1:1A-D	[m.1:1A-B, & m.1:3A-B]			
A1	[m.1:1A-B]			
A2-B		m.1:1A-B		
C1	[m.1:3A-B]			

2.   Neusner's taxonomy distinguishes Tosefta passages as either commenting on, complementing or supplementing Mishnah. For Neusner, "supplementary cognitive units . . . do not directly relate, and sometimes scarcely relate at all, to Mishnah's pericopae". A Tosefta passage which is Mishnah commentary "may cite and then gloss Mishnah or respond to problems clearly raised by Mishnah in a way which clearly depends upon Mishnah". Complementary units in Tosefta "do not cite and gloss Mishnah, [but] "clearly are intended to augment and complement the main ideas of Mishnah's equivalent and corresponding pericopae" (Neusner, 1986e:202). My own categories of Tosefta as explication and as complement of Mishnah differently distinguish between those toseftan materials which in Neusner's categorization would be found in his toseftan commentary and complement taken together. No doubt, some of his commentary as well as his complementary units I classify as explicative, for example. My own categorization appears better suited to this work's particular purpose, namely, relating substantive relationships with Mishnah and Tosefta's rhetorical features.

() = explicates; [] = complements; {} = supplements

Tosefta	relates to our m., t.	cites our m.	cites other m., t.	relates to other m., t.
C2-D		**m.1:3A-B**		
1:1E-H	**(m.1:3E-G)**			
E-G1		m.1:3E-G		
G.2-H	same			
1:1I-M	**[m.1:3E-G & t.1:1E-G]**			
I	same			
J-K5	same			
K2			m.3:6	
K5			same	
L-M	[t.1:1I-M]			[.3.5]
1:1N-O	**[m.1:1G-I]**			
N1	same			
N2		m.1:1G		
O	same			
P		m.1:1I		
1:2A-1:3D	**(m.1:3 & m.1:1 // t.1:1A-D)**			
1:2A-B	same			
C		m.1:1A-B=t.1:1A-B		
D		m.1:3C		
E	same			
1:3A-B		m.1:3A-B=t.1:1C-D		
C	(m.1:3C)			
D		m.1:3D		
1:3E-M	**[m.1:3D]**			
E	same			
F		m.1:3D		
G-M	same			
1:3N-O	**(m.1:2A.3-B)**			
N		m.1:2B		
O	same			
1:3P-X	**[m.1:3A-D // t.1:3A-D]**			
1:4A-E	**(m.1:5A-E)**			
A-B	same			
C-E		m.1:5C-E		
1:4F-Q	**(m.1:5F-K)+[K]**			

() = explicates; [] = complements; { } = supplements

Tosefta	relates to our m., t.	cites our m.	cites other m., t.	relates to other m., t.
F-G		m.1:5F-G		
H-Ia	(m.1:5F-J)			
Ib		m.1:5I		
- - - - - - - -	- - - - - - - - - -	- - - - - - - -	- - - - - - - - - -	- - - - - - - - - -
J-P	(m.1:5K)			
J-M	same			
N		m.1:5Kb		
O-P	same			
- - - - - - - -	- - - - - - - - - -	- - - - - - - -	- - - - - - - - - -	- - - - - - - - - -
Q	[m.1:5K]			
1:5A-L	**(m.1:6F-L)+[m.1:6F-L]**			
A-F	(m.1:6F-L)			
A1b-A2		m.1:6F		
B		m.1:6G		
C-Da	same			
Db		m.1:6Jb		
E-Fa		m.1:6Ha+Ib		
- - - - - - - -	- - - - - - - - - -	- - - - - - - -	- - - - - - - - - -	- - - - - - - - - -
G-L	[m.1:6F-L]			
Gb-I			t.Ter.10:3	
J-L	same			
1:6-1:9	**[m.1:6O,B,P-Q]**			
1:6A-1:7C	[m.1:6O,B]			
A		m.1:6A,M,O		
A-D	same			
E			m.6:1//t.4(6):1	
E-G	same			
G		m.1:6B		
H-I	same			
1:7A-C	same			
- - - - - - - -	- - - - - - - - - -	- - - - - - - -	- - - - - - - - - -	- - - - - - - - - -
D-G	[m.1:6P-Q]			
D		m.1:6P		
D-E	same			
F-G	same			
- - - - - - - -	- - - - - - - - - -	- - - - - - - -	- - - - - - - - - -	- - - - - - - - - -
1:8A-E	[m.1:6O,B]			
A			m.6:1//t.4(6):1	
B			t.4(6):1	
C-E	same			
- - - - - - - -	- - - - - - - - - -	- - - - - - - -	- - - - - - - - - -	- - - - - - - - - -
F-J	[m.1:6P-Q]			
F-G	same			
H-I	same			
J	same	m.1:6Q		
- - - - - - - -	- - - - - - - - - -	- - - - - - - -	- - - - - - - - - -	- - - - - - - - - -

() = explicates; [] = complements; { } = supplements

Tosefta	relates to our m., t.	cites our m.	cites other m., t.	relates to other m., t.
1:9A-I	[m.1:6P-Q]			
A-G	same			
A			t.4(6):2b	
B			same	
C			same	
H-I	same			
2:1A-H	**[m.2:1A-D]**			
A		m.2:1A//m.1:1A//m.1:3E		
B	same			
C		m.2:1B-C//m.1:1B//m.1:3F		
D-H	same			
2:2A-H	**{t.2:1A-H}**			
A-C	same			
D	[t.2:2A-C]			
E-H	same			
G-H			t.2:1G-H	
2:2I-N	**(m.2:1Q)**			
I-N		m.2:1K-O,Q		
2:2O-Q	**(m.2:2K,L-O)**			
O		m.2:2A		
P		m.2:2B		
Q		m.2:2G		
2:2R-W	**[m.1:3A-B]+[m.1:1A-B]**			
R-S	same			
T		m. 1:1B		
U-W	same			

The first and most basic observation borne out by Chart 1 is that our attempt to apply our classification of mishnaic rhetorical traits to t. Gittin 1:1-2:2 has been extraordinarily "successful." This was not the case at all when, in our work on the Bavli, methods developed for the documentation of rhetorical character of the Babylonian Talmud were applied to Mishnah, Tosefta, and Halakic Midrash (see Lightstone, 1994, chapter 5). Matters appear otherwise in the case at hand, when applying Mishnah-based methodologies to t. Gittin 1:1-2:2. The vast majority of the language of Tosefta is easily subsumed in columns 1 through 7, just like Mishnah. The eighth column, reserved for language that is not an instance of Mishnah-like rhetorical features, is relatively devoid of material, just like Mishnah. The joining/concatenating formulae, "and," "that," "says," "lo," are prominent in column 1, just as in Mishnah. Much of column 2, reserved for formulae with which logical and analogical arguments are constructed, is, like Mishnah, largely empty. Like Mishnah, the repetition of similar phrases with or without paired opposites (e.g., "fit" vs. "unfit," or x vs. "not" x) abounds in columns 5, 6, and 7. Sustaining verb morphology within pericopes and across the opening protases of several pericopae seems entirely Mishnah-like and helps give an air of unity and coherence to a larger composition defined by its subject matter, like a Mishnah "chapter." Moreover, certain homophonic/homosemantic markers, in particular "in my presence it was written [and] in my presence it was signed," appear regularly throughout, giving further rhetorical definition to the Toseftan "chapter." Not only does this resemble Mishnah rhetorically, m. Gittin 1:1-2:2, the Mishnah "chapter" with which our toseftan passages correlate in subject matter, uses the very same homophonic/homosemantic markers throughout. Finally, like Mishnah, t. Gittin 1:1-2:2 shows at several junctures the systematic, lyrical repetition *cum* permutation of terms and phrases to generate and "spin out" cases for legal adjudication. Several quite elegant examples are t. 1:3G-M (complementing m. 1:3D = t. 1:3C and F), t. 2:2R-W (complementing m. 1:1A-B and m. 1:3A-B) and especially the extended construction of 1:6-1:9 (complementing m. 1:6O.B,P-Q).

All this being said, much about t. Gittin 1:1-2:2 seems decidedly different than Mishnah. First, both Chart 1 and Chart 2 document the sustained literary dependence of Tosefta on Mishnah, in particular on the Mishnah "chapter" *ad locum* (as shown in Chart 1 by the appearance of text in capital letters). In addition, Tosefta remains at many junctures logically dependent upon the Mishnah "chapter" *ad locum* to be *fully* intelligible. Some toseftan perciopes logically require Mishnah without having cited it at all, or after having only partially cited Mishnah. Take, for example, t. 1:1Iff ("they used to say . . ."); it appears to "come from nowhere" (to use a colloquial expression), unless the reader is aware of m. Gittin 1:1A-B. Even t. Gittin 1:1A-D, which fully cites m. 1:1A-B and m. 1:3A-B, has a strong *non-sequitur* air about it, if read without knowledge that t. 1:1A2-B and t. C2-D in fact quote an antecedent mishnaic text that is Tosefta's object of analysis and amplification. This alone serves to show that Tosefta, from a rhetorical perspective, presents itself as a *derivative and dependent exercise*. In dramatic contrast, Mishnah, rhetorically speaking, presents itself as a highly independent, self-contained text, despite Mishnah's obvious logical dependency at many junctures on Pentateuchal law.

The derivative, dependent nature of Tosefta is communicated in yet another way, again evident in its contrast to Mishnah. As noted, Mishnah takes great pains to rhetorically join individual pericopes to a "chapter's" shank. Take, for example, the use of both repetition of phrases and morphology to join m. Gittin 1:4,5 and 6 to one another and to the shank of the Mishnah chapter at m. 1:3. The list that follows aptly demonstrates the point.

Chart 3.3: Morphological and phrase repetition unifying
m. Gittin 1:3-1:6

m. 1:3 [part of shank]

One who
> brings
>> a writ [of divorce] . . .

One who
> brings
>> a writ [of divorce] . . . .

m. 1:4

. . .

> writs of [divorce of] women
> manumission papers of slaves . . .

one who
> takes

one who
> brings
>> writs of [divorce of] women
>> manumission papers of slaves . . . .

m. 1:5

. . .

> writ . . .
> writs of [divorce of] women and
> manumission papers of slaves. . .

> writ of [divorce of] a woman . . .

> writs of [divorce of] women and
> manumission papers of slaves . . . .

m. 1:6

one who
> says:
> give
>> this
>> writ of [divorce of] to my wife and
>> this
>> manumission paper to my slaves . . .

>> writs of [divorce of] women . . .
>> not . . . manumission papers of slaves . . . .

one who
> says:
> give
>> this
>> writ of [divorce of] to my wife and
>> this
>> manumission paper to my slave . . .

> give
>> this

maneh
to so-and-so.

Throughout this section of the Mishnah "chapter," the mishnaic authors have carefully managed to reflect at every juncture some salient aspect of the language of
the antecedent section, even though by the end of m. 1:6 the subject matter has
wandered quite far from the concerns of the chapter's shank, as represented at m.
1:3. By contrast, consider t. 1:6, which commences the longest, most elegant and,
with respect to its rhetorical character, seemingly the most Mishnah-like composition (t.1:6-9) in our Toseftan "chapter." Aside from the morphology of the verb
which opens 1:6 (ה + 3rd person sing. part.), absolutely nothing in the language of
t. 1:6 (or t. 1:7,8 and 9) reflects the language of the preceding part of the Tosefta
"chapter," t. 1:1-5. However, the language of t. 1:6 (and, therefore, of t. 1:7-9)
extensively reflects the language at several junctures of m. 1:6. On the basis of
such evidence I suggest that *at the level of the rhetorical use of language, and
quite apart from legal substance,* Tosefta implicitly communicates that *the unity
and coherence of Tosefta resides in, and derives from, Mishnah, and not in itself.*
Of this aspect of Tosefta's rhetorical character, Tosefta 1:6-9 provides a blatant
example. But a similar analysis of t. 1:4 and 1:5 gives a similar result.

We are faced, in the end, with an interesting paradox. At first glance it
appeared that, in attempting to reinforce and represent the unity and coherence of
its "chapter," t. Gittin 1:1-2:2 has used the repetition of the very same phrases that
Mishnah has used to aid in the demarcation of its larger substantive unit (i.e., "in
my presence it was written and in my presence it was signed"). Yet Tosefta's use
of Mishnah-like rhetorical techniques and devices shows that Tosefta's authors,
by comparison, are either less skilled in, or less concerned with, using these
devices to effect anywhere near the same level of internal integrity as is evident in
Mishnah. What, then, does one make of Tosefta's use of "in my presence it was
written and in my presence it was signed?" In light of the foregoing discussion, I
suggest that by this means as well Tosefta implicitly represents itself as derivative
of, and dependent upon, Mishnah.

Tosefta not only presents itself as an exercise that is derivative of and
dependent on the correlative Mishnah "chapter," but also as assuming a vantage
point that looks beyond the horizon of the immediate correlative Mishnah passage, the analysis and amplification of which Tosefta represents as its purpose and
the basis of its own organization of materials. Our toseftan "chapter" cites what it
considers relevant material from elsewhere in both Mishnah and Tosefta (e.g., m.
Gittin 3:5, 6:1, t. Gittin 4(6):1-2, t. Ter. 10:8). The long composition at t. 1:6-9 is
an interesting case in point, precisely because in a highly Mishnah-like manner, it
uses repetition and permutation to "spin out" a series of cases for adjudication.
The operative verb of the first protases in t. 1:6 and t. 1:7 ("give") is taken from
m. 1:6. The operative verbs of protases in t. 1:8 and t. 1:9 ("take," "make receive,"
"make benefit," "carry," "bear," and "let be") are taken from m. 6:1 and t. 4(6):1-
2. They appear in our Tosefta composition in exactly the same order as in t.
4(6):1-2, although the rest of the language of the composition is clearly dependent
upon our Mishnah pericope *ad locum* (m. 1:6).

In effect, Tosefta achieves two things at t. 1:6-9. Most obvious, it produces a rather elegant "Mishnah chapter" of its own, provided one understands a pericope reconstructed from m. 1:6 (O,B,P-Q) as its opening "Mishnah section." More subtly, it breaks any exclusive focus on the Mishnah "chapter" *ad locum* and implicitly represents the legitimacy of a process of culling "snippets" of material from elsewhere in both Mishnah and Tosefta in the construction of "new, additional knowledge" of the ordered world created by halakah. However, in Mishnah the process of creating and defining this world is rhetorically represented as constructed out of nowhere, or rather, out of a self-contained contemplation of a halakically defined world. I suggest that in Tosefta, by contrast, we see a shift to a view that one can contribute to Mishnah-like world definition by contemplating authoritative texts, elements of which may be excised and recombined. In other words, it appears that in its rhetorical features Tosefta represents a kind of authoritative virtuosity which is founded upon (1) knowledge and contemplation of authoritative texts, especially, but not exclusively, of Mishnah, in order to (2) expand upon and proffer a finer and more precise "resolution" (in the optical sense) of Mishnah's world. Consistent with this claim is the dependency of Tosefta on Mishnah, and the paradoxical Mishnah-like character of much of Tosefta's pericope, contrasted with the total lack, at the level of rhetorical characteristics, of a Mishnah-like, self-contained coherence and unity.

This "explicative" virtuosity reflected and modelled by Tosefta may help account for some other features evident in Charts 1 and 2, which we have yet to discuss. Despite, or in addition to, Tosefta's imitation of Mishnah-like rhetoric, there is as well a tendency to overcome Mishnah's laconic character. As I have noted, Mishnah's rhetorical features give rise to a curious mixture of redundant repetition, on the one hand, and an obvious laconic character, on the other. Because of the latter, it is often not, grammatically speaking obvious what a mishnaic pericope must mean. Tosefta at several junctures attempts merely to remediate Mishnah's laconic nature, within certain limiting parameters–coming up with a pericope which, in all other respects. is rhetorically Mishnah-like. To illustrate this point, let me take just one example, t.1:1E-H, and contrast it with the Mishnah pericope which it cites and explicates, m. 1:3E-G.

Chart 3. 4: Synopsis of m. Gittin 1:3E-G
and t. Gittin 1:1E-H

m. Gittin 1:3E-G	t. Gittin 1:1E-H
1. One who	One who
2. brings	brings
3. a writ	a writ
4. from a Mediterranean province	from a Mediterranean province
5. and	[and]
6. cannot say:	cannot say:
7. In my presence it was written	In my presence it was written
8. and	and
9. in my presence it was signed—	in my presence it was signed—
10. if	
11. - - - - -	he is able to make it

12. there are upon it witnesses,	- - - - -
13. it shall stand upon its signatures.	stand upon its signatures,
14. - - - - -	it is fit
15. - - - - -	and
16. - - - - -	if
17. - - - - -	not
18. - - - - -	it is unfit.

In terms of meaning, I do not see how Tosefta adds anything new to Mishnah. M. 1:3E-G is formulated to parallel the language of what precedes it at m. 1:3A-D. Tosefta has no such constraints; its focus is solely m. 1:3E-G, which Tosefta cites almost in full and then glosses. With the gloss we have a rather nice Mishnah-like pericope, concluding with a well-balanced apodasis. But substantively Tosefta equals Mishnah. What is achieved? All that has happened is a reduction by Tosefta of the laconic character of Mishnah.

T. 1:2C-1:3D is another exercise in explicative virtuosity. In this case Tosefta brings this expertise to bear on m. 1:1A-B and m. 1:3A-B, now melded into a single pericope, and provided with a prefatory structure (t. 1:2A-B) which is rare but not unknown for Mishnah "chapters."[3]

Chart 3.5: Synopsis of m. Gittin 1:1A-B and 1:3A-B
and t. Gittin 1:2C-E and 1:3A-D

m. Gittin 1:1A-B	*t. Gittin 1:2C-E*
1. One who	One who
2. brings	brings
3. a writ	a writ
4. from	from
5. a Mediterranean province—	a Mediterranean province—
6. it is required	it is required
7. that	that
8. he should say:	he should say:
9. In my presence it was written	In my presence it was written
10. and	and
11. in my presence it was signed.	in my presence it was signed.
12. - - - - -	Even though
13. (see m. line 29)	there are
14. (see m. line 30)	challengers
15. (see m. line 31)	to it,
16. - - - - -	it is fit.
m. Gittin 1:3A-B	*t. Gittin 1:3A-D*
17. One who	One who
18. brings	brings
19. a writ	a writ
20. within	from
21. the Land of Israel—	the Land of Israel—

---

3.   See, for example, m. Shabbat 1:1 and m. Bekhorot 8:1.

22. it is not required	it is not required
23. that	that
24. he should say:	he should say:
25. In my presence it was written	In my presence it was written
26. and	and
27. in my presence it was signed.	in my presence it was signed.
28. If	If
29. there are	there are
30. challengers	- - - - -
31. to it,	- - - - -
32. - - - - -	upon it
33. - - - - -	witnesses,
34. it	it
35. shall stand	shall be established
36. upon	upon
37. its	its
38. signatures.	signatures.

Once again, Tosefta has added little or nothing to the substance of Mishnah, other than to explicate what most readers would have easily concluded from Mishnah upon reflection. Tosefta has gone about its work by bringing m. 1:1A-B and m. 1:3A-B together and, for the most part, by using the language of the latter to make explicit what is implicit in the former but eclipsed by Mishnah's typical laconic rhetorical character.

Similarly, t. 1:4A-E and t. 1:4F-P are explicated versions of m. 1:5A-E and m. 1:5F-K respectively.[4] T. 1:5A-F, moreover, is a less laconic version of the "debate" at 1:6F-L in Mishnah. Relative to Tosefta, Mishnah contains significantly fewer, and rather short, "debates." T. 1:5G-L, then, provides an additional rebuttal for one of the parties. Perhaps because of this relative movement away from Mishnah's more extreme laconic character, Tosefta, interestingly, introduces more formulae that help construct argument. Hence column 2 of our scored charting of t. 1:5 contains more material than we have ever seen in that column in our chartings of Mishnah.

Our analysis of the rhetorical features of t. Gittin 1:1-2:2 has been far from exhaustive or comprehensive. Time and space do not allow it. Moreover, the focus of the analysis is not the rhetorical study of Tosefta, but of Mishnah. This analysis should help this endeavour by providing a meaningful point of comparison. Notwithstanding, what social definitions of authority and authoritativeness are modelled in Tosefta's particular rhetorical character?

---

4.   The only net substantive addition to m. 1:5 lies in adding more attributions to named rabbinic figues. The substance of Mishnah is largely anonymous (see Neusner, 1981 and subsequent works on Mishnah). Despite the addition of attributions in this Tosefta passage, Tosefta shows no decided tendency to attributions in comparison with Mishnah, as shown by Neusner (1986e).

III
Tosefta's rhetoric and models of authoritative virtuosity in the post-mishnaic rabbinic guild

To broach this issue let me rehearse what I have previously argued with respect to Mishnah, the text which is obviously Tosefta's focus. I have characterized Mishnah's rhetoric as the lyrical, permutative, list-like concatenation of cases and rulings in which the inner logic remains ever implicit and in which "lyrical" completeness is sometimes in itself sufficient, implicit justification for including a case in a list. Moreover, rhetorical markers (as opposed to, or in addition to, substantive completion) mark off "chapters" of Mishnah as whole and complete in themselves. Finally, Mishnah's rhetorical characteristics give it a highly self-referential and self-contained air. What immediate realm in social formation may have been served by rhetorically depicting such expertise or virtuosity as "normal," "appropriate," and "authoritative?"

The question is so framed as to imply an answer: the ability to compose and spin out such lists in such a lyrical fashion was in and of itself a principal *hallmark* and *mode* of authoritativeness constituting the "mastery" of the "mishnaic" rabbi (lit. "my master"). By their very appearance in such a lyrical, permutative list, the rules for specified cases and the "system" which these rules comprise gain an air of self-evident appropriateness. That is to say, the rhetorical form bespeaks the authority of the list-maker-lyricist "master" and lends authority to individual items in the list, to the list as a whole, and to the emerging legal system contained in a series of topically related lists. However, the system or world which is the focus of attention, and partially mapped out, in such lyrical, baroque-like list-making is an imagined, utopian, ideal one. In that imagined world a Temple and its related institutions still stand and occupy the centre, 130 or so years after the historical Temple state's demise. Thus the Mishnah rhetorically reinforces and reflects a portrayal of elite, authoritative virtuosity that may be characterized as a mastery of guardianship of the old priestly-scribally stewarded social and cultic order, an order that is self-contained, complete, and entirely self-referential.[5]

Is the authoritative virtuosity, the mode of "being a rabbi," implicitly reflected in Tosefta's rhetorical features a mere simulation of that modelled in Mishnah's? To a degree, the answer is yes—this insofar as many Toseftan pericopes undertake the same type of repetitive, permutative exercise to generate lists of cases for which rulings must be supplied. In this respect Toseftan "rabbis'" virtuosity appears to be an attempt to perpetuate Mishnah's.

Here, however, is precisely where and why the similarity breaks down. An analysis of Tosefta's rhetorical features against the backdrop of the rhetoric of Mishnah, brings to the fore two dominant features of Toseftan rhetoric. First, it is

---

5. I have made this case previously on more limited evidentiary grounds, simply by comparing Mishnah's tendency to use joining language to the Babylonian Talmud's penchant for formulae that pose challenges and questions and that support logico-deductive arguments. See Lightstone, 1994:253-59, and, although also based on the comparative perspective supplied by the Talmud, the more fully developed argument in Lightstone, 1995b.

highly derivative of, and dependent upon, Mishnah. Any unity, coherence and, often, intelligibility of a larger Toseftan unit derives from, and requires constant attention to, another text, which is its principal object of focus and attention. Second, Tosefta's rhetoric, relative to its object of analysis, Mishnah, is largely explicative of the latter, spelling out in only quasi-mishnaic-like rhetoric that which must remain only implicit in Mishnah because of its own rhetorical tendencies. Again the focus of the Toseftan "master" is Mishnah. And as we have now demonstrated, this is the case not only in that Tosefta has been organized with respect to Mishnah's topical divisions. It is so as well at the level of the rhetorical characteristics of individual units, in the very choice of language and implicit rules governing a unit's formulation. In all, the toseftan "master's" focus, the object of a toseftan "rabbi's" exercise of authoritative virtuosity, which on the surface seems so Mishnah-like, is not so much the ideal Temple world (as in Mishnah) as Mishnah itself. The mishnaic rabbi imagines a Temple state created in the self-contained, self-referential rhetorical world of Mishnah-making. The toseftan rabbi contemplates a privileged object, Mishnah, which ever lies outside as an external referent of Tosefta-making.[6]

In the final analysis, in the move from Mishnah's to Tosefta's rhetoric, we see the reflection of, and the model for, a drift in the mode of exercising rabbinic virtuosity, that is, in the social definition within the rabbinic guild of "being a rabbi." For a tosefta-formed rabbi, that elite, authoritative virtuosity involved being a close, incisive reader and explicator of a text, specifically Mishnah. If the mishnaic rabbi is more a priestly scribe, then the toseftan master has begun the social transformation toward an exegetical scribe, on the road toward, but still far from, the image of the scholastic philosopher reflected in the Babylonian Talmud's diatribe-like rhetoric.

The drift in the model of "being a rabbi" represented in Tosefta's dissimulation of Mishnah evidences, perhaps, yet another transformation, a change in the imagined or ideal social venue of the exercise of quintessential rabbinic virtuosity. Mishnaic rabbis "imagine" themselves to be priestly scribes, Temple bureaucrats (albeit without a "real" Temple as an institutionalized base for their profession). Toseftan rabbis, as argued, value above all the close reading and explication of text, or, at least, of an authoritative text, the Mishnah. As persons operating in the social climate of the Late Roman, eastern Mediterranean world and espousing such activity as the hallmark of their virtuosity and authority, in what authoritative institutionalized setting, real or imagined, do they locate themselves? As I have noted elsewhere (Lightstone, 1995b:n.1), in that social world persons and groups dedicated to study and analysis, valued to some significant degree for their own sake, of received texts and traditions expressed an ethos associated, not with Temples and civic bureaucracies and administrations, but with guilds or colleges

---

6.   Any reader familiar with J. Neusner's conclusions about the structure and formal traits of Tosefta (see Neusner, 1986e:201-249), will find that my own claims to complement his own, although this study has reached its conclusions asking quite different questions and adopting a methodology substantially different from Neusner's. In all, my own conclusions bear out his.

of scholars, schools, and academies of various types and sizes (Saldarini, 1982:79-82; see also Downey, 1960:147-64). Interestingly, the earliest material evidence for rabbinic schools is for late-third-century Galilee (Levine, 1985), a matter to which we return in Chapter 5. Of course, one does not require a physical schoolhouse to have the social institution.

In sum, what may well be reflected in, and/or facilitated by, the rhetorical drift from Mishnah to Tosefta is a social-institution-in-(re)formation—the slow metamorphosis of rabbinic guild virtuosity from priestly scribe toward the exegete schoolmaster—later to find its more complete statement in the rhetoric of the Talmud(s). Or perhaps what we see is some pale historical reflection of the beginnings of differentiation of social roles or specialization(s) within the third-century Galilean rabbinic guild, wherein the civic bureaucratic rabbi is complemented by the exegete schoolmaster in whose hands lies specifically the training of the guild's *relève*. With these conclusions in view we turn to the next point of comparison, Maseket Semahot.

4

Semahot's Remaking of Mishnah's Rhetoric

I
Gaining more comparative advantage

Earlier I articulated two claims. The notion of "fit" is key to both of them. First, the cultural and social world is experienced by their inhabitants as coherent (and therefore as real) because of the fit or integration which obtains *synchronically* across the many socially constructed spheres comprising that world. Second, complete coherence and integration is an ideal that is never achievable– is, in fact, increasingly unattainable with the passage of time. Internal and external forces impinging upon the elements of the social and cultural world constantly elicit uncoordinated and uneven transformations and experimentation.

While this is true of society or the socially constructed world as a whole, it is also the case within a more circumscribed group, guild or association. For example, some members may transform and/or augment the core expertise constituting the guild mastery. In their view, these changes may better enable them to carry out their role as guild masters. In such transformations and experimentation, *diachronic* fit with the already established and legitimated models of guild expertise becomes an issue. In other words, the past tends to lay claim to authority over the present in all societies, especially in traditional ones.

The degree of elasticity of both synchronic fit and diachronic continuity in any given society or association will determine whether conflict and separation, or variety and accommodation, will emerge as preferred routes to social transformation and experimentation. In terms of a professional guild, such as that of the early rabbis, will the guild permit new and different guild competencies to accrue to some (or all) members, or will schism and the emergence of competing associations of masters result in each group peddling its distinctive set of expertise to society? Will traditional, core expertise persist alongside new complementary forms of virtuosity; will the former give way before the latter; or will claims regarding the exclusivity of the former dominate within the guild? This admixture of synchronic and diachronic issues regarding social fit and social persistence are lived in any professional guild, whether that of the ancient rabbis, or that of the modern college of physicians.

What is the significance of the above for our larger project? The production and promulgation of Mishnah, with its particular rhetoric, in our view, reflects and helps define *the* authoritative guild expertise that was core to the social formation of the early rabbinic guild. To be sure, other associated or supplementary professional competencies may have been present. But from the *prima facie* evidence listed earlier nothing had the pre-eminence of Mishnah and the study of Mishnah in the early rabbinic guild. How long did that core expertise persist unchanged? How was it modified or augmented? In what directions?

Let me be clear about my precise focus of interest in asking these questions. I am not concerned here with supplementary expertise, which is quite different from that reflected in Mishnah's rhetoric and which might have originally been present or been nurtured within the early rabbinic guild. The earliest rabbinic guild might have valued those with theurgic prowess, or members who know the praxis of mystical ascent, or rabbis capable of midrashic exposition of scripture. Rather my concern focuses on the transformation of the mishnaic (core) expertise itself as initially represented in the foundational document of the guild, the Mishnah. The body of evidence that permits us this focus is found in documents which bear a closer, rather than further, family resemblance to Mishnah. The most obvious of these is Tosefta, for example. (Indeed, the family resemblance of Tosefta and Mishnah is such that pre-modern and a number of modern scholars– up to 1975 or so– saw Tosefta as a collection of some of the "raw materials" Mishnah's editors had in hand.)

The method for tracing persistence and transformation of mishnah-like core expertise in the early rabbinic movement is systematic comparison of mishnaic rhetoric and the rhetorical characteristics of these more mishnah-like texts. More specifically, the precise taxonomy developed to "chart" or "score" the constituent elements of Mishnah's rhetoric is applied to other documents. The results of the latter exercises are compared to those resulting from analysis of Mishnah.

In addition to the aforementioned theoretical and conceptual reasons for undertaking systematic comparison, there is as well a simpler methodological reason for doing so. The nature of one social (arti)fact is brought into high relief by systematic comparison with other apparently similar or parallel social (arti)facts. To serve these "perceptual" needs, end comparisons can be cross-cultural, or intra-cultural across time. The attendant theoretical concerns will determine the choice. Because of this work's interest in addressing the aforementioned questions about the persistence and transformation of core expertise within a professional guild, comparative analyses stay within the historical and social frame of the early rabbinic guild.

I have already compared Tosefta with Mishnah. If Toseftan evidence[1] bespeaks the latter half of the third century, as is generally accepted, then toseftan rhetoric, I have argued, gives evidence of a "drift" in early rabbinic guild expertise to a type of commentary by gloss and supplementation of mishnaic materials. That is why Toseftan pericopes look so mishnah-like, but fuller in their articulation, to those who (mistakenly) maintained that Tosefta preserved much of Mishnah's source materials. In *The Rhetoric of the Babylonian Talmud, Its Social Meaning and Context*, I argued that the Palestinian Talmud[2] (mid- to late-fifth century) in

---

1.   My choice of this wording deliberately finesses the question of the date of redaction of Tosefta. However, Neusner's analyses of Tosefta and my own (episodic) analyses of toseftan parallels in halakic midrash, in the Palestinian Talmud, and in the Babylonian Talmud are consistent with the hypothesis that toseftan materials are third century.
2.   I refer here specifically to the non-midrashic sections of the Palestinian Talmud.

many respects represents a further development of the expertise reflected in Tosefta's rhetorical features.

In this chapter, I submit two of the 14 chapters of Maseket Semahot (the Tractate Mourning) to an analysis using the identical rhetorical taxonomy developed for Mishnah, just as I did for Tosefta in the previous chapter. Semahot may seem at one and the same time both an obvious and an inappropriate choice. It is obvious, because, as with Tosefta, the literary traits of Semahot are closest in family resemblance to those of Mishnah, as indeed we shall see.

Semahot may seem to some scholars an inappropriate choice, because according to many it dates from the seventh or eight century CE. However, the reasons adduced for this late dating seem odd to me. Let me rehearse them. Maseket Semahot seems never to have been among the core authoritative texts of the early rabbinic movement. Relative to other texts, Semahot was infrequently studied in antiquity or in the medieval period. It has not attracted the body of commentary that other more seminal documents have. All of these arguments can also be made concerning Tosefta. Indeed, they had been by Solomon Zeitlin. And they are no more probative with respect to Semahot than they are as regards Tosefta. Dov Zlotnick was the first modern scholar to attract some significant support for a late-third-century dating of Semahot. Today, very few would support Zeitlin's dating of Tosefta, and Zlotnick's reasons for an earlier dating of Semahot bear a resemblance to those of Zeitlin's detractors regarding his late dating of Tosefta. My own purpose is quite other than to contribute to this debate. Nevertheless, the results of this chapter's rhetorical analysis of Semahot would seem to lend weight to Zlotnick's dating;[3] I shall return to this claim near the end of the chapter.

II
A rhetorical "scoring" of Semahot 1-2

Let me turn now to the rhetorical analysis of Semahot, chapters 1 and 2, using the identical taxonomy developed for the description of Mishnah's principal rhetorical features. As in the preceding chapter, I first provide my segmented translation of the text. The rhetorical "scoring" of the same text follows.

1:1
a. One who is dying—lo, he is like a living [person] with respect to (ל) all matters.
b. He must [fulfill obligations to enter into] levirate marriage.
c. And he causes [his dependents to be eligible] to eat heave offering [if he is a priest].
d. And he renders [his dependents] unfit [to eat] from heave offering [if he is a priest].

---

3. Moreover, when in the preparation of my translation of chapters 1 and 2 of Semahot I checked parallels in the Babylonian Talmud, I saw no probative evidence that Semahot's pericope was dependent upon the Babylonian Talmuds's. Indeed, the literary formulation of such pericopes seemed far more consistent with their literary setting in the chapter of Semahot than with their context in the Babylonian Talmud.

e.	And he inherits [property].
f.	And he causes [others] to inherit [property].
g.	[If] a limb is separated from him, [the limb] is like [i.e., is subject to the laws concerning] a limb from a living [being].
h.	[If] flesh, [the flesh] is like [i.e., is subject to the laws concerning] flesh from a living [being].
i.	And they sprinkle for him the blood of his purification offering and the blood of his guilt offering.
j.	[All of the above applies] until such time that he dies.

1:2
a.	They do not tie his jaws.
b.	And they do not stop up his orifices.
c.	And they do not lay upon him a metal vessel, and not something that cools upon his abdomen,
d.	until such time that he dies.

1:3
a.	They do not move him.
b.	And they do not bathe him.
c.	And they do not carry him—
d.	not upon [a bier covered with] sand,
e.	and not upon [a bier covered with] salt,
f.	until such time that he dies.

1:4
a.	They do not close his eyes.
b.	One who touches him
c.	and [one] who moves him—
d.	lo, he spills blood.
e.	R. Meir used to liken him [i.e., dying person] to a shimmering candle/lamp;
f.	Since someone touched it, immediately, one extinguished it.
g.	So too they who close the eyes of a dying person.
h.	They account him as though he loosens his, [the dying person's soul, from his body].

1:5
a.	They [the relatives of the dying person] do not tear [their garments as one does for a deceased.]
b.	And they do not loosen [clothing to bare their shoulders, as one does for a deceased].
c.	And they do not eulogize [the dying man].
d.	And they do not bring into the house with him a coffin
e.	until such time that he dies.

1:6
a.	They do not acclaim him
b.	And they do not recount in regards to him his [noteworthy] deeds [until such time that he dies.]
c.	R. Judah says: If [the dying person] was a sage, they do recount in regards to him his [noteworthy] deeds [even before such time that he dies.]

1:7
a.	[At such time that he dies], they do not inquire after the well-being in a small city.
b.	With respect to what [circumstances] is this stated?

c.   In a small village.

d.   But (אבל) in a large city, it is permitted.

1:8

a.   A severed [foetus],

b.   a breech-birth [foetus who does not survive],

c.   a miscarried [foeti],

d.   one at eight months [gestation] [born] alive [that then dies],

e.   and one at nine months [gestation] [born] dead—

f.   they do not attend to [Israelite funerary and mourning rites with respect to] it in any manner.

1:9

a.   Gentiles and slaves [who die]—they [the Israelites] do not attend to [pagan rites] together with them [the pagan mourners] in any manner.

b.   But (אבל) (pres. part. pl.) they [the Israelites] do call out [publicly] together with them [the pagan mourners]: Woe, [departed] lion; woe, [departed] hero.

c.   R. Judah says: [Also] [they, the Israelites, do] [call:] Woe [departed] faithful witness, who consumed the outcome of his labour.

d.   They said to him: If so, what have you left [as an approbation] for the fit [i.e., Israelite, departed]?

e.   He said to them: If he [or she] were fit [i.e., an Israelite], wherefore (מפני מה) do they [the Israelites] not call out [publicly] in regards to him [or her]?

1:10

a.   They [the Israelites] do not (emend: negative particle, אין) receive condolences on account of [the death of] slaves.

b.   And it once transpired that when (ומעשה כש) the handmaiden of R. Eliezer died, his disciples entered to console him.

c.   He [then] entered before them into the courtyard [to avoid them].

d.   They entered after him.

e.   [He then entered] into the house.

f.   They entered after him.

g.   He said to them: It seemed to me that you would be scalled with warm [water], and [by contrast] you are not scalded [even] with hot [water];

h.   Thus have I not taught you—

i.   that they [the Israelites] do not receive condolences on account of [the death of] slaves,

j.   because (מפני ש) slaves are considered to be like animals [i.e., living property]?

k.   And when (וכש) Tevi, the slave of R. Gamaliel, died,

l.   he received condolences on account of him.

m.   Said to him his disciples:

n.   And have you not taught us—

o.   that they [the Israelites] do not receive condolences on account of [the death of] slaves?

p.   He said to them: Tevi, my slave, is not like other slaves; as (ש) he was fit.

q.   Also (אף) he [R. Gamaliel] permitted him to put on phylacteries.

r.   They said to him: Have you not instructed us that slaves are exempt from [the obligation of putting on] phylacteries?

s.   He said to them: Tevi, my slave, is not like other slaves; since (כי) he is fit.

1:11

a.   They [the Israelites] do not (emend: negative particle, אין) call out [publicly] on account of (ל) [the death of] male slaves and on account of (ל) female slaves: Father so-and-so and Mother so-and-so.

b.   And [on account of] those [slaves] from (של-) the House of R. Gamaliel, they used to call out [publicly] on account of [the death of] his slave: Father Tevi and Mother Tevita (as

emended by Elijah, Gaon of Vilna on the basis of parallel in b. Ber. 16b; as noted in Zlotnick, ed., 1966, p. 100, n.11).

1:12

a. They [the Israelites] do not (emend: אין) call out [publicly] on account of (ל) [the death
of] Fathers [that is, recognizing the deceased as an ancestor of the people]: Our Father
[so-and-so], except (אלא) on account of (ל) [memorializing the death of] the three Fathers
[of the people, Abraham, Isaac and Jacob];

b. and [they do] not [call out publicly] on account of (ל) [the death of] Mothers [that is,
recognizing the deceased as an ancestor of the people]: Our Mother [so-and-so], except
(אלא) on account of (ל) [memorializing the death of] the four Mothers [of the people,
Sarah, Rebecca, Rachel and Leah].

2:1

a. One who commits suicide with forethought—they [the Israelites] do not attend to
[funerary and mourning rites] in regards to him in any manner.

b. R. Ishmael says: They do call out [publicly] in regards to him: Woe, one drawn away;
woe, one drawn away.

c. Said to him R. Aqiva: Leave him in his undefined state; Do not praise him, and do not
curse him.

d. They [the relatives] do not tear [their garments, as one does for other deceased Israelites].

e. And they do not loosen [clothing to bare their shoulders, as one does for other deceased
Israelites].

f. And they do not eulogize [as one does for other deceased Israelites] in regards to him

g. But (אבל) they do stand in a line in regards to him,

h. and they do say in regards to him the blessing of the mourners.

i. because (שׁ מפני) it is an honour [due] to the living [i.e., the surviving relatives].

j. [This is] the general principle of the matter (כללו שׁל דבר):

k. everything that (כל שׁ) is an honour [due] to the living—they do attend to [funerary and
mourning rites] in regards to it;

l. everything that (כל שׁ) is not an honour [due] to the living—the majority [i.e., members of
the community] at large do not attend to [funerary and mourning rites] in regards to it.

2:2

a. Who is [considered] one who commits suicide with forethought?

b. Not one who climbed to the top of the tree, and he fell, and he died.

c. And not [one who] [climbed] to the top of the roof, and fell, and died.

d. Rather [אלא] they saw [that] he climbed to the top of the tree, and he fell and he died,

e. and to the top of the roof, and he fell and he died.

f. Lo (הרי), this one is (זה ב) assumed [to be] one who commits suicide with forethought.

g. And they [the Israelites] do not attend to [funerary and mourning rites] in regards to him
in any manner.

2:3

a. They found him strangled and hung in a tree;

b. slain and cast upon a sword—

c. lo (הרי), this one is (זה ב) assumed [to be] one who commits suicide not with forethought.

d. And any- (כל) one who commits suicide not with forethought—they [the Israelites] do not
withhold [funerary and mourning rites] from him in any manner.

2:4

a. And it once transpired [with respect to] (כ ומעשׁה) the son of Gorgios that (שׁ) he fled from
the schoolhouse (בית הספר)

b.   and his father [threatened to] cuffed him in his ear,

c.   and he was fearful of his father,

d.   and he committed suicide [by casting himself] in a pit.

e.   And they inquired of R. Tarfon [what the law was].

f.   And he said: they do not withhold [funerary and mourning rites] from him in any manner.

2:5

a.   And, again, it once transpired [with respect to] (כ ושוב מעשה) a child from Bnei Brak that (ש) he smashed a bottle

b.   and his father [threatened to] cuffed him in his ear,

c.   and he was fearful of his father,

d.   and he committed suicide [by casting himself] in a pit.

e.   And they inquired of R. Aqiva [what the law was].

f.   And he said: they do not withhold [funerary and mourning rites] from him in any manner.

g.   And on this basis they said: One shall not [threaten to] cuff a child in his ear.

h.   Rather one should strike him immediately or one should remain silent (שותק אותו) and one does not say anything.

i.   R. Simeon b. Eleazar says: [Concerning one's] [sexual] inclination, a child, and a wife—let the left [hand] push away, and draw near [with] the right hand.

j.   And R. Nathan says: There is nothing that distinguishes laughing from crying.

2:6

a.   Those [who have been] executed [on the order] of the [Jewish] court—they do not attend to [funerary and mourning rites] in regards to them in any manner.

b.   Their siblings and their [other close] relatives come, and they inquire after the well-being (שואלין שלום) of the witnesses and [after] the well-being of the judges.

c.   As in saying (כלומר) that: (ש) "There is nothing in our hearts [against you]."

d.   [and] that: "You have made a truthful judgment."

e.   And they do not mourn;

f.   Rather they grieve,

g.   since grief is only (אין...אלא) in the heart.

h.   And they do not prepare the funerary meal [for mourners] in regards to them [i.e., these relatives],

i.   as it is said [in scripture]: You shall not eat in the presence of (על) the blood (Lev. 19:26).

j.   [On the basis of this verse] the court which executed [someone, that is, condemned someone to death] would not taste [anything] all that same day.

2:7

a.   And they do not allow him to speak with his siblings and his relatives in order to delay [his execution].

b.   And they make him drink wine

c.   so that (כדי ש) he shall not suffer.

d.   And they instruct him to confess [his sins],

e.   since whosoever (כל) confesses [his sins prior to death] has a share in the world to come.

f.   For thus we have found with respect to (שכן מצינו ב) Akan— that Joshua said to him: "My son, do honour to the Lord, God of Israel, and give him thanks, and please tell me what you have done; do not withhold [anything] from me. And Akan answered Joshua, and he said: I have sinned before the Lord, God of Israel, and such and such I have done" (Josh. 7:19-20).

g.   And why does scripture say (מה תלמוד לומר): "And such I have done (Josh. 7:20)" [a second time]?

h.   It [thereby] teaches that (מלמד ש) he committed sacrilege with respect to the banned [i.e., taboo] property twice.

i.   [Scripture says:] "I have sinned"— and not my household— "I have sinned"— and not my children—

j.   teaching that (מלמד ש) he confessed in sincerity (lit., in truth).

k.   And whence [do we learn] (מניין) that his confession atoned for him?

l.   As it is said (שנאמר): "And Joshua said: You have vexed me; may the Lord vex you this very day"—

m.   [meaning] this very day you are vexed, and you are not vexed in (ל) the world to come.

n.   And [Scripture furthermore] says: "And the sons of Zerah [were] Zimri [aka. Akan], and Ethan, and Heman, and Kalkal, and Darda— five in all" (I Chron. 2:6).

o.   But is it not the case that (וכי אין) we know [that they number] five in all?

p.   Rather (אלא) [scripture] teaches that Akan b. Zerah is with them in the world to come.

2:8

a.   Anyone (כל) who abandons (פורש) the norms [for behavior] of the community (דרכי ציבור), [and subsequently dies]—they [the Israelites] do not attend to [funerary and mourning rites] in regards to him in any manner.

b.   Their siblings and their [other close] relatives wear white,

c.   and they wrap themselves [in outer garments] of white,

d.   and they eat,

e.   and they drink,

f.   and they rejoice,

g.   since (ש) they have lost one who hates (שונאיו) [the people] of the locale,

h.   as it said (שנאמר) [in scripture]: Lord, shall I not hate those that hate you, and shall I not dispute those who rise up against you? With complete hatred I hate them, I have made them my enemies (Ps. 139:21-22).

2:9

a.   One who is executed [on the order] of the [non-Jewish] state—they [the Israelites] do not withhold [funerary and mourning rites] from them in any manner.

b.   From when (מאימתי) do they count [the days of mourning] on account of them?

c.   From the hour that (emend: משעה ש) they abandoned [their] expectation [of a positive response] to (-מל) requesting [the return of the body for burial rites],

d.   but [they have] not [abandoned their expectation of success in attempting] to (-מל) steal [back the body for burial rites].

e.   Anyone (כל) who steals [a body under normal circumstances]—lo, this one [is like one who] sheds blood.

f.   And not only [is this one] like one who sheds blood.

g.   Rather (אלא), [this one is] like one who engages in idolatry,

h.   and engages in consanguineous sexual relations,

i.   and profanes the sabbaths.

j.   [And] so too [is] (כיוצא בו) one who steals the [imperial] taxes—lo, this one [is like one who] sheds blood.

k.   And not only [is this one] like one who sheds blood.

l.   Rather, (אלא) [this one is] like one who engages in idolatry,

m.   and engages in consanguineous sexual relations,

n.   and profanes the sabbaths.

o.   [And] so too [is] (כיוצא בו) one who steals banned [i.e., taboo] property—lo, this one [is like one who] sheds blood.

p.   And not only [is this one] like one who sheds blood.

q.   Rather, (אלא) [this one is] like one who engages in idolatry,

r.   and engages in consangineous sexual relations,

s.   and profanes the sabbaths.

2:10

a.   Someone that fell [overboard] into the sea,

b.   or that a river swept away,

c.   or that a vicious beast devoured—

d.   they [the Israelites] do not withhold [funerary and mourning rites] from him in any manner.

e.   From when (מאימתי) do they count [the days of mourning] on account of them?

f.   From the hour that (emend: שׁ משׁעה) they abandoned [their] expectation: [of a positive result] to (מל-) seek [the remains].

g.   They found him limb by limb—they do not count [the days of mourning] until (עד שׁ-) his head and the greater part [of his body] will have been found.

h.   R. Judah says: the spinal column and the skull— lo, these are the greater part [of his body].

2:11

a.   Someone whose husband was crucified, with her [present] in the [self same] city,

b.   [and someone] whose wife was crucified, with him [present] in the [self same] city,

c.   [and someone] whose father and whose mother were crucified, with him [present in the self same city]—

d.   he [or she] shall not remain in the self same city,

e.   except if (אלא אם כן) it was a large city, like Antioch.

f.   [In the latter case] he [or she] shall not remain in this side [of self same city, i.e., the side in which the crucifixion occurred].

g.   But rather (אבל) he [or she] shall remain in the other side [of self same city].

h.   Until when is it said [i.e., until when does this ruling apply] (עד מתי הוא אמור)?

i.   Until (עד שׁ) the flesh [of the corpse] (3rd imperf. sg.) shall be wasted away, and there is no recognizable figure on the bones.

2:12

a.   The House of Hillel say: One who divorces his wife—he shall not remain with her:

b.   not in [the same] alley;

c.   and not in [the same] courtyard.

d.   And if it was the alley of both of them, he switches his door to another side [on the adjacent alley].

e.   And if it was the courtyard of both of them, one cedes [the courtyard] in favour of (מפני) the other (זה ... זה).

f.   The woman cedes in favor of the man.

g.   With respect to what [precise circumstances] is this said (במה דברים אמורים)?

h.   At such time as (בזמן שׁ-) they have [each re]married,

i.   and [also] with respect to (ב) the priesthood [i.e., the former husband is a priest], even though they have not [each re]married.

j.   He who performs the rite of loosening the sandal of his levirate wife [i.e., refuses to marry his dead brother's childless widow] shall not cede [the courtyard in favor of the levirate wife],

k.   because (מפני שׁ) he does not pine for her [since they had no prior intimate relationship].

[translation my own from ed. Zlotnick, 1966]

Chart 4.1: Rhetorical "Scoring" of Semahot 1-2

Column 1 = Conjunctive/Coordinating formulae (CC)
Column 2 = Logical/Analogical formulae (LA)
Column 3 = Other Formulae (OF)
Column 4 = Morphological markers (M)
Column 5 = Homophonic-Homosemantic/antisemantic markers, level 1 (HH1)
Column 6 = Homophonic-Homosemantic/antisemantic markers, level 2 (HH2)
Column 7 = Homophonic-Homosemantic/antisemantic markers, level 3 (HH3)
Column 8 = Other Content (OC)

CC	LA	OF	M	HH1	HH2	HH3	OC
1:1							
			A. (ה+pres. part. sg.) One who				
							is dying—
lo,							
						he	
						is like a living [person]	
					with respect to (ל) all matters.		
			B. (pres. part. sg.) he				
							must [fulfill obligations enter into] levirate marriage.
C. And							
			(pres. part. sg.) he				
							causes [his dependents to be eligible] to eat
					heave-offering [if he is a priest].		
D. And							
			(pres. part. sg.) he				
							renders [his dependents] unfit [to eat] from
					heave-offering [if he is a priest].		
E. And							
					he inherits [property].		
F. And							
			(pres. part. sg.) he				
					causes [others] to inherit [property].		
							G. [If]
					a limb		
							is separated from him, [the limb]
					is like		
					[i.e., is subject to		

CC	LA	OF	M	HH1	HH2	HH3	OC

the laws concerning]
a limb
from a living [being]

H. [If]
flesh,

[the flesh]
is like
[i.e., is subject to
the laws concerning]
flesh
from a living [being]

I. And

(pres. part. pl.)
they

sprinkle for him

the blood of
(3rd sg. pronominal suffix)
his
purification offering

and

the blood of
(3rd sg. pronominal suffix)
his
guilt offering.

J. [All of the above applies]
until such time that he dies.

1:2

A. (negative particle, אין,
+ pres. part. pl.)
They do not

tie

(3rd sg. pronominal suffix)
his

jaws.

B. And

(negative particle, אין,
+ pres. part. pl.)
They do not

stop up

(3rd sg. pronominal suffix)
his

orifices.

C. And

(negative particle, אין,
+ pres. part. pl)
They do not

lay upon

(3rd. sg. pronominal suffix)
him

a metal vessel,

and

(negative particle, לא)

CC	LA	OF	M	HH1	HH2	HH3	OC

M: not

OC: something that cools upon

M: (3rd sg. pronominal suffix)
his

OC: abdomen,

D. until such time that he dies.

1:3

A. (negative particle, אֵין, + pres. part. pl.) They do not

OC: move

(accusative particle, אֶת,+ 3rd. sg. pronominal suffix) him.

B. And

(negative particle, אֵין, + pres. part. pl.) They do not

OC: bathe

(accusative particle, אֶת,+ 3rd. sg. pronominal suffix) him.

C. And

(negative particle, אֵין, + pres. part. pl.) They do not

OC: carry

(accusative particle, אֶת,+ 3rd. sg. pronominal suffix) him—

D. (negative particle, לֹא) not upon

OC: [a bier covered with] sand,

E. and

(negative particle, לֹא) not upon

OC: [a bier covered with] salt,

F. until such time that he dies.

1:4

A. (negative particle, אֵין, + pres. part. pl.) They do not

OC: close

(accusative particle, אֶת,+

CC	LA	OF	M	HH1	HH2	HH3	OC
			3rd sg. pronominal suffix)				
				his			
							eyes.
			B. (ה+ pres. part. sg.) One who				
							touches
			(dative particle, ב,+ 3rd person pronominal suffix)				
				him			
C. and							
			(pres. part. sg.) [one] who				
							moves
			(3rd person pronominal suffix)				
				him—			
D. lo,							
			(pres. part. sg.) he				
							spills blood.
							E. R. Meir used to
			(pres. part. sg.)				
							liken
			(3rd person pronominal suffix)				
				him			
				[i.e., dying person]			
							to a shimmering candle/lamp;
	F. Since						
							someone touched it, immediately, one extinguished it.
	G. So too						
							anyone
			(ה+ pres. part. pl.) they who				
							close the eyes of a dying person.
			H. (pres. part. pl.) They				
							account
			(על+3rd person pronominal suffix) him				
					as though		
			(pres. part. sg.) he				
							loosens his [the dying person's soul, from his body].

CC	LA	OF	M	HH1	HH2	HH3	OC
1:5							
			A. (negative particle, אין, + pres. part. pl.) They [the relatives of the dying person] do not				
							tear [their garments as one does for a deceased]
B. And			(negative particle, לא +pres. part. pl.) They do not				
							loosen [clothing to bare their shoulders, as one does for a deceased].
C. And			(negative particle, לא +pres. part. pl.) They do not				
							eulogize [the dying man].
D. And			(negative particle, אין +pres. part. pl.) They do not				
						bring into the house with	
			(3rd person pronominal suffix) him				
							a coffin
			E. until such time that he dies.				
1:6							
			A. (negative particle, אין, + pres. part. pl.) They do not				
							acclaim
			(dative particle, על+ 3rd person pronominal suffix) him				
B. And			(negative particle, אין, +pres. part. pl.) They do not				
						recount	
			(dative particle, על,+ 3rd person pronominal suffix) in regards to him				
			(3rd person pronominal suffix) his				
							[noteworthy] deeds
			[until such time that he dies.]				

CC	LA	OF	M	HH1	HH2	HH3	OC
							C. R. Judah
C. says:							
If							
							[the dying person] was a sage,
			(pres. part. pl.) They do				
							recount
			(dative particle, עַל,+ 3rd person pronominal suffix)				
							in regards to him
			(3rd person pronominal suffix)				
							his
							[noteworthy] deeds
						[even before such time that he dies.]	

1:7

CC	LA	OF	M	HH1	HH2	HH3	OC
						A. [At such time that he dies],	
			(negative particle, אֵין, + pres. part. pl.) they do not				
							inquire after the well-being in a
						small city.	
B. With respect to what [circumstances] is this stated?							
							C. In a small village.
D. But (אבל)							
						in a large city,	
							it is permitted.

1:8

CC	LA	OF	M	HH1	HH2	HH3	OC
			(pres. pass. participle sg.)				
							a severed [foetus],
			(pres. pass. participle sg.)				
							a breech-birth [foetus who does not survive],
			(pres. pass. participle pl.)				
							a miscarried [foetus],
						one at eight months [gestation] [born] alive [that then dies],	
and							
						one at nine months [gestation] [born] dead—	
			(negative particle, אֵין, + pres. part. pl.) they do not				
							attend to [Israelite funerary and mourning rites with respect to] it

CC	LA	OF	M	HH1	HH2	HH3	OC
					in any manner.		
1:9							
			A.(ה + pl. noun)				
							Gentiles
and							
			(ה + pl. noun)				
							slaves [who die]—
			(negative particle, אין, + pres. part. pl.) they [the Israelites] do not				
						attend to [pagan rites]	
			(dative particle, עם,+ 3rd person pronominal suffix)				
						together with them [the pagan mourners] in any manner.	
B. But (אבל)							
			(pres. part. pl.) they [the Israelites] do				
						call out [publicly]	
			(dative particle, עם,+ 3rd person pronominal suffix)				
						together with them [the pagan mourners]:	
						Woe,	
							[departed] lion;
					woe,		
							[departed] hero.
							C. R. Judah
	says: [Also]						
			[they, the Israelites, do]				
							[call:]
					Woe		
							[departed] faithful witness, who consumed the outcome of his labour.
D. They said to him: If so, what							
							have you left [as an approbation] for
						the fit [i.e., Israelite, departed]?	
E. He said to them: If							
							he [or she] were
						fit	

CC	LA	OF	M		HH1	HH2	HH3	OC

[i.e., an Israelite],

wherefore (מפני מה)

(negative particle, אין,
+ pres. part. pl.)
do they [the Israelites]
not

call out [publicly]

(dative particle, על,+
3rd person pronominal suffix)

in regards to
him [or her]?

1:10

A. (emend: negative particle, אין,
+ pres. part. pl.)
They [the Israelites] do not

receive
condolences
on account of
[the death of]

slaves.

B. And it once
transpired that
when (ומעשה כש)

the handmaiden of
R. Eliezer
died,

B. his disciples
entered
to console
him.

C. He [then]
entered

before them
into

the courtyard
[to avoid them].

D. They
entered
after him.

E. [He then
entered]
into

the house.

F. They
entered
after him.

G. He said to them:

CC	LA	OF	M	HH1	HH2	HH3	OC
							It seemed to me that
						you would be scalded with warm [water],	
and							
							[by contrast]
						you are not scalded [even] with hot [water];	
							H. Thus
						have	
							I
						not taught	
							you—
I. that							
			(negative particle, אין, + pres. part. pl.) they [the Israelites] do not				
						receive condolences on account of [the death of] slaves,	
	J. because (מפני שׁ)						
						slaves	
							are considered to be like animals [i.e., living property]?
K. And when (וכשׁ)							
							Tevi, the slave of R. Gamaliel, died,
							L. he
						received condolences on account of	
							him.
M. Said to him							
						his disciples:	
N. And							
						have	
							you
						not taught	
							us—
O. that							
			(negative particle, אין, + pres. part. pl.) they [the Israelites] do not				
						receive condolences	

CC	LA	OF	M	HH1	HH2	HH3	OC
						on account of [the death of] slaves?	
P. He said to them:							
					not (אין)	Tevi, my slave, is	
						like other slaves;	
	as (ש)						
						fit.	he was
Q. Also (אף)							
							he [R. Gamaliel] permitted him to put on
						phylacteries.	
R. They said to him:							
							Have you not instructed us
that						slaves	
							are exempt from [the obligation of putting on]
						phylacteries?	
S. He said to them:							
					not (אין)	Tevi, my slave, is	
						like other slaves;	
	since (כי)						
						fit.	he is
1:11							
			A. (emend: negative particle, אי, + pres. part. pl.) They [the Israelites] do not				
							call out [publicly]
						on account of (ל) [the death of]	
						male slaves	
and							
						on account of (ל)	
						female slaves:	
						Father so-and-so	

CC	LA	OF	M	HH1	HH2	HH3	OC
and						Mother so-and-so.	
B. And [on account of] those [slaves] from (-שֶׁל) the House of R. Gamaliel,							
			(past part. pl.) they used to				
							call out [publicly]
							on account of [the death of]
							his slave:
							Father Tevi
and							Mother Tevita [B. as emended by Elijah, Gaon of Vilna on the basis of parallel in b. Ber. 16b; as noted in ed. Zlotnick, 1966, p. 100, n.11].
1:12							
			A. (emend: negative particle, אֵין, + pres. part. pl.) They [the Israelites] do not				
							call out [publicly]
							on account of (לְ) [the death of]
							Fathers [that is, recognizing the deceased as an ancestor of the people]:
							Our Father [so-and-so],
except (אֶלָּא)							
							on account of (לְ) [memorializing the death of]
							the three Fathers [of the people, Abraham, Isaac, and Jacob];
B. and							
			(negative particle, לֹא)				

CC	LA	OF	M	HH1	HH2	HH3	OC
			[they do] not				
							[call out publicly]
							on account of (ל) [the death of]
							Mothers [that is, recognizing the deceased as an ancestor of the people]:
							Our Mother [so-and-so],
except (אלא)							
							on account of (ל) [memorializing the death of]
							the four Mothers [of the people, Sarah, Rebecca, Rachel, and Leah].
2:1							
			A. (ה+pres. part. sg.) one who				
				commits suicide with forethought—			
			(negative particle, אין, + pres. part. pl.) they [the Israelites] do not				
					attend to		
					[funerary and mourning rites]		
			(dative particle, עם,+ 3rd person pronominal suffix)				
				in regards to him			
					in any manner.		
							B. R. Ishmael
says:							
			(pres. part. pl.) They do				
						call out [publicly]	
			(dative particle, על,+ 3rd person pronominal suffix)				
				in regards to him:			
						Woe,	
							one drawn away;
					woe,		

CC	LA	OF	M	HH1	HH2	HH3	OC
							one drawn away.
C. Said to him							
							R. Aqiva: Leave
			(accusative particle, ל, + 3rd person pronominal suffix)	him			
							in
			(3rd person pronominal suffix)		his		
							undefined state; Do not praise him,
							do not curse him.
and							
			D. (negative particle, אין, + pres. part. pl.) They [the relatives] do not				
					tear [their garments, as one does for other deceased Israelites].		
E. And							
			(negative particle, אין, + pres. part. pl.) They do not				
					loosen [clothing to bare their shoulders, as one does for other deceased Israelites].		
F. And							
			(negative particle, אין, + pres. part. pl.) They do not				
					eulogize [as one does for other deceased Israelites]		
			(dative particle, על,+ 3rd person pronominal suffix)		in regards to him		
G. But (אבל)							
			(pres. part. pl.) they do				
							stand in a line
			(dative particle, על,+ 3rd person pronominal suffix)		in regards to him,		
H. and							
			(pres. part. pl.) they do				
							say
			(dative particle, על,+				

CC	LA	OF	M	HH1	HH2	HH3	OC
			3rd person pronominal suffix)				
					in regards to him		
							the blessing of the mourners.
	I. because (מפני שֶׁ)						
					it is an honour [due] to the living [i.e., the surviving relatives.]		
J. [This is] the general principle of the matter (כללו של דבר):							
					K. everything that (כל שֶׁ) is an honour [due] to the living—		
			(pres. part. pl.) they do				
				attend to [funerary and mourning rites]			
			(particle, בּ, + 3rd person pronominal suffix)				
					in regards to it;		
					L. everything that (כל שֶׁ) is not an honour [due] to the living—		
			(negative particle, אין, + pres. part. pl.)				
						the majority [i.e., members of the community at large]	
			do not				
				attend to [funerary and mourning rites]			
			(particle, בּ, + 3rd pronominal suffix)				
					in regards to it.		
2:2 Who is [considered]							
			A. (pres. part. sg.) one who				
					commits suicide with forethought?		
			B. (negative particle, לֹא, + relative pronoun, שֶׁ, + 3rd perf. sg.)				

CC	LA	OF	M	HH1	HH2	HH3	OC
			Not one who				
						climbed to the top of the tree,	
and							
			(3rd perf. sg.) he				
						fell	
and							
			(3rd perf. sg.) he				
						died.	
C. And							
			(negative particle, לא,) not [one who]				
						[climbed] to the top of the roof,	
and							
			(3rd perf.t sg.) he				
						fell	
and							
			(3rd perf. sg.) he				
						died.	
D. Rather [אלא]							
			(3rd perf. pl. + 3rd sg. pronominal suffix) they				
							saw [that]
			(3rd perf. sg.) he				
						climbed to the top of the tree,	
and							
			(3rd perf. sg.) he				
						fell	
and							
			(3rd perf. sg.) he				
						died.	
E. And							
						to the top of the roof,	
and							
			(3rd perf. sg.) he				
						fell	
and							

CC	LA	OF	M	HH1	HH2	HH3	OC
			(3rd perf. sg.) he				
						died.	
F. Lo (הרי), This one is (זה ב)							
							assumed [to be]
			(pres. part. sg.) one who				
						commits suicide with forethought.	
G. And							
			(negative particle, אין, + pres. part. pl.) they [the Israelites] do not				
					attend to [funerary and mourning rites]		
			(accusative particle, ב,+ 3rd person pronominal suffix)				
					in regards to him		
					in any manner.		
2:3							
			A. (3rd person perfect pl. + 3rd person sg. pronominal suffix) They				
							found
					him		
			(past part. sg.)				
							strangled
and							
			(past part. sg.)				
							hung in a tree;
			B. (past part. sg.)				
							slain
and							
			(past part. sg.)				
							cast upon a sword—
C. lo (הרי), This one is (זה ב)							
							assumed [to be]
			(pres. part. sg.) one who				
						commits suicide not with forethought.	

CC	LA	OF	M	HH1	HH2	HH3	OC
D. And					any- (כל)		
			(pres. part. sg.) one who			commits suicide not with forethought—	
			(negative particle, אֵין, + pres. part. pl.) they [the Israelites] do not			withhold [funerary and mourning rites]	
			(particle, הֵימִן, + 3rd person pronominal suffix)			from him	
						in any manner.	
2:4 A. And it once transpired [with respect to] (ומעשׂה כ)							the son of Gorgios
that (שׁ)			(3rd person perf. sg.) he				fled from the schoolhouse (בית הספר)
B. and			(3rd person perf. sg.)				his father
						cuffed him in his ear,	
C. and			(3rd person perf. sg.) he			was fearful of his father,	
D. and			(3rd person perf. sg.) he			committed suicide [by casting himself] in a pit.	
E. And			(3rd person perf. pl.) they				

CC	LA	OF	M	HH1	HH2	HH3	OC
						inquired of	
							R. Tarfon
						[what the law was].	
F. And he said:							
			(negative particle, אֵין, + pres. part. pl.) they do not				
					withhold		
					[funerary and mourning rites]		
			(particle, הֵימִין, + 3rd person pronominal suffix)				
					from him		
					in any manner.		

2:5

CC	LA	OF	M	HH1	HH2	HH3	OC
A. And, again, it once transpired [with respect to] (וְשׁוּב מַעֲשֶׂה כ)							
					a child		
							from Bnei Brak
that (שֶׁ)							
			(3rd person perf. sg.) he				
							smashed a bottle
B. and							
					his father		
			(3rd person perf. sg.)				
					cuffed him in his ear,		
C. and							
			(3rd person perf. sg.) he				
					was fearful of his father,		
D. and							
			(3rd person perf. sg.) he				
					committed suicide [by casting himself] in a pit.		
E. And							
			(3rd person perf. pl.) they				
					came		
and							

CC	LA	OF	M	HH1	HH2	HH3	OC
			(3rd person perf. pl.) they				
							inquired of R. Aqiva [what the law was].
F. And he said:			(negative particle, אי, + pres. part. pl.) they do not	withhold [funerary and mourning rites]			
			(particle, המין, + 3rd person pronominal suffix)		from him		
					in any manner.		
G. And on this basis they said:			(negative particle, אל, + 3rd person imperf. sg.) one shall not		cuff a child in his ear.		
H. Rather							one should strike him immediately
or							one should remain silent (שותק אותו)
and							one does not say
					anything.		
							I. R. Simeon b. Elazar
says:							
							[concerning one's] [sexual] inclina- tion, child,
and							wife—
				let the left [hand] push away			
and							

CC	LA	OF	M	HH1	HH2	HH3	OC
						draw near [with] the right hand.	
J. And							
says:							R. Nathan
			(negative particle, אין) There is not				
						anything	
							that distinguishes laughing from crying
2:6							
			A. (passive part. pl.) Those [who have been]				
						executed [on the order] of the court—	
			(negative particle, אין, + pres. part. pl.) they do not				
					attend to [funerary and mourning rites]		
			(accusative particle, ב, + 3rd person pl. pronominal suffix)				
					in regards to them		
					in any manner.		
						B. Their siblings	
and							
						their [other close] relatives	
			(pres. part. pl.)				
							come
and							
			(pres. part. pl.) they				
							inquire after the well-being (שואלין שלום) of the witnesses
and							
							[after] the well-being of the judges.
C. As in saying (כלומר) that (שׁ)							
							"there is nothing in our hearts

CC	LA	OF	M	HH1	HH2	HH3	OC
							[against you]"
D. [and] that							"you have made a truthful judgment."
E. And			(negative particle, לֹא, + 3rd pl. pronoun, הם, + pres. part. pl.) they do not				mourn;
F. Rather			(pres. part. pl.) they				grieve,
	G. since						grief is only (אין...אלא) in the heart.
H. And			(negative particle, אין, + pres. part. pl.) they do not				prepare the funerary meal [for the mourners]
			(dative particle, על,+ 3rd person pl. pronominal suffix) in regards to them,				
I. as it is said [in scripture]:							You shall not eat in the presence of (על) the blood (Lev. 19:26).
J. [On this basis]							the court which executed [someone, that is, condemned someone to death] would not taste [anything] all that same day.

2:7

CC	LA	OF	M	HH1	HH2	HH3	OC
A. And			(negative particle, אין, + pres. part. pl.) they do not				
							allow
			(אותו: accusative, את,+ 3rd person pl. pronominal suffix)				
				him			
							to speak with
					his siblings		
					his relatives		
and							
in order to (בשביל)							
							delay [his execution].
B. And							
			(pres. part. pl.) they				
							make
			(אותו: accusative, את,+ 3rd person pl. pronominal suffix)				
				him			
							drink wine
C. so that (כדי ש)							
							he shall not suffer.
D. And							
			(pres. part. pl.) they				
							instruct
			(אותו: accusative, את,+ 3rd person pl. pronominal suffix)				
				him			
				to confess [his sins],			
E. since							
							whosoever (כל)
			(ה + pres. part. sg.)				
				confesses [his sins prior to death]			
							has a share in
					the world to come.		
	F. For thus we have found with respect to (שכן מצינו ב)						
							Akan—
that							

CC	LA	OF	M	HH1	HH2	HH3	OC
							Joshua said to him: "My son, do honour to the Lord, God of Israel, and give him thanks, and please tell me what you have done; do not with-hold [anything] from me.
							And Akan ans-wered Joshua, and he said:
						I have sinned	
							before the Lord, God of Israel, and such
						and such I have done" (Josh. 7:19-20).	
G. And							
	why does scripture say (מה תלמוד לומר):						
							"And such I have done (Josh. 7:20)" [a second time]?
	H. It [thereby] teaches that (מלמד ש)						
							he committed sacrilege with respect to the banned [i.e., taboo] property twice.
	I. [Scripture says:]						
						"I have sinned"— and not my household—	
						"I have sinned"— and not my children—	
	J. teaching that (מלמד ש)						
							he confessed in sincerity (lit. in truth).
	K. And whence						

CC	LA	OF	M	HH1	HH2	HH3	OC
	[do we learn] (מניין) that (שׁ)						
							his confession atoned for him?
	L. As it is said (שנאמר):						
							"And Joshua said: You have
						vexed	
							me; may the Lord
						vex	
							you
						this very day"—	
	M. [meaning]						
						this very day you are vexed,	
						you are not vexed	
and							
						in (ל) the world to come.	
N. And	[Scipture furthermore] says:						
							"And the sons of Zerah [were] Zimri [aka. Akan], and Ethan, and Heman, and Kalkal, and Darda—
						five in all" (I Chron. 2:6).	
	O. But is it not the case that (וכי אין)						
							we know [that they number]
						five in all?	
	P. Rather (אלא) [scripture] teaches that						
							Akan b. Zerah is with them in
						the world to come.	

2:8

CC	LA	OF	M	HH1	HH2	HH3	OC
						A. Any- (כל)	
			(ה+pres. part. sg.) one who				
							abandons (פורש) the norms [for behaviour] of the community (דרכי ציבור), [and subsequently dies]—
			(negative particle, אי, + pres. part. pl.) they [the Israelites] do not	attend to	[funerary and mourning rites]		
			(dative particle, עם,+ 3rd person pronominal suffix)	in regards to him			
					in any manner.		
						B. Their siblings	
and						their [other close] relatives	
			(pres. part. pl.)			white,	wear
C. and			(pres. part. pl.) they				wrap themselves [in outer garments] of
						white,	
D. and			(pres. part. pl.) they				eat,
E. and			(pres. part. pl.) they				drink,
F. and			(pres. part. pl.) they				rejoice,
G since (ש)			(3rd person perf. pl.) they have				lost

CC	LA	OF	M	HH1	HH2	HH3	OC

CC **LA** **OF** **M** **HH1** **HH2** **HH3** **OC**

one who hates
(שׂונאיו) [the
people]
of the locale,

H. as it said (שׁנאמר)
[in scripture]:

Lord, shall I not
hate those that hate
you, and shall I not
dispute those who
rise up against you.
With complete
hatred I hate them,
I have made them
my enemies (Ps.
139:21-22).

2:9

A. (pres. part. sg.)
one who **is**

executed
[[on the order]
of the [non-Jewish]
state—

(negative particle, אין,
+ pres. part. pl.)
they [the Israelites] do not
withhold
[funerary and mourning rites]

(particle, המין, +
3rd person pronominal suffix)
from them

in any manner.

B. From when (מאימתי)

(pres. part pl.)
do they

count
[the days of
mourning]

(accusative part., ל, +
3re person pl. pron. suffix)
on account of
them?

C. From the hour that
(emend: שׁ משׁעה)

they abandoned
[their] expectation
[of a positive
response]

to (מל-)

CC	LA	OF	M	HH1	HH2	HH3	OC
							requesting [the return of the body for burial rites],
D. but							
							[they have] not [abandoned their expectation of success in attempting]
						to (-מל) steal [back the body for burial rites].	
					A. Any- (כל)		
			(ה+pres. part. sg.) one who				
						steals	
							[a body under normal circumstances]—
lo,							
						this one [is like one who]	
			(pres. part sg.)				
						sheds blood.	
E. And not only (ולא ... בלבד)							
						[is this one] like one who sheds blood.	
F. Rather, (אלא)							
						[this one is] like one who	
			(pres. part. sg.)				
						engages in idolatry,	
G. and							
			(pres. part. sg.)				
						engages in consanguineous sexual relations,	
H. and							
			(pres. part. sg.)				
						profanes the sabbaths.	
I. [And] so too [is] (כיוצא בו)							
			(ה+pres. part. sg.) one who				
						steals	

CC	LA	OF	M	HH1	HH2	HH3	OC
							the [imperial] taxes—
lo,							
							this one [is like one who]
			(pres. part sg.)				
							sheds blood.
J. And not only (ולא ... בלבד)							
							[is this one] like one who sheds blood.
K. Rather, (אלא)							
							[this one is] like one who
			(pres. part. sg.)				
							engages in idolatry,
L. and							
			(pres. part. sg.)				
							engages in consanguineous sexual relations,
M. and							
			(pres. part. sg.)				
							profanes the sabbaths.
N. [And] so too [is] (כיוצא בו)							
			(ה+pres. part. sg.) one who				
						steals	
							banned [i.e., taboo] property—
lo,							
							this one [is like one who]
			(pres. part sg.)				
							sheds blood.
O. And not only (ולא ... בלבד)							
							[is this one] like one who sheds blood.
P. Rather, (אלא)							
							[this one is] like one who
			(pres. part. sg.)				
							engages in

CC	LA	OF	M	HH1	HH2	HH3	OC
						idolatry,	
Q. and			(pres. part. sg.)				
						engages in consanguineous sexual relations,	
R. and			(pres. part. sg.)				
						profanes the sabbaths.	

2:10

CC	LA	OF	M	HH1	HH2	HH3	OC
A. Someone that (-שׁ מי)			(3rd perf. sg.)				fell [overboard] into the sea,
B. or that			(3rd perf. sg. + 3rd. sg. pronominal suffix)				a river swept away,
C. or that			(3rd perf. sg. + 3rd. sg. pronominal suffix)				a vicious beast devoured—
			D. (negative particle, אין, + pres. part. pl.) they [the Israelites] do not	withhold	[funerary and mourning rites]		
			(particle, המין, + 3rd person pronominal suffix)		from him		
						in any manner.	
E. From when (מאימתי)			(pres. part pl.) do they		count [the days of mourning]		
			(accusative part., ל, + 3re person pl. pron. suffix)			on account of them?	
F. From the hour that (emend: שׁ משׁעה)						they abandoned [their] expectation	

CC	LA	OF	M	HH1	HH2	HH3	OC
						[of a positive result] to (מל-)	
							seek [the remains].
			G. (3rd perfect pl. + 3rd sg. pron. suffix) They				
					him		
							found
							limb by limb—
			(negative particle,אין, + pres. part. pl.) they do not				
							count [the days of mourning]
	until (-עד ש)						
and							his head
						the greater part [of his body]	
			(3rd imperf. pl. pass.)				
							will have been found.
							H. R. Judah
says:							
and							the spinal column
Lo,							the skull—
							these are
						the greater part [of his body].	
2:11 A. Someone (-מי ש)							
			(3rd perf. sg.) (noun + 3rd sg. fm. suffix)				
						whose husband	
			(passive part. sg.)				
						was crucified,	
			(ablative prep., עם+ 3rd. sg. fm. suffix)				
						with her [present]	
						in the [self same] city,	
B. [and someone whose]							

CC	LA	OF	M	HH1	HH2	HH3	OC
			(noun + 3rd sg. masc. suffix)			whose wife	
			(passive part. sg.)			was crucified,	
			(ablative prep., עמ+ 3rd. sg. masc. suffix)			with him [present]	
						in the [self same] city,	
C. [and someone]							
			(noun + 3rd sg. masc. suffix)			whose father	
and			(noun + 3rd sg. masc. suffix)			whose mother	
			(passive part. pl.)			were crucified,	
			(ablative prep., עמ+ 3rd. sg. masc. suffix)			with him [present]	
						[in the self same city]—	
			D. (negative particle, לא, + 3rd imperf. sg.) he [or she] shall				
				not remain			
						in the self same city,	
E. except if (אלא אם כן)							
			(3rd perf. sg.) it				
				was			a large
						city,	
like (כ)							Antioch.
			F. (negative particle, לא, + 3rd imperf. sg.)				

CC	LA	OF	M	HH1	HH2	HH3	OC
			He [or she] shall				
						not remain	
						in this side	
						[of self same city].	
G. But rather (אבל)							
			(negative particle, לא, + 3rd imperf. sg.) he [or she] shall				
						remain	
						in the other side	
						[of self same city].	
H. Until when is it said [i.e., until when does this ruling apply] (עד מתי הוא אמור)?							
I. Until (עד ש)							
							the flesh [of the corpse]
			(3rd imperf. sg) shall				
							be wasted away,
and							
							there is no recognizable figure on the bones.
2:12							
							A. The House of Hillel
say:							
			(ה + pres. part. sg.) One who				
							divorces
			(noun + 3rd sg. masc. suffix)			his wife—	
			(negative particle, לא, + 3rd imperf. sg.) he shall				

CC	LA	OF	M	HH1	HH2	HH3	OC
						not remain	
			(ablative prep., עם+ 3rd. sg. fm. suffix)				
						with her:	
						B. not in [the same]	
						alley;	
C. and							
						not in [the same]	
						courtyard.	
D. And if (ואם)							
			(3rd perf. sg.) it				
						was the alley	
						of both of them,	
			(pres. part. sg.) he				
							switches
			(noun + 3rd sg. pron. suffix)				
						his	
							door to another side.
E. And if (ואם)							
			(3rd perf. sg.) it				
						was the courtyard	
						of both of them,	
			(pres. part.) one				
						cedes [the courtyard] in favour of (מפני)	
							the other (זה ... זה).
						F. The woman cedes	

CC	LA	OF	M	HH1	HH2	HH3	OC
							in favour of the man.
G. With respect to what [precise circumstances] is this said (במה דברים אמורים)?							
H. At such time as (בזמן ש-)			(3rd perf. pl.) they have			[re]married,	
I. and with respect to (ב)						the priesthood [i.e., the former husband is a priest],	
even though			(3rd perf. pl.) they have			not [re]married.	
			J. (ה + pres. part. sg.) He who				performs the rite of loosening the sandal of his levirate wife [i.e., refuses to marry his dead brother's childless widow]
			(negative particle, לא, + 3rd imperf. masc. sg.) shall			not cede [the courtyard in favour of the levirate wife],	
K. because (מפני ש)							he does not pine for her.

[trans. and scoring my own, based on text of Zlotnick, ed., 1966.]

III
The rhetoric of Semahot and Mishnah compared

III.i. How much of the language of Semahot 1-2 is captured by the rhetorical taxonomy developed for Mishnah?

As a general observation, and as was the case with Tosefta, the application of the rhetorical taxonomy design to document Mishnah's rhetorical features has been relatively successful in accounting for the language of Semahot 1-2. The evidence of that success is that a great deal of the language of these two chapters can be classified under columns 1 (concatenating language), 4 (morphological repetition), and 5-7 (the repetition of identical or similar-sounding phrases, or the alternation of semantic opposites). There is still relatively little in the way of logico-deductive formulae (column 2), the hallmark of many other post-mishnaic rabbinic texts. Moreover, like Mishnah, terms which in these other documents are the logical "operators" of stock dialectical formulations (e.g., which/that, lo, except, since, as it is said) are more often joining/concatenating language in Semahot.

　　All this being said, there is substantially more in column 8 (other content) in the scored chart of Semahot 1-2 than was the case in either Mishnah or Tosefta. For both the Mishnah and the Tosefta chapters analyzed earlier, column 8 was substantially empty. Not so at first glance for Semahot 1-2. What this means is that some significant proportion of the language in column 8 is not "captured" by the mishnaic rhetorical taxonomy. More specifically, the language in column 8 was not "captured" in columns 5 through 7 (homophonic, homosemantic, and antisemantic markers).

　　At this point, I should note that I have deliberately "inflated" the amount of material in column 8, so as not to prejudice the case in favour of Semahot appearing Mishnah-like. How did I do this? All verbs in Semahot 1-2 which repeat the same morphological form (a very mishnah-like rhetorical trait) but which do not repeat the same verbal root (or its semantic opposite) I have located in column 8. Therefore, what we really have in most of these instances is not "autonomous" content, that is, language whose formulation is independent of Mishnah-like rhetorical requisites. Rather at these junctures we have *lists* of activities or practices, with all of the verbs in the list cast in exactly the same form (present participle plural) and, save one, preceded by the negative particle אֵין. In addition, in most cases the verb is followed by a substantive or particle with a masculine singular pronominal suffix. "And" serves as concatenating/joining language. Finally, the clause "until such time as he dies" punctuates the list at several junctures. Isolating only these elements from the scored chart, one "hears" the following:

Chart 4.2: Rhetorical markers unifying Semahot 1:2-7

1:2

	They do not	tie	his ....
And	they do not	stop up	his ....
And	they do not	lay upon	him ... until such time that he dies.

1:3

	They do not	move	him ....
And	they do not	bathe	him ....
And	they do not	carry	him ... until such time that he dies.

1:4

| | They do not | close | his .... |

1:5

	They do not	tear	
And	they do not	loosen	
And	they do not	eulogize ...	
And	they do not	bring...him ...	until such time as he dies.

1:6

	They do not	acclaim	him ...
And	they do not	recount ...	him ... his ...
			[until such time that he dies].
		recount ...	him ... his ...
			[even before such time as he dies].

1:7

| | | | [At such time that he dies]. |
| | They do not | inquire.... | |

The foregoing extractions from the scored chart of Semahot 1:2-7 makes clear that the verbs I prejudicially assigned to column 8, that is, content seemingly unrelated to Mishnah-like rhetorical requisites, are nothing of the sort. What we have is a beautifully spun-out list, the items of which are identically formulated, unifying six of the 10 pericopes (1:2-1:7) of Semahot chapter 1. The result is quintessentially mishnaic. It is worth noting at this juncture that the verb sequence in 1:1-1:7 is not the only such sequence in Semahot chapters 1 and 2, if one examines the chart. No other sequence, however, is nearly as long.

With our concatenated list of verbs removed from the "catch-all" category represented in column 8, a vertical perusal of the score from Semahot 1:8 on shows much less language assigned to column 8. Later I will have occasion to speculate as to how this language "escaped" the formulation in accordance with Mishnah-like canons of rhetoric. Therefore, to state my conclusion thus far, the mishnaic rhetorical taxonomy captures the vast majority of the language of Semahot 1-2, especially when one reconsiders the classification of quite elegant lists of similarly formulated verbs.

III.ii. Are mishnaic rhetorical strategies used to define, integrate, and mark off larger intermediate subdivisions of the tractate?
Among the principle traits of Mishnah is the use of morphological and/or repetition of phrases as markers of a larger intermediate subdivision of a tractate. In this manner Mishnah rhetorically marks off its topical "chapters." J. Neusner (1981) was the first to notice this, particularly as regards morphology. And our analyses of Mishnah's rhetorical traits demonstrate that fuller array of mishnaic rhetorical strategies is also used to these ends.

While Tosefta uses all of Mishnah's rhetorical techniques, we have already demonstrated that Tosefta tends not to use them to define, integrate, and mark off larger intermediate divisions ("chapters") of a toseftan tractate. This is so because Tosefta deliberately and self-consciously presents itself rhetorically as a type of commentary on Mishnah. Therefore, its larger intermediate subdivisions are not defined by some *autonomous* inner-Toseftan means, but rather by its direct *dependence* on the language and sequence of the pericopes of the Mishnah "chapter" with which it deals. What now of Semahot? As is evident from the scored chart, Semahot 1-2 stands much closer to Mishnah than to Tosefta in these respects.

The first topical "chapter" deals with someone just on the borderline between life and death (Semahot 1:1-1:7). The "chapter" commences with a substantive in the form of *heh* plus present participle singular (הגוסס). As we have already seen, Semahot 1:1-1:7, is set off not only by its topical frame, introduced by the aforementioned substantive, but also by the use of a defined set of literary markers:

1) concatenating conjunction, "and";
2) "until such time that he dies";
3) the negative particle, אין;
4) verb in the present participle plural;
5) 3rd person masculine singular pronominal suffix.

The repetition of some critical mass of these five markers at regular junctures throughout the topical subdivision serves to set off the shank of the "chapter" by means quite distinct from legal content.

Semahot 1:8 through 2:12 constitutes the second "chapter" of the tractate; again, this larger intermediate division is again defined both topically and by means of literary markers evincing typical mishnaic rhetorical traits. The concluding two percicopes, 2:11 and 2:12, are somewhat tangential both topically and rhetorically to the "chapter's" shank. These final two pericopes are supplemental postscripts—a not uncommon technique in Mishnah for signalling the end of a major intermediate unit. With respect to rhetorical markers, 2:11 and 2:12 are well joined to one another and to 1:10 (still part of the shank) by picking up several of 1:10's phrases and morphological forms—again typical of Mishnah.

Topically, this "second chapter's" shank considers whether the full array of funerary rites normally observed for the "natural" death of an Israelite (male?), should be observed for persons whose status as Israelites is questionable, or whose death is in some way abnormal. The list of persons in this category are generally given as substantives in participial form (with or without the *heh-hayediah* as grammatically needed). The rhetorical markers establishing the shank of the chapter are the following:

Element A
1) participial substantive(s) (with one exception)

Element B
2) (negative particle, אין, + verb in present participle plural:) "They do not,"

plus
3)   "attend to [rites] ... (third person pronominal suffix) it/him/them in any manner,"

Element C
sometimes plus
4)   "but (אבל)," "and" or "rabbi x says/said"
plus
5)   (verb in present participle plural:) "they do"
or
      marker (2)

Element D
or
      marker (2)
plus
5)   "withhold [rites] .... from (third person pronominal suffix) it/him/them in any manner."

Element A presents the subtopic of the "chapter" and is followed by the rhetorical markers of either Element B or Element D. The markers of Element C allow the authors to spin out further the particular subtopic—all within the shank of the "chapter." Chart 3 documents the use of these elements and constituent rhetorical markers in Semahot 1:8-2:12.

Chart 4.3: Rhetorical markers of the shank of the second "chapter" of Semahot (1:8-2:12)

1:8

severed [foetus]					
breach birth					
miscarried [foetus]					
one 8 months					
one 9 months	they do not		attend to	it	in any manner

1:9

gentiles					
slaves	they do not		attend to	them	in any manner
But	they do	call out		them	

1:10

[And]	they do not	receive condolences	

1:11

[And]	they do not	call out

1:12

[And]		they do not	call out			

2:1

	one who commits suicide	they do not		attend to	him	in any manner
says		they do	call out		him	
and		they do not	tear			
and		they do not	loosen			
and		they do not	eulogize		him	
but		they do	stand in line		him	
and		they do	say ...		him	
		they do		attend to	it	
		they do not		attend to	it	

2:2

Who is
one who
commits
suicide ...

This is ...
one who
commits
suicide

and		they do not		attend to	him	in any manner

2:3

Lo, this is ...
one who
commits
suicide
not ...

And	any one who commits suicide not ...	they do not		withhold	him	in any manner

2:4

And it once transpired ...

and he said		they do not		withhold	him	in any manner

2:5

And
again it once transpired ...

and he said		they do not		withhold	him	in any manner

2:6

	those executed ...	they do not		attend to	them	in any manner
and		[they]	come			

and		they	inquire		
and		they do not	mourn		
rather		they	grieve		
and		they do not	prepare meal		them

2:7

And		they do not	allow speak		him
And		they	make drink		him
And		they	instruct confess		him

2:8

	any one who abandons	they do not		attend to	him	in any manner
		[they]	wear			
and		they	wrap			
and		they	eat			
and		they	drink			
and		they	rejoice			

2:9

	one who is executed ...	they do not	withhold	them	in any manner.

2:10

	someone that fell				
or	that ... swept away				
or	that .... devoured	they do not	withhold	him	in any manner.

2:11

someone ... was crucified
... was crucified
... were crucified

2:12

say	one who divorces

The use of Element-A, Element-B and Element-D markers is clearly evident in the foregoing. These three sets of rhetorical markers help define "chapter" 2 of Semahot; Element-C markers function to spin out a list of permitted or forbidden rites once Elements A plus B or Elements A plus D have provided the occasion. Whether Element C uses "and" or "but" depends simply upon whether what follows is logically conjunctive or disjunctive with what preceded; for example, the prohibition of a rite will be joined by "but" to an antecedent prescription to observe a rite. Together Elements A, B, D, and C identify pericopes or parts thereof constituting the "chapter's" shank. As was mentioned, 2:11 and 2:12 are clearly not part of the shank as defined by rhetorical markers; nor are they integral topically to the "chapter." However, they provide atypical "tangential" postscripts with which many mishnaic chapters typically mark their conclusion.

In all, then, the second "chapter" of Semahot comprises a topical unit whose shank and boundaries are carefully marked by means of rhetorical techniques entirely within the bounds of normalcy for a mishnaic "chapter."

III.iii. Are mishnaic-like rhetorical techniques used to attach materials to the shank of the "chapter" and to integrate elements of individual pericopes?

The very same techniques used by Mishnah to rhetorically mark out the shank of a Mishnah tractate's larger intermediate divisions, that is, replication of morphological form coupled with repetition of phrases (sometimes while also alternating paired semantic antonyms) is used within a mishnaic "chapter" to join materials to that shank and to unify the resulting pericopes. Again a perusal of our scored chart of Semahot 1-2 demonstrates the Mishnah-like character of Semahot. Since the object of our larger study is Mishnah, not Semahot, I shall not here perform a comprehensive analysis of how all of the elements of Semahot 1:1-7 and 1:8-2:12 are joined to their respective chapter's shank. For purposes of comparison with Mishnah, permit me an example or two.

The case of 1:9-1:12 will prove instructive and will suffice for our purposes. As demonstrated above, 1:9 is part of the shank of the second "chapter." Three primary markers join materials in 1:10-12 to that chapter's shank. They are:

1)   (present participle plural, with or without the preceding negative particle,אין) "They do/they do not";
2)   "call out";
3)   "slave(s)".

A fourth marker substitutes for "call out" throughout 1:10; it is

4)   "receive condolences."

If one returns to Chart 2 above at Semahot 1:9, one sees that the first usage of "call out" (formulated in the present participle plural) falls within the category of Element-C markers helping to define the shank of the "chapter." The subsequent appearances of it help join materials to that shank. Similarly with the first appearance of "slaves" is, an Element- A marker, at the beginning of 1:9. Its repetition integrates subsequent subsections and joins them to the shank. Chart 4 documents these markers' use in 1:9-1:12.

Chart 4. 4: Appearance of markers joining 1:9-1:12 to the shank of Semahot's second "chapter"

1:9

	slaves	they do not	
But		they do	call out

1:10

		they do not		receive condolences
	slaves			

that		they do not		receive condolences
	slaves			
that		they do not		receive condolences
	slaves			
because				
	slaves			
that		they do not		receive condolences
	slaves			
said	slave			
	slaves			
that	slaves			
said	slave			
	slaves			

1:11

		they do not	call out	
	male slaves			
and	female slaves			
			call out	
	slave			

1:12

		they do not	call out	

On the whole, three of the four markers appear with regular periodicity throughout 1:9-12, just as one would expect in Mishnah when markers are used to join pericopes to a "chapter's" shank. A perusal of the scored chart in the Appendix indicates that similar mishnah-like results would arise from analyses of how other pericopes are joined to the shank of the chapter.

III.iv. How does Semahot differ from Mishnah?

The sum total of the analyses of the preceding sections indicates that Semahot 1-2 replicates Mishnah's rhetorical traits to a significant degree. Indeed, Semahot is far closer in this regard to Mishnah than is Tosefta. And as with Mishnah, we must conclude that the rhetorical requisites informing Semahot's authors required them to recast significantly the language of any written sources upon which they may have been dependent for content.

Perhaps the fundamental factor accounting for the difference between Semahot and Tosefta is that the latter formally presents itself as a type of commentary on Mishnah. Tosefta is constantly dependent upon Mishnah for an agenda and (for at least two-thirds of Tosefta's materials) for an intelligible context. Semahot, by contrast, is structured as an autonomous document, intelligible on its own, and organized according to the logic of its own subtopics. Semahot rhetorically attempts to convey a sense of exhaustively treating each subtopic before moving on to the next. Each chapter is constructed as a self-contained, self-standing whole. It is fundamentally this substantive trait of Semahot, together with its Mishnah-like literary/rhetorical techniques, that makes Semahot so much like Mishnah, in contrast to Tosefta.

Notwithstanding the foregoing, Semahot 1-2 has not fully replicated Mishnah's rhetorical style. One indication of this is already present in Chart 3 at 1:10. What I have called a "substitution" of marker 4 for marker 2 indicates a weakening of the link between 1:10 and 1:9. Moreover, toward the end of 1:10 we are limited to a single marker, "slave(s)" joining 1:10 to the shank and to the subsections that precede and follow it. Only with 1:11 do we return to the type of "critical mass" of rhetorical markers one would expect to see in Mishnah's efforts to join pericopes to a "chapter's" shank. In effect, 1:10 is, relatively speaking, disjointed from the shank of the chapter and from the materials preceding and following 1:10– even if 1:10 taken on its own displays wonderful unity and coherence and achieves this by means of mishnah-like techniques. In this respect, 1:10 (and other pericopes displaying the same strong internal unity, but rhetorically weak links to the "chapter") begins to look somewhat more like toseftan pericopes which function to supplement Mishnah rather than to explicate and complement Mishnah. I believe that the significant number of pericopes in Semahot that resemble 1:10 in these specific respects in part led earlier scholars to the conclusion that Semahot was a late "compilation" of independently formulated and independently circulating materials. In fact, we have proven that matters are quite otherwise. However, at these junctures in Semahot 1-2, Semahot is not as faithfully mishnaic in character.

Further to this same point, Semahot 1:10, the rhetorically 'weakly connected' pericope by mishnaic standards, is a series of three "precedent stories" (which typically begin with the formula מעשׂה ב/שׁ, "it was transpired"). This weak connection to 1:9 is contrasted with quite elegant literary coherence and unity within and across the three stories themselves. Another series comprising two precedent stories and a concluding appendix appears at Semahot 2. Here rhetorically, the precedent stories have been integrated into the shank of the chapter with the marker, "they do not withhold [rites] from him in any manner" attributed as direct discourse to the rabbinic authorities "acting" in the stories. However, this marker aside, the internal coherence and unity across the stories and concluding appendix is strong.

Such precedent stories, fairly frequently used in Semahot, are not typically mishnaic. Or, more precisely, series of two or more similarly formulated precedent stories are not mishnaic; Tosefta, by contrast, more frequently makes use of them. That being said, precedent stories do appear in Mishnah, but they are by far the exception, not the rule. More important still, precedent stories in Mishnah tend to be quite concise, serving either to bolster an antecedent ruling or to substitute for an alternative and opposing ruling attributed to a named authority. In the latter instance, casting the alternative ruling as a precedent story seems simply an alternative to the common mishnaic dispute form. Indeed, one often can easily recast such a pericope in typical dispute form with little change or omission in the language of the story.[4] M. Gittin 1:5, previously scored and analyzed, is a case in point.

A.	Any writ that has upon it [the signature of] a Samaritan witness–
B.	is unfit,
C.	except writs [of divorce] of women and manumission papers of slaves.
D.	It once transpired that they brought before R. Gamaliel in Kefar Otnai
E.	a writ [of divorce] of a women, and its witnesses were Samaritan witnesses,
F.	and he declared [it] fit.

[Mishnah Gittin 1:5]

M. Gittin 1:5D provides the literary requisites of casting matters as a story precedent: the formula "it once transpired that" + name of rabbinic authority + setting. The remainder of the "story" in E and F replicates the language of A, B, and C. M. Gittin 1:5 proffers quite a sharp contrast indeed to the series of precedent stories at Semahot 1:10 or 2:4-5. By mishnaic standards, these series of precedent stories "loosen" the rather tight rhetorical cohesiveness of the chapter.

Another aspect of Semahot 1-2 which is not typical of Mishnah is the "aggadic (narrative/homilectic) midrash" at Semahot 2:7F-P. Indeed, Semahot as a whole proffers "aggadic-midrashic" materials quite regularly. The composition of entire works of aggadic midrash became a major genre of the rabbinic movement in the late fourth and subsequent centuries. Individual aggadic-midrashic pericopes appear periodically (but not frequently) in Tosefta (mid- to late-third century), and more often in the Palestinian and Babylonian Talmuds. Avot de Rabbi Nathan, the "Tosefta" to Avot, is aggadic in character and much of it is midrash as well. But aggadic-midrashic pericopes are a rarity in Mishnah. From a rhetorical perspective, they are more difficult to integrate into a mishnaic chapter than a (concise) precedent story.

Another strong rhetorical trait of Mishnah seems less prevalent in Semahot 1-2. Mishnah not only repeats the same or similar phrases as a technique, but permutes them to spin out "cases." The greater the number of phrases permuted the more precise and refined the "cases" for which Mishnah seeks to determine the rule of halakah. In this respect m.Gittin 2:1 is typical, given the following pattern, as previously seen:

	one	says	in my presence it was		written
and			in my presence it wasnot		signed
			in my presence it wasnot		written
and			in my presence it was		signed
			in my presence it was	in entirety	written
and			in my presence it was	in part	signed
			in my presence it was	in part	written
and			in my presence it was	in entirety	signed

---

4.   I argued this point more thoroughly elsewhere (Lightstone, 1985: 53-58).

	one	says	in my presence it was		written
and [another]	one	says	in my presence it was		signed
	two	say	in our presence it was		written
and	one	says	in my presence it was		signed.
	one	says	in my presence it was		written
and	two	say	in our presence it was		signed.

This permutation of phrases is less evident in Semahot, indeed, absent in Semahot 1-2. The closest one comes in Semahot 1-2 to Mishnah-like spinning out of circumstances through repetition of phrases is in sections like Semahot 2:2. A sequence of operative verbs (climbed, fell, died) is repeated four times. The last two times the list is preceded by "Rather they saw that," thus differentiating the two cases that preceded from the two which follow. The effect, although elegant in terms of its use of Mishnah-like repetition, is not the permutative spinning out of ever more finely differentiated "cases," but the more simple contrasting of two sets of circumstances: a + b + c give one ruling, but d + a + b + c gives another. Mishnah, in contrast, might give us: a + b + c give ruling ...; not a + b + c give ruling ...; a + not b + c gives ruling ...; a + b + not c give ruling ...; not a + not b + c gives ruling ...; and so on.

IV
The persistence and transformation of mishnaic rhetoric
as reflected in Semahot 1-2

The upshot of the foregoing section is that Semahot, like Tosefta, attempts to replicate many of the features characteristic of Mishnah's rhetoric. Indeed, because the authors of Semahot have cast the document as an autonomously intelligible treatment of its subject matter, like a mishnaic tractate, they have been better able than Tosefta's authors to adopt Mishnah's rhetorical techniques of "marking" topical "chapters." Given the fact that Tosefta is formulated as a kind of "commentary" on Mishnah, it is hard to see how Tosefta could have done this without undermining its self-representation as a "commentary/supplement" to another "authoritative" document.

On the other hand, Semahot, again like Tosefta, simply does not *replicate* faithfully the rhetorical features consistently characteristic of Mishnah. Indeed, leaving aside the principle aforementioned difference distinguishing Tosefta and Semahot, it is the penchant of both documents to supplement and complement which distinguishes them from Mishnah. Furthermore, the increased use of precedent stories and other 'non-mishnaic' literary genres to meet these ends is evident in Semahot and in Tosefta.[5]

---

5.   My impression is that the use of aggadic midrash is far more pronounced in Semahot than in Tosefta. Tosefta, however, frequently uses halakic midrash to complement Mishnah.

In sum, as was the case with our previous analyses of Tosefta, a close reading of Semahot's use of mishnaic rhetorical techniques serves to bring into sharper relief the rhetorical nature of Mishnah and the distinctive type of guild expertise or professional virtuosity reflected in that rhetoric. It is the expertise to *imagine* a social and cultic world capable of being closely defined according to the finest and most tight "grid" which accounts for even the slightest independent variation of multiple possible factors characterizing a situation. Central to that virtuosity, at least as reflected in Mishnah, is not external authority, whether in precedent set by some court or rabbi's decision or in some other authoritative text. To be sure, biblical law is assumed by Mishnah's authors. But, as we have confirmed in previous analyses, and as Neusner demonstrated in the late 1970s, Mishnah is not at all an exegesis of the legal sections of the Hebrew Bible. Rather, with biblical law as an antecedent given, it is the inner logic of the law as ramified and discovered by the permutation of cases to spin out series of minutely differentiated cases which is at the heart of Mishnah's rhetoric and of mishnaic-rabbinic virtuosity—and which seems to be at the heart of the self-definition of members of the newly (re)fashioned rabbinic guild at the end of the second century after reaching an accommodation and partnership with the Galilean Patriarchy.

With Semahot, as with Tosefta, the authority of Mishnah's rhetoric and associated virtuosity is evidently strong. But it has succumbed as well to other developments both in terms of literary genres/rhetoric and associated forms of inner-guild expertise. These complementary and supplementary forms of expertise will at the literary level constantly undermine attempts of guild masters to replicate exactly a mishnaic tractate. If it quacks like a duck, it is a duck. A parrot cannot sustain quacking like a duck; it will quite soon give itself away by sounding like a parrot (who can also quack like a duck).

As argued earlier, comparisons of the literary/rhetorical features of Tosefta and Semahot with those of Mishnah help us better understand Mishnah's rhetorical characteristics and the professional virtuosity which Mishnah both reflects and promotes as the foundational feature of the membership of the early rabbinic guild. These comparisons also give us some sense of the persistence and transformation of that core guild virtuosity in the century or so following the formation of the guild.

5

Summary and Conclusions:
Rhetoric and Role–
Mishnah, Material Evidence, and the Emergence
of the Rabbinic Guild in the Late-Second-Century Galilee

This book began by offering a socio-rhetorical analysis of Mishnah. I argued that such an approach provides some theoretical and methodological leverage on two longstanding issues: the problem of reconstructing a description of the early rabbinic guild's social formation, and the question of the "social meaning" of that guild's foundational text, the Mishnah. In chapter 1, the Introduction, I proposed such an approach as useful, because "rhetoric" is more than a stylized way of communicating with others. It must, in addition, be recognized by those authors' audience as authoritative or persuasive. This can occur only within a specific social context which deems that rhetorical style, and therefore what is thereby conveyed, as normal, appropriate, and particularly legitimate. Hence rhetorical styles reflect, embody, and inform social institutions, and especially social definitions of power and authority within those institutions. Rhetoric, I argued, is the art of *creatively* using *appropriate* language to *persuade* in such public spheres as the court, the council, the academy, and other such fora of debate and decision in antiquity and late antiquity–and by extension in texts which "recall" or "recreate" these fora. The appropriateness and effectiveness of the modes of expression and argument are a function of social definition and convention, context, and situation—that is, social definitions regarding who is speaking to whom, about what, and where. The existence of a legitimated, authoritative rhetoric bespeaks socially legitimated and supported institutions and social formations.

Within this conceptual frame, chapter 2 undertook an extensive rhetorical analysis of a "typical" mishnaic "chapter." In order better to grasp salient features of Mishnah's rhetorical character, chapters 3 and 4 subjected sections of Tosefta and Semahot, two arguably "mishnah-like" early rabbinic documents, to analyses using the same rhetorical-analytical categories used in chapter 2 for Mishnah. Both the successes and failures of this attempt to apply to Tosefta and Semahot those rhetorical-analytical categories that served so well to capture Mishnah's pervasive rhetorical features have proven useful. The exercise has highlighted Tosefta's and Semahot's appropriations of, and departures from, Mishnah's rhetoric, helping us both to see Mishnah's features in full relief and to view Mishnah, its framers, and its receivers in the broader context of the development of the early rabbinic guild.

Now, with the analysis and the interim findings of chapters 2 through 4 in hand, this concluding chapter will summarize and extend those findings. It will also afford the occasion to return to matters of social formation of the early rab-

binic guild and the social location of guild members in the Land of Israel from the
second to the turn of the third centuries CE.

I
Reviewing characteristic features of Mishnah's rhetoric

In the Introduction and at the beginning of chapter 2, I attempted to anticipate
what analyses of Mishnah in chapter 2 would reveal. I stated that Mishnah's
authors rely most heavily on three techniques:

(1)   morphological repetition, which itself provides a kind of alliteration and
        assonance

(2)   the repetition of similar or identical words and phrases, or of paired
        opposites, which provide a kind of rhyme, rhythm, and metre, and at times
        a kind of mechanistic permutative quality to the text

(3)   the linking of items with the above-mentioned qualities by means of
        several repeated, stock conjunctive formulae ("and," "which/that," "ex-
        cept," and perhaps "says") which give the text not only a list-like quality
        but a litany-like one.

These techniques are used to produce nested sets of literary or rhetorical
"markers" which (1) establish the rhetorical unity and coherence of a Mishnah
"chapter's" shank. Such "markers" also serve (2) to rhetorically cement other
pericopes to that shank, and, finally, (3) to effect rhetorical unity and coherence
within a pericope. Using in particular the first and second of these three techniques often produces a baroque/lyrical-like structuring of a Mishnah chapter and of
its pericopes as morphological forms, words, and phrases are repeated, inverted,
reversed and shuffled. The language already abstracted in chapter 1 from m. Gittin
2:1-2:2 (demonstrating the second above-mentioned technique) will remind us of
what we have seen, or more accurately "heard," in the analyses of chapter 2.
(Given the decided "aural" quality to Mishnah's rhetoric).

> is required to say:
> in my presence it was written;
> in my presence it was signed.
>
> cannot say:
> in my presence it was written;
> in my presence it was signed.
>
> said:
> in my presence it was written;
> not in my presence it was signed.
> said: in my presence it was signed;
> not in my presence it was written.
>
> in its entirety,
> in part;
> in part,

in its entirety

one, one;
two, one;
one, two

day, day;
night, night;
night, day;
day, night

Equally significant, the effect of the aforementioned rhetorical-literary techniques is not only aesthetic, but also legal-substantive in nature. Such use of the techniques themselves, first, produce different legal "cases" for which rulings must be supplied and, second, serve to help effect substantive closure of a chapter's content. That is to say, the subject of the chapter or major subunit has been exhausted when one has "run through" the rhetorical permutations. Perhaps, that is in part why Tosefta can so easily complement and extend Mishnah's content, as we have seen in chapter 3. Tosefta's authors have not rhetorically limited themselves as assiduously as Mishnah's, despite the obvious and frequent instances of Tosefta's replication of the rhetorical features of a Mishnah passage in composing its own interpretive or complementary pericope.

In order to review our findings about Mishnah–findings from which the reader is now several hundred pages removed–so as to commence a discussion of the place of Mishnah in the social formation of the early rabbinic guild, I present here a brief analysis of yet another passage from Mishnah, m. Bekhorot 1:2-1:4a. And for those readers not already intimately familiar with Mishnah, this analysis will provide yet more exposure to a not atypical Mishnah text before venturing into issues of social meaning and social formation.

Mishnah Tractate Bekhorot 1:2-1:4a

1:2

A. (1) A cow which gave birth [to an offspring] like [one] from an ass,
A. (2) or an ass which gave birth [to an offspring] like [one] from a horse—
B. [the offspring] is exempt from the law of the firstling,
C. since it is said, "The firstling of an ass" (Ex 13:13), "The firstling of an ass" (Ex. 34:20),
D. two times, [meaning the offspring is not liable to the law of the firstling] until it shall be [the case that] that which gives birth is an ass and that which is born is an ass.
E. And what are they with respect to eating?
F. A clean animal which gave birth [to an offspring] like [one] from an unclean animal—
G. [the offspring] is permitted with respect to eating.
H. And an unclean animal which gave birth [to an offspring] like [one] from a clean animal—
I. [the offspring] is prohibited with respect to eating
J. Since what comes forth from an unclean [animal] is unclean and what comes forth from a clean [animal] is clean.
K. An unclean fish which swallowed a clean fish—
L. [the fish swallowed] is permitted with respect to eating
M. A clean fish which swallowed an unclean fish—
N. [the fish swallowed] is prohibited with respect to eating,
O. because it is not its offspring

1:3
A.   An ass which had not given birth to any offspring and it gave birth to two males [and it is not known which came out first]—
B.   [the owner] gives one [redemption] lamb to the priest;
C.   a male and a female—
D.   [the owner] separates one lamb for himself
E.   Two asses which had not given birth to any offspring and they gave birth to two males—
F.   [the owner] gives two [redemption] lambs to the priest;
G.   a male and a female,
H.   or two males and a female—
I.   [the owner] gives one [redemption] lamb to the priest;
J.   two females and one male,
K.   or two males and two females—
L.   there is nothing here for the priest

1:4a
A.   One [ass] had given birth to offspring, and one [i.e., another ass] which had not given birth to any offspring, and they gave birth to two males—
B.   [the owner] gives one [redemption] lamb to the priest;
C.   a male and female—
D.   [the owner] separates one lamb for himself.

The assumed legal background required to deal with the subject matter of m. Bek. 1:2-1:4a is not complex. Pentateuchal law stipulates at several junctures that the first male offspring of humankind and domestic animals is holy; it belongs to God, and by proxy to the priesthood (see Ex. 13:2, 11-13; 22:28-29; 24:19-20; Lev. 27:26; Num. 3:13; 18:15-18; Deut. 14:23; 15:19-23; 21:15-17). The firstlings of species that are fit for consumption and the altar (i.e., "clean" species) are sacrificed. The firstlings of domestic animals not fit for consumption or the altar ("unclean" species) are redeemed with a lamb or goat which is then consigned to the priest. This much is relatively clear and unambiguous in biblical law. That which is less clear need not concern us, as it does not bear upon understanding m. Bek. 1:2-1:4a, with one notable exception. Mishnaic law assumes that the requirement to redeem the firstling of an unclean animal pertains to the firstling of an ass only, a stipulation which certainly limits the financial liability of the owners.

Suffice it to say that, from a rhetorical perspective, the authors assume that the reader of Mishnah either already commands the aforementioned legal background or has immediate and ongoing access to someone who does (namely, a "master"). In any case I shall not here delve into the legal substance of the Mishnah passage at hand. Let me turn rather to the passage's rhetorical features.

As I have already claimed for Mishnah passages examined in chapter 2, little in this passage from m. Bek. would count as argument, that is, the active attempt to convince one's audience (and possible detractors) of the appropriateness of one's claims. The closest one comes to such a concern in the passage is the scriptural proof-texting and exegesis at 1:2, sections C-D. In addition, J and O of 1:2 might seem at first glance to offer arguments intended to persuade. This type of truncated, supporting scriptural exegesis is not uncommon in Mishnah. However, the vast majority of Mishnah's rulings go unsupported by any accompanying scriptural prooftexting (with or without exegesis). With respect to the (alleged) "arguments" or "reasons" provided at J and O, in reality, they merely make explicit as a general ruling that which is already (implicitly) communicated in the preceding rulings on specific cases. That is, J and O merely spell out the contrast already made in adducing the cases at F-I and at K-N. In the former that which emerges is an offspring. In the latter, it is not. Spelling out in general terms what is contained in several specific case rulings is not an aberration in Mishnah, although it is not frequent.

What, now, is left in 1:2-1:4a without 1:2:C-D and 1:2:J,O? We have a list of cases and of circumstances made up of individual cases joined by "and" and "which." We have very laconic rulings for each, in truth the replication several times over of a very limited number of contrasting rulings, often repeating identical language save for the use of lexical opposites (e.g., permitted, prohibited) or lexical progressions (e.g., one, two) to achieve the contrast. Following is the language of the rulings (apodises) only:

1:2

B.	is exempt from the law of the firstling;
G.	is permitted with respect to eating;
I.	is prohibited with respect to eating;
L.	is permitted with respect to eating;
N.	is prohibited with respect to eating;

1:3

B.	gives one lamb to the priest;
D.	separates one lamb for himself;
F.	gives two lambs to the priest;
I.	gives one lamb to the priest;
L.	there is nothing here for the priest;

1:4

B.	gives one lamb to the priest;
D.	separates one lamb for himself.

I now turn to the "cases" (protases) for which the rulings are given. What follows abstracts from the passage cited only the language constituting the cases

1:2

A.(1)	a cow which gave birth [to an offspring] like [one] from an ass:
A.(2)	an ass which gave birth [to an offspring] like [one] from a horse:
D.	which gives birth is an ass and that which is born is an ass;
F.	a clean animal which gave birth [to an offspring] like [one] from an unclean animal;
H.	an unclean animal which gave birth [to an offspring] like [one] from a clean animal
K.	an unclean fish which swallowed a clean fish;
M.	a clean fish which swallowed an unclean fish;

1:3

A.	an ass which had not given birth to any offspring and it gave birth to
A.	two males;
C.	a male and a female;
E.	two asses which had not given birth to any offspring and they gave birth to
E.	two males;

G.   a male and a female;
H.   or two males and a female;
J.   two females and one male;
K.   or two males and two females;

1:4a
A.   one [ass] had given birth to offspring, and one [i.e., another ass] which had not given birth to any offspring, and they gave birth to
B.   two males;
C.   a male and female

Once again the reader is reminded that, in Mishnah, the language in which the cases are formulated is laconic in the extreme. Again the same language is reused in case after case. This includes not only simple lexical repetition but also repetition of entire phrases and clauses and of morphology and syntax. New cases are generated by:

- changes in one or two operative terms (cow, ass)
- the use of lexical opposites (clean, unclean)
- simple inversion or negation (has given birth, has not given birth)
- progressions (an ass, two asses)
- permutations (two males and a female, a male and two females).

As in chapter 2, one sees how by these techniques the author spins out lists of contrasting cases, often of increased complexity—all from an economy of words and phrases.

We are reminded, too, how little there is that is discursive-prose-like about this text's use of language to define circumstances that are to be the object of rulings. Earlier in this book and elsewhere (Lightstone 1997: 275-95), I have repeatedly described the use of language in Mishnah as lyric-like and have spoken of Mishnah formulations as baroque-like, in the sense of baroque music's penchant for spinning out musical movements by inversion, progression, and permutation of musical theme. All this is to imply that in this respect, as in so many others, Mishnah does not restrict itself to real circumstances, but rather displays a strong tendency to define and rule upon hypothetical and increasingly complex circumstances in a theoretical or imagined world (just as, for most of Mishnah's tractates, the Jerusalem Temple, destroyed some 130 years earlier, still stands with its institutions of national cult and governance in full operation). The increased complexity and the strong sense of the hypothetical/theoretical derives from the multiplication of defining factors and their systematic permutation, progression, inversion, and augmentation. I do not know whether it is ironic or highly appropriate that the hypothetical and fictive cases generated by Mishnah's rhetorical machinery treat matters so often pertaining to a Temple-centred Israelite "world," itself a fiction, even if a compellingly legitimate one, at the close of the second century CE when Mishnah was authored.

As noted several times earlier in this volume, the literary-aural qualities of Mishnah's lyric-like permutative rhetoric has served to efface the idiomatic antecedent language of any of Mishnah's sources, whether literary or oral. In addition, it has equally expunged the idiomatic speech of any individual masters, despite Mishnah's frequent use of named attributions to late first- and second-century rabbinic personages. Indeed, the rhetorical requisites of Mishnah will have necessarily wiped out a fair degree of the idiomatic content of antecedent sources, as both W.S. Green (1983) and J. Neusner (1981) have already argued on slightly different evidentiary grounds. More important still, in doing so Mishnah's rhetoric reflects, projects, promotes, and legitimates a unitary and coherent method of going about one's business, the business of being a mishnaic rabbi. With the foregoing statement, I have conceptually returned to the issues with which I began this volume.

(1) What social definitions, institutions, and formations representing the "inner social life" of the early rabbinic guild are aided and abetted by the production of Mishnah, with its particular rhetorical features, its specific model of legitimate rabbinic guild "mastery," and by its promulgation as *the* core text within the early rabbinic movement?

(2) What "extra-guild" social spheres and contexts sustained these inner-guild definitions and formations—indeed, paid for them—since expertise must be "bought and paid for" somewhere within society to be sustainable?

II
Rhetoric, core expertise, inner-guild formation, and rabbinic origins

II.i. The mastery to imagine highly differentiated "grids"
The reader has by now attended in chapters 1 and 2 enough formulations of the answer to the first question, that in this chapter it will now seem commonplace and obvious. Therefore, I shall only summarize matters here in order to prepare for a more extensive treatment of the second question.

Recall my general definition of rhetoric: formal modes of speaking, writing, or evincing a formalized expertise which are socially defined as authoritative within a given social sphere, community or group. We know, as mentioned, that from the late second and early third centuries the study of Mishnah was deemed among the rabbis to be a lifelong pursuit. From that pursuit, rabbinic disciples were validated by their masters as worthy of the title of "master." In that pursuit, masters maintained their master-status in the eyes of their disciples and peers. Study of Mishnah was a key element in the social formation, definition, maintenance, and perpetuation of the rabbinic guild, professional order, or "college of masters." No doubt other key elements have to do with the social, political, cultural, and economic order of late-second and early third-century Galilee (which I shall discuss at greater length later in this chapter). But what is characteristic of Mishnah defined the core expertise characteristic of the rabbi as understood within the inner life of the professional order or guild, apart from other, complementary social definitions of the role and expertise of the rabbi which may have existed outside the guild in the marketplace, court or council.

What is that inner-guild, defining, core expertise that is reflected, inculcated, and perpetuated in Mishnah and by its perpetual study? Reformulated simply, and in the terms of Mary Douglas's *Natural Symbols* (Douglas, 1973), masters of the rabbinic guild are a class of persons who have the training to imagine, conceptualize or define a sphere of reality in accordance with a highly, indeed evermore highly, differentiated grid. For that stipulated, bounded sphere, the rabbi is the one who can multiply and ramify defining and differentiating factors in order to better distinguish one case from another, where others can perceive or create no differentiation at all. In stating that one (divinely sanctioned) rule applies in one such differentiated case but not another, the rabbi is stating that the master's perceptions of these differences matter in the utmost. Moreover, in applying one rule rather than another to circumstances which the non-rabbinic eye cannot differentiate, the rabbi claims the ability and authority to lay a highly-differentiated, divinely-sanctioned, world-ordering grid on sphere after sphere of our otherwise undifferentiated, chaotic world.

The theoretical and conceptual framework and attendant methods of socio-rhetorical analysis provide distinctive insights into the nature and social formation of the earliest rabbinic guild. These sometimes differ from and sometimes complement what is suggested by other scholarly approaches. Other scholars of the history of early rabbinism have focused on the rabbi as tradent, preserving and ramifying the legal traditions of Judean society from the period before its destruction in two wars with Rome. They see the formation of the rabbinic movement or guild and the production of Mishnah as a concerted effort to preserve these endangered traditions. But our analyses offer another vantage.

I have attempted to show that a particular core expertise seems reflected and promoted in Mishnah, and now claim that the definition of that expertise was formative for the rabbinic movement at the end of the second century and beginning of the third. Does the production and promulgation of Mishnah mark the beginning of that expertise or of the rabbinic movement? The answer is both yes and no.

On the one hand, Mishnah is the first document authored and promulgated within the rabbinic movement as authoritative for all. More to the point, Mishnah was the first text successfully promulgated as authoritative for all by some group of rabbis who eradicated (or assimilated to themselves) other rabbinic groups which may have competed with them for primacy within nascent rabbinism. Hence, the very production and successful promulgation of Mishnah represents some massive formation or reformation of the early rabbinic movement. In this regard, it is worth noting that, as Neusner has demonstrated in his numerous works on Mishnah (especially Neusner, 1981), Mishnah's authors have largely eradicated the language of any antecedent sources or tradents the substantive legal teachings of which may have been incorporated into Mishnah. The power to do so should not be taken for granted, politically or sociologically.

On the other hand, Mishnah preserves the names of some one hundred rabbinic tradents, to whom are attributed legal rulings (Cohen, 1992: 157-74), now cast in Mishnah's authors' language and rhetorical style (Lightstone 1997: 275-95). These named tradents span, for the most part, the approximately one hundred years from the destruction of Jerusalem in 70CE to about the last quarter of the second century. In sheer volume, however, attributions to four masters (Judah, Yosi, Meir, and Simeon) from the period of ca135 to 165CE outstrip enormously all others (Goodblatt, 1994: 264). I shall not venture into the debate concerning the reliability of these attributions (Neusner, 1981; Goodblatt, 1994: 147). Surely, it was not in the interest of the rabbinic circle that produced Mishnah to portray itself as a self-creation *ex nihilo*. And much myth-making is to be expected from them in order to place their authority upon an older foundation. That foundation will have had to be recognized as legitimate within the group and within the circles of those whom they aspired to assimilate to their group. But this does not mean that all attributions are necessarily without substance or basis.

More to the point of this book, it is improbable that the guild expertise modelled and promulgated in the Mishnah is created *ex nihilo* near the end of the second century. More likely, that expertise revives and transforms one which had some institutional base and functionality (and had therefore been bought and paid for) within Palestinian society in some era not too far removed from the date of Mishnah's authors. However, the production and promulgation of Mishnah, with its modelling of a particular core rabbinic expertise, must reflect the emergence of some contemporary, late second-century institutional/functional venue in which mishnah-like expertise was (once again?) bought and paid for.

II.ii. The likely institutional origins of core rabbinic guild expertise
Briefly at the end of chapter 1 and more extensively in chapter 2, I argued that Mishnah, in its lyrical, clockwork rhetoric, models a priestly-scribal virtuosity of comprehensively mapping the world, and implicitly lays claim to priestly-scribal authority for the guild of rabbinic Sages. I have stressed that this transpires not only at the level of the legal substance of Mishnah, which defines aspects of an ideal Temple-centred state, but also by means of implicitly communicated, non-discursive knowledge of how things really are given in Mishnah's pervasive rhetorical traits, which model the requisite mastery of the guild. But is the implicit claim to priestly-scribal virtuosity more than self-justificatory invention of late second century persons? Is there some historical validity to the claim as regards the origins or antecedents of the late-second-century rabbinic guild? In other words, can we reasonably formulate an answer to the question, Whence the rabbis?

In truth, I can acknowledge as valid no direct historical evidence, either from early-rabbinic or extra-rabbinic sources, which provides a firm basis for answering the question, if the query is understood in its most straightforward sense. Pre-70 Pharisees and/or Scribes are commonly adduced as the font of Rabbinism. In addition, Hasideans, a pietistic or quietistic group alleged to have arisen in Hasmonean times, "reformed" Essenes, and members of the Priestly castes, have all been identified by one scholar or another as elements party to the founding and crystalization of the rabbinism movement just prior or immediately subsequent to the Great Revolt. In chapter 1, I assessed the methodological problems associated with the attribution of the rabbinic guild's origins to some centuries-old (occupational?) group called by many historians *"the* Sages" (of which pre-70 Pharisaism is usually touted to be the most faithful (although by no means the only) expression before the establishment of the rabbinic movement. Aside from using, with the requisite caution, the nascent rabbinic guild's episodic, somewhat late, ever ambiguous, and, whenever it is made, entirely self-serving claim to be the rightful heirs of the Pharisees, no reliable historical evidence can be adduced to substantiate any clear identification of principal historical ancestors of the rabbinic movement near the time of the Great Revolt, if one takes the exercise's goal to be ascribing rabbinic origins to named Second-Temple Judaic movements, singly or in combination. And the problem with evidence in this respect is twofold. Not only does the evidence permit us only the haziest reconstruction of historical events pertaining to the development of the rabbinic movement itself at the end of the first or the beginning of the second century. The evidence also permits us to say only very little about the historical development of such groups as the Pharisees, Sadduccees, or the Scribes (if indeed the latter may be similarly characterized as a movement/group at all). It is altogether easy to identify group "a" with group "b," when one knows too little about either. In such instances the practical value, let alone the historical validity, of the identification is minimal. The reviews of scholarship on this question by A.J. Saldarini (1986) and L. Grabbe (1992) amply bear out this conclusion.

However, I can propose a response to the question of rabbinic origins from my particular theoretical and methodological viewpoint if I restate the question in quite different terms: Whence in late-first-or second-century Roman Judea and/or Galilee came the virtuosity or expertise modelled in Mishnah's pervasive rhetorical traits? Who, in all likelihood, would possess this expertise so as to be able to train others in its intricacies? It is unlikely that such expertise was hatched spontaneously at the end of the second century by some bright ambitious persons "off the street." Far more likely, expertise of this type resided historically in some group or class, even if their (would-be) successors further refined and redefined the character of such expertise before passing it on to others. Such professional guild traits usually come from an institutionalized social setting where expertise is bought and paid for.

Given what I have argued in the preceding sections, the most likely institutional point of origin for such expertise would be somewhere within the Temple-state's administration itself, before its demise in 70CE. As David Goodblatt argues in his extensive treatment of Second Temple and Early Rabbinic political institutions, during the entire Second-Temple period Judea was first and foremost, a high-priestly monarchy; the high priests' administration was the central government, not only of the Temple, but of the Israelite homeland (Goodblatt, 1994: 6-29). The evidence for other institutions of national political and religious power, such as a national *gerousia* or *sanhedrin*, is weak and equivocal (Goodblatt, 1994: 77-130). Not so with respect to high-priestly national governance.

I suggest that those persons who are at the largely veiled origins of Rabbinism are refugees from the Temple state's national bureaucracy and administration, who, having lost their institutional base, first tried to preserve and pass on their professional guild expertise.[1] I cannot perceive another more likely venue for

---

1.　　I do not want the weight of my use of the word "first" to be downplayed. What I suggest is that preservation of the guild, thorough preservation of its characteristic virtuosity, "drove" the development of the earliest rabbinic movement— more than any motivation to define a

the origins of the rabbinic movement. Similarly, the very production and promulgation of Mishnah, the first "canonical" rabbinic document, suggests that they finally managed to create or to find at the end of the second century a new institutional home for the exercise and perpetuation of that guild expertise. No wonder that, time and with a new institutional setting, the implicit claim to be Temple-priestly administrators would seem increasingly less germane. With time, their new setting would have gained its own legitimacy, or the rabbinic guild would not have survived Late Antiquity.[2] Therefore, it is to a discussion of this contemporary social context and its institutions at the end of the second century that we devote the remainder of this concluding chapter. That setting, I will argue, was the emergent Patriarchate, the allegedly Roman-sanctioned institution of limited home-rule for the ethno-religious community (*civitas*) of Jews living in the Land of Israel and, perhaps, in southern Syria as well at the end of the second century (see Goodblatt, 1994: 131-231).

III
The rabbinic guild, the Palestinian Patriarchy, and the material evidence of late Roman Galilee

III.i. The extra-guild institutional venue for the exercise of Mishnah-like rabbinic expertise

The evidence of Mishnah would, therefore, have us look to not one but two institutional/functional venues for a guild expertise partially modelled in mishnaic-like rhetoric. One would be an earlier venue, perceived as the historical, even historic, origin for that professional guild expertise. The other would be a venue contemporary with Mishnah's authors. I propose that Mishnah's attributions, be they mere myth-making or more, point to the Mishnah authors' perception of the interval between these social-institutional venues. The lion's share of Mishnah's attributions span approximately one century, ending with the last quarter of the second century CE. The importance to the Mishnah's authors of spanning these one hundred years with a tradental line is all the more evident when one considers that the overwhelming number of attributions in Mishnah are to Yosi, Judah, Meir, and Simeon of the post-Bar-Kohkba era. Making attributions to masters believed to have been active before the Bar-Kohkba rebellion seems a challenge for Mishnah's authors. Yet they appear committed to the enterprise.

Judaism without a functioning Temple and Temple state, or to preserve the legal traditions of that Temple state. Alas, the psychological states and motivations of persons long gone cannot be probatively established, a methodological caveat too often ignored in many historical works about early Rabbinism.

2. Indeed, the comparison of Mishnah's rhetorical features with those of post-mishnaic rabbinic texts should, and in my own research does appear to, confirm that gradual transformation over the several subsequent centuries. See above, chapter 3; see also Lightstone (1994: 173-281).

Likely possibilities, real or perceived, for appropriate institutional venues for the employment of Mishnah-rhetoric-like expertise at either end of these one hundred years are not numerous. The Temple-centred national administration of Roman Palestine is surely at the earlier end. The Galilee-centred Patriarchate of Judah I is at the other. In both semi-autonomous religious/administrative governments, persons with expertise akin to that reflected in Mishnah's rhetoric would have furnished what A. Saldarini (following G. Lenski) has called a retainer class of administrative officials (Saldarini, 1988).

I propose that the creation and promulgation of Mishnah reflects the formation or major reformation of the Patriarchate at the time of Judah I and the formation or reformation of the rabbinic guild as a retainer class within the Patriarchate of Judah I near the end of the second century.[3] In other words, a new stage in the development and institutionalization of the rabbinic class correlates with the use of the rabbinic class as retainers in Judah I's administration. The Patriarchy itself probably underwent a major transformation at this time, if indeed the Patriarchate does not actually begin with Judah I (see Goodblatt, 1994: 131-231; Levine, 1979; 1985: 90-127; 1996). Mishnah (1) models, in its pervasive rhetorical style,the professional expertise paid for by Judah I's administration in its use of members of the rabbinic class as retainers; and (2) reflects the attempt to unify and control members of the class by imposing its model upon all members of the rabbinic class and (retroactively) upon all antecedent tradental circles.

However, in its content (the ideal, Temple-centred world of Mishnah's rulings), Mishnah claims for the class origins as retainers in the Temple priesthood's govenment.

In these respects, Mishnah is indeed a watershed document. It reflects an idealized past, in order to model a formative expertise for a new social formation. Tosefta (ca. 250-300), the first post-mishnaic rabbinic legal work and first Mishnah commentary, lies beyond that watershed moment, as I believe a systematic

---

3.   With respect to a different set of issues and on quite different evidentiary grounds, Cohen makes a similar claim about the late-second-century rabbinic movement and the Patriarchy of Judah I (Cohen, 1992: 157-74). Goodblatt offers a rather different view (Goodblatt, 1994: 131-231). At issue, in part, is the dating of the foundation of the Patriarchy itself. Goodblatt proposes that its foundation dates from Gamaliel II prior to the Bar-Kohkba rebellion, with a re-establishment of the institution after 135 under Simeon b. Gamaliel II. Hezser's view is intermediary between my own and Goodblatt's in that she tends to date evidence, in particular so-called "tannaitic" evidence, in post-mishnaic works to the period in which the masters named therein flourished. However, she believes that the Patriarchate in Roman Palestine was established in the time of Judah I, who was its first incumbent (Hezser, 1997: 406). Still further on the continuum of views about the establishment or powers of the Partriarchy is M. Goodman, who claims that only in the latter half of the third century is such power attested by the evidence (Goodman, 1983; see also Goodman, 1992: 127-39). L.I. Levine also offers an interpretation of the evidence concerning the Patriarchy in third-century Roman Palestine, but without prejudice to its status or foundation in the second (Levine, 1979: 649-88; 1985: 90-129; 1996: 1-32). Levine, like Goodblatt, sees the origins of the Patriarchy with Gamaliel II, but asserts that some major reformation of the institution, reflected in significant redefinition of its power and authority, occurred with Judah I at the beginning of the third century.

comparison of the rhetorical features and content of the two texts will demonstrate. Despite Tosefta's dependence upon Mishnah's agenda and literary formulations, Tosefta registers in concrete ways the rabbinic class's involvement and interest in issues faced by the guild members in fulfillment of their duties as retainers.[4] Indeed, I suspect that a study of extra- or para-mishnaic legal concerns registered in Tosefta and in earlier sources preserved in the Palestinian Talmud will parallel the evidence we have for the responsibilities and powers of the Patriarchate in third-century Palestine.[5] In any event, the strong dependency of the rabbinic class upon the Patriarch, or, perhaps more accurately, the co-dependency of the rabbinic retainers and the Patriarch registers clearly in Tosefta and in "earlier" sources preserved in the Talmuds (Goodblatt, 1994: 131-231; Levine, 1979; 1985: 90-127; 1996).

What then may be said of the powers and responsibilities of the Palestinian Patriarchate from the onset of the third century, the period of Mishnah's promulgation and of the social (re)formation of the rabbinic guild of masters? I review here the main lines of L. I. Levine's catalogue of third-century Patriarchal powers as portrayed in rabbinic sources. (However, unlike Levine, I view rabbinic references in third-century and later texts to the state of affairs in the first half of the second century as, more likely, a combination of anachronistic retrojection and self-serving myth-making.) Here, then, is a summary of Levine's list (Levine, 1996).

1. representative to imperial authorities;
2. focus of leadership in the Jewish community:
    2.1. receiving daily visits from prominent families;
    2.2. declaration of public fasts;
    2.3. initiating or abrogating the ban (*herem*);
3. appointment of judges to Jewish courts in Palestine;
4. control of the calendar;
5. issuing enactments and decrees with respect to the applicability or release from legal requirement, e.g.:
    5.1. use of sabbatical year produce, and applicability of sabbatical year injunctions;
    5.2. repurchase or redemption of formerly Jewish land from gentile owners;
    5.3. status of Hellenistic cities of Palestine re: purity, tithing, sabbatical year;
    5.4. exemptions from tithing;
    5.5. conditions in divorce documents;

---

4. Again I believe results reported by S.J.D. Cohen are a harbinger of this (Cohen, 1992: 157-74).
5. Interestingly, I have already demonstrated that when Tosefta does not replicate Mishnah's rhetorical style, Tosefta's rhetorical repertory anticipates that of the Palestinian Talmud (Lightstone, 1994: 173-245). S.J.D. Cohen (1992) states that in J. Neusner's view, Palestinian Talmud is "about" Jewish society, whereas Mishnah is about a utopian Temple-centred world (Neusner, 1983, b and c).

5.6. use of oil produced by gentiles;

6. dispatching emissaries to Diaspora communities;

7. taxation: both the power to tax and the authority to rule/intervene on the disposition of taxes raised for local purposes by local councils.

Several of these third-century Patriarchal powers, which Levine argues are evidenced in rabbinic documents, are attested in Roman legal decrees about Patriarchal powers. Alas, Roman evidence derives from sources from the last decade (only) of the third century through the first quarter of the fifth. Contemporary non-Jewish literary, as opposed to legal, sources confirm and complement the evidence from Roman legal documents. As Goodblatt shows (Goodblatt, 1994: 132-39; see also Goodman, 1992), these Roman decrees concern in particular:

1. the judicial powers of Jewish courts under Patriarchal control, or Jewish courts to which the Patriarch appoints judges;

2. the prerogative of the Patriarch to appoint (and remove) Jewish communal officials, such as, *archisynágogos*, local patriarchs, presbyters, and others, in addition to appointments to judicial benches;

3. the power of the Patriarch to levy taxes (including tithes and first fruits) so that local communities can defray the costs of his administration;

4. the practice of sending emisaries (apostles) to local communities to speak for or represent the interests of the Patriarch.

The sources adduced by Goodblatt and others clearly indicate that, by the end of the fourth century, the Palestinian Patriarch exercises many of these powers outside the Land of Israel as well as with respect to Jewish communities in Roman lands.

From the list, and the sources from which they are culled, it is clear that a two-tiered system of "Jewish" government existed in Roman Palestinian Jewish communities from the late second or early third century on. To some degree, this two-tiered structure was later replicated beyond Palestine in the Roman Diaspora. One tier operated at the local level, under the authority of the council (*boulē*) of local aristocratic families. This level, in Goodblatt's view, existed prior to the ascendancy of the Palestinian Patriarchate (Goodblatt, 1994: 131-231). The other level, which by the onset of the third century came to overlay, but not replace, local Jewish administration, was that of the Patriarch. Both Goodblatt and Levine agree that no national council existed. Therefore, none could serve as a venue for Patriarchal power or for the exercise of the expertise or authority of members of the rabbinic class. The Patriarch did seem to have his own judicial court (*bet din*).[6]

---

6.   This seems remarkably consistent with what we know transpired in the Land of Israel, including the Galilee from the mid-second century on, as Rome reorganized the structure of administration in the area from one which was based on hierarchical, centralized governance of nomes and toparchies to one based on roman-style urbanization such as that instituted by Pompey the Great and Augustus elsewhere in the Roman East outside of Palestine, Southernmost Syria, and Egypt. Later in this chapter we shall talk more about Roman-style urbanization in the Galilee and Land of Israel in the latter part of the second century. At this juncture it is important to note that Roman-style urbanization tended to divide all territory into "cities" under the rule of a city centre. While provincial and

However, evidence does not point to that court possessing general trans-local power.

Where does this leave the rabbinic retainer class? They are clearly associated with the Patriarchate. They are agents, not of local communal government, but of the Patriarch's delimited interventionist powers. On a day-to-day basis that power would surely be most powerfully expressed in the local courts, the principal local institution over which the Patriarch seems to have had the power to directly appoint officials. Powers of judicial courts in ancient Palestinian society also included enforcement and administration of compliance. These are bureaucratic-legal functions which today we associate with a civil service functionary class, not with judicial courts per se. Here, at both levels of the judicial bench and of court agent/functionary, the rabbinic class or guild of retainers provided a cadre of persons with appropriate "professional" expertise.

But as the sources by Levine indicate, the power held by the Patriarch was judiciously used, with appropriate sensitivity to the aspirations and traditional power of members of the local Jewish aristocracy. The Patriarch's need to retain the favour of the latter was sometimes exercised to the dismay of would-be appointees to local benches from the rabbinic retainer class.

To conclude, there is no better summary of non-Jews' perception of the power and status of the Patriarch in mid-third-century Palestine than a passage from Origin's Letter to Africanus. Goodman (1992: 128), Goodblatt (1994: 131) and Levine (1996: 22) cannot resist citing it. Neither can I.

> Now that the Romans rule and the Jews pay the two drachmas to them, we, who have had experience of it, know how much power the ethnarch [Patriarch of the Jews] has among them and that he differs in little from a king of the nation. Trials are held according to the [Jewish] law [as determined by the Patriarch], and some are [even] condemned to death. And though there is not full permission for this [i.e., the trial of capital cases], still it is not done without the knowledge of the [Roman] ruler (trans. Goodman, 1992: 128; additions in square brackets are my own).

imperial Roman officials meddled in the governance of these cities, cities were self-governing under constitutions given them by the roman crown, with the exception of judicial, military, provincial-imperial taxation and levies and other trans-city affairs, in which the various levels of imperial administration "above" that of the city retained hegemony. Another feature of Roman-style urbanization, was the emergence of an hereditary decurion class in each city that was inferior to the Roman senatorial and equestrian orders but possessed a senator-like status, authority, and responsibilities within the local, home "city." The Patriarch's powers and responsibilities, including the limits of those powers in the face of local town aristocrats, seems entirely commensurate with the Patriarch and his administration occupying a place in the provincial-imperial administrative echelon (just?) above that of the "cities" in the Land of Israel. The place of "cities" in late second-and third-century Roman Galilee seems a very fruitful topic of research. I argued this in a paper delivered to the Canadian Society of Biblical Studies (Edmonton, June 2000). And one possibly appropriate sequel to this book might well be a study of the "city" and its governance in late second- and third-century Galilee and the Land of Israel as reflected in Mishnah and Tosefta.

III.ii. Venues of the court of the Patriarch and of the rabbinic class, and Palestinian Jewish settlement in the Galilee and adjacent territories

Rabbinic evidence points to the southern Galilee as the principal base in Roman Palestine of the rabbinic guild or class after the Bar Kohkba rebellion. Indeed, early third- through fifth-century Palestinian rabbinic sources consistently portray that principal base as co-located with the court of the Patriarch at Usha (with Simeon B. Gamaliel II, if Patriarchal powers are not anachronistically assigned to Simeon by rabbinic sources), at Bet She'arim and subsequently at Sepphoris (both with Judah I), and finally at Tiberias (with Judah I's successors through the first quarter of the fifth century).

Certainly after (and largely as a result of) the failed Bar-Kohkba rebellion, Jewish settlement in Palestine shifted northward to Upper Galilee (including the Golan) and Lower Galilee (including the Jezreel, Bet Shean, and Jordan valleys). Jewish settlements remained, indeed likely increased, in cities of the Palestinian coastal plain (such as Caesarea) as Jews left the Judean hill communities which had surrounded Jerusalem. But the material remains of Jewish settlement from the end of the second through the sixth centuries covering several dozens of towns and cities in the Galilee is prodigious by comparison (Tsafrir, 1984). Vivid indications of this claim derive from the distribution in the Land of Israel of the remains of synagogues dated to the Roman and Byzantine eras. L.I. Levine and A. Kroner taken together show about three dozen cities and towns with the remains of about 60 synagogues in the north, including the Golan. They show less than half that number in the towns and cities in the remainder of the Land of Israel (Levine, 1981: 1-10, cf. 2; Kloner, 1981: 11-18; Safrai, 1986: 210; Foerster, 1986 [reprint]: 63-68, cf. 64). The location of the Patriarch's headquarters in Lower Galilee, Jezreel, and the adjacent Jordan valleys, close to this concentrated settlement, but still within reasonable travel distance from Caesarea, seems eminently functional. Given, as I have argued, the (unequal) co-dependency of the Patriarch and the members of the rabbinic guild of masters, it is in the north, in Galilee, that the leadership of the rabbinic class would reside and in the north that their retainer functions would especially be used (see Cohen, 1992).[7]

III.iii. The material evidence for the exercise of rabbinic power in Roman Palestine

At this point a perennial question begs to be asked. What evidence have we of the effective exercise of the power and authority of the members of the rabbinic guild in late second- or early third-century Galilee or Palestine? Mishnaic and toseftan literature does not provide much reliable evidence. Non-rabbinic literature, whether Roman or Christian, is virtually silent about rabbinic office. Since the debates between and about Kraeling (1956) and Goodenough (1956-68), material evidence, imperfect and indirect as it is, has necessarily filled the gap. Has, then, the power and authority, or the prestige of members of the rabbinic guild, a

---

7.   On the rabbinic sources concerning purported rabbinic interest in regulating synagogue functions, see Levine (1992: 201-22).

Patriarch-sanctioned retainer class, registered on the material evidence for Roman Palestine, in particular in the Galilee? The short answer is, apparently not. The salient points are simple.

1.   The basic architecture of synagogues[8] for the late second through fifth centuries does not accord with rabbinic dicta. For example, synagogues, according to Palestinian rabbinic sources were to be oriented east-west, like the Jerusalem Temple, toward the rising sun (see. e.g., Tosefta Megillah 3:22; 4:22 in ed. Lieberman). No Roman- or Byzantine-period synagogues in the Galilee or adjacent territories are so oriented (Levine, 1992; Foerster, 1992). This is all the more striking given that many were rebuilt one or several times over this period, sometimes with reorientation of the building-never in accordance with rabbinic dicta. Before the fourth century, northern Palestinian synagogues had a monumental facade and entrance facing south, toward Jerusalem. On the interior of the monumental facade were one or more aedicula(e) (probably for the display of the Torah scroll) beside the entrance. The assembled faced south, not east.

In synagogues built or rebuilt in the fourth or fifth centuries, the Torah Shrine and entrance(s) were no longer on the same wall, but the shrine in these later synagogues is still on the southern wall, with the assembled congregation, still facing south to Jerusalem. If one hypothesizes that rabbinic power over the course of Late Antiquity was consolidated and increased in Roman Palestine, this is a significant negative result (see essays in Urman and Flesher, 1995 and in Fine, 1996a; see also Fine, 1996b; 1998).

2.   The art found in Late Roman and Byzantine Galilean synagogues does not accord with even the most stalwart attempts to interpret Palestinian rabbinic sources so as to render them more lenient, and hence more consistent with the material evidence (Levine, 1992; Foerster, 1992).[9] Before the fourth century, Galilean synagogues did not generally have mosaic floors. The evidence shows that some interior synagogue walls were plastered and painted. These could have had murals or frescoes. But no such paintings have survived, if they existed. Nothing found in Galilee parallels the murals and frescoes found in the Dura-Europos synagogue. Their preservation was a fortuitous find. The synagogue abutted the city wall. City defenders, anticipating a siege, buttressed the inner side of the city wall with sand fill. The fill remainded until the synagogue was excavated in modern times. However, many Galilean synagogues from the fourth

8.   For a good, up-to-date bibliography on scholarship concerning ancient synagogues, see Binder (1999)

9.   The list of publications debating the question of the consistency or inconsistency of rabbinic dicta, on the one hand, and ancient synagogue art, on the other, is extensive. The "classic" debate by modern scholars over the second half of this century begins just after World War II with Kraeling's reports on the Dura-Europos synagogue (see Kraeling, 1956), progressing through Goodenough's subsequent critique of Kraeling, Goodenough's famous 12 volume work on Jewish symbols in the Graeco-Roman Period in the 1950s and 1960s (see Goodenough, 1956-68), and the numerous participants in the debate over Goodenough's work, including Jacob Neusner, Ephraim E. Urbach, Morton Smith, Eric M. Meyers, and many others. Following this debate and documenting it bibliographically would be a study in its own right.

and fifth centuries have elaborate mosaic floors. Animal and human figures are liberally and ubiquitously portrayed, especially in depictions of the zodiac, of the personified seasons, and of Helios on his chariot. Scholarly interpretation of rabbinic laws concerning idolatrous images and the second commandment must be creatively stretched to account for this, if the hypothesis of the authority of rabbinic law over synagogue builders is to be maintained.

Mosaic floors in fourth- and fifth-century Galilean synagogues also tend to have some representation of the Torah Shrine, and these are typically flanked by depictions of Temple-cult paraphernalia. These include incense shovels, shofar, palm branch (lulav), citron (etrog) (originally Temple-cult objects), and the seven-branched candelabra (menorah). As L.I. Levine points out, rabbis decried the use of explicit Temple symbolism in the synagogue, with special mention of the menorah interdicted (Levine, 1992: 216; again, see essays in Urman and Flesher, 1995 and in Fine, 1996a; see also Fine, 1996b; 1998).

3. "Jewish" inscriptions on public buildings in the Galilee, almost exclusively synagogues, tend to refer to two types of persons: benefactors whose generosity made mosaics or monumental architectural features possible; and artisans who performed the work (Foerster, 1992: 298, 306; Naveh, 1981; Urman, 1981; Ben-Dov, 1981; Lifshitz, 1967). Most are in Aramaic, a few in Hebrew or bilingually in Aramaic and Hebrew, fewer still in Greek. Curiously there appears no tendency to refer to synagogue officials in these inscriptions. Generally missing is reference to members of the rabbinic class/guild.[10]

There are two particularly notable exceptions to the above. One is the lengthy synagogue mosaic epigraph in the synagogue at Rehob, south of Bet Shean (Sussman, 1981). It concerns the boundaries of the Land of Israel with respect to the application of sabbatical-year prohibitions and tithing. A number of aspects of the epigraph should be noted. First, the epigraph is an halakic text dependent upon known rabbinic sources. Second, it makes reference to Patriarch Judah I by his usual title in early rabbinic literature (simply "Rabbi," without the designation of either his or his father's name). Third, while some of the rabbinic sources upon which the epigraph appears dependent bear attributions to named rabbinic figures, these attributions do not appear in the epigraph. The only attribution is to "Rabbi." Fourth, the synagogue in which the epigraph appears dates no earlier than near the end of the Byzantine period. The epigraph sheds no light on the role and authority of members of the rabbinic class or guild in the third or fourth century. However, it may well indicate the ascendancy of rabbinic law and

---

10. In passing, it is worth noting that the trend in Diaspora synagogues may differ somewhat in regard to reference to synagogue officials. But the paucity of the evidence from Diaspora synagogue inscriptions, relative to Palestine, makes the comparison meaningless (see Foerster, 1981). Kraabel (1981) sums up matters. However, when he states that "elders, the *archisynágogos*, archons and scribes are well attested in Jewish inscriptions in the Diaspora generally" (Kràabel, 1981: 84) he refers not so much to evidence from synagogues as from tomb inscriptions. In Palestine and Galilee, too, funerary inscriptions provide far richer evidence for the social/organizational structures of synagogues than that which comes from synagogue sites themselves (see Kant, 1987).

legal literature after the demise of the Palestinian Patriarchate in the period following the first quarter of the fifth century. Therefore, the Rehob epigraph represents the exception which proves the rule.

The second exception is an inscription that comes from Dabbura in adjacent Golan. Inscribed in Hebrew, it translates as, "this is the study house of (*bet midrasho shele*) Rabbi Eliezer HaQappar" (see Urman, 1981: 155). The inscription appears on a lintel of a building, now lost, dating from the third century. The juxtaposition of a reference to *bet midrash* (an institution frequently mentioned in Tosefta) and the title "rabbi" makes this inscription unique in providing clear reference from the remains of a Galilean Jewish institutional building to a member of the rabbinic guild/class of masters. A Rabbi Eliezer HaQappar (sometimes referred to as Bar-Qapparah in Aramaic) is known from third-century rabbinic texts. The textually attested Rabbi Eliezer flourished in the time of Judah I. I distinguish the HaQappar inscription from the *bryby* inscriptions or epigraphs, some of which appear on public Jewish buildings. Since the remainder of the bryby inscriptions/epigraphs appear on tombs, I deal with them below when discussing funerary inscriptions.

Finally, one inscription (in Greek) from level IIA (early fourth century) of the synagogue at Hammath Tiberias honours one Severus, "a student of the illustrious Patriarchs" for his support in completing the (re)construction of the synagogue (Dothan, 1981). We do not require such an inscription to lend weight to conclusions about Patriarchal power and prestige in fourth-century Galilee. For the fourth century, Patriarchal authority is well represented in rabbinic sources, Roman legal documents, and non-Jewish literary works. It is noteworthy that the term "illustrious Patriarchs" offers the Greek equivalent of the term usually used in Roman legal compendia for the Palestinian Patriarch.

In sum, synagogue inscriptions and epigraphs offer only slight hints of the powerful role played by named members of the rabbinic class (and this situation differs in no way from the literary evidence from non-Jewish sources).

4.   Funerary inscriptions from the Galilee provide the richest material evidence for social roles in late Roman Jewish Galilee (and for other Jewish communities as well). In the late Roman period, the necropolis at Bet Shearim was a preferred burial site for many of those who were wealthy enough to transport their dead and to have tombs hewn in Bet Shearim's catacombs (Weiss, 1992; Van der Horst, 1991; Frey, 1952; cf. Cohen, 1981-2; Kant, 1987: cf. 697; Schwab and Lifshitz, 1974). The terms *rby, brby, ryby,* and *bryby* appear. Here, and in other Palestinian epigraphs (several in synagogues) in both Aramaic and in Greek transliteration. Unlike the Dabbura inscription concerning the "house of study" of "Rabbi Eliezer bar HaQappar," there is little basis for concluding that the persons so designated were members of the rabbinic guild of masters. As S.J.D. Cohen (1981-82) in particular has argued, the term tends be an honorific used for those who materially support the institutions of the Jewish community, that is, the wealthy local Jewish aristocrats. These honorifics do not seem to be used for persons with formal leadership functions in the synagogue or community, such as *archisynágogos* or *gerousiarch*. I surmise that the latter titles placed one at the apogee of the local aristocracy, with *rby/ryby* providing a generic honorific for

others in this social class. It appears, then, that members of the rabbinic guild of masters appropriated this honorific also for themselves. At the very least, guild masters used "rabbi" as an honorific in their inner-guild social relations. Thereby, they would have made explicit claims, among themselves, to aristocratic status on grounds of their torah-mastery. Since there is little or no epigraphic or extra-rabbinic literary evidence that anyone else used this honorific when referring to members of the rabbinic class, it seems that the "true blue" Jewish aristocrats and their "clients" either did not know of the inner-guild use of the honorific, or viewed it as pretentious.

III.iv. When silence indeed speaks volumes
It is hard to see in the foregoing anything other than a negative result. If we did not have early rabbinic literature, we would not have concluded from the material evidence that the early rabbinic class or guild of masters flourished at the dawn of the third and during subsequent centuries CE in Roman Galilee. At this point, however, a shift in perspective is helpful in understanding the relationship between the evidence given in Part I and that which has been presented thus far in Part III.

In Part II I argued that the administration of the Palestinian Patriarch, for which the members of the rabbinic guild or class were retainers, would not have displaced a strong tradition of local Jewish government by aristocratic families. Indeed, the material evidence for the Galilee largely represents the initiatives of this local elite. And the material evidence confirms that our rabbis, *qua* rabbis, were not part of local synagogue leadership and did not belong to the local aristocracy or their councils. Local Jewish judicial bodies, on the other hand, have left no material evidence. So the appointment of members of the rabbinic class to local courts, suggested by evidence adduced in Part I, would not have registered in the material remains.

In sum, the material evidence is consistent with the hypothesis that the expertise of members of the newly (re)formed rabbinic guild was "bought and paid for" by the Patriarch's administration specifically, for which they served as a retainer class. Retainers are rarely members of the highest echelon of leadership and power. Retainers are their (senior) functionaries and agents. Again, the material evidence is consistent with this depiction. Our aforementioned negative result seems, at least, not a contradictory one. And while the preceding smacks of being an argument from silence, one must consider that the confirmation of continued communal and synagogue administration by local aristocracy during the third- and fourth-century Patriarchy is not at all such an argument from silence.

III.v. The forces of urbanization in late second- and early third-century Galilee
There is one final perspective shift in approaching the material evidence that may make the latter better speak to the literary evidence for the social (re)formation both of the rabbinic guild or class of masters and of the Patriarchy at the end of the second century. Yoram Tsafrir (1984), Shaye J.D. Cohen (1992), and Lee I. Levine (1985), to name a few scholars writing on the topic during the last 15 years have all stressed the importance of the social and economic transformation which

occurred in second- to fourth-century Galilee as a result of massive urbanization. Cohen and Levine explicitly relate the effects of urbanization to the rise of the rabbinic class and the emergence of the Patriarchy. Catherine Hezser (1997), on the other hand, rejects this line of reasoning. She maintains that major urbanization began over a century earlier. While, in her view, the process continued into the second and third centuries CE, she sees nothing remarkable in second- or third-century developments. Therefore, Hezser does not concede that urbanization of either Roman Palestine or the Galilee might be a factor in the appearance and development of the rabbinic class.

I side with Cohen, Tsafrir, and Levine, for a number reasons. However, I note at the outset that the disagreement between Hezser and the others may reflect different emphases given to material evidence in relation to literary testimony. Hezser rejects the opposing view largely by pointing to literary evidence. Indeed, the literary evidence indicates and speaks unequivocally about the founding of cities in Palestine in the earlier period, as per Hezser's position. However, the material evidence for the Galilee demonstrably supports the hypothesis that something new and different in magnitude, even if not in kind, happened with respect to urbanization and related developments from the mid-second century and into the third.

Ironically, in order to elaborate on this claim, I offer the remarks of Eric M. Meyers and James F. Strange (1981). They decry the value of material evidence for elucidating the culture of first-century Galilee, their principal interest.

> While one of the predominating concerns of the authors has been the recovery of data that would help reconstruct Galilee of the first century C.E., it has become abundantly clear that a large body of material from this period may never become available. The overwhelming bulk of all materials, both architectural and other, coming out of Galilee thus dates from the Middle-Late Roman period and later, that is, the second to fourth centuries CE (Meyers and Strange, 1981: 34).

To what do Meyers and Strange attribute this near complete material reconstruction of the Galilee? Not to its cataclysmic destruction, but to a massive social migration which required, it would seem, a total remake of the physical infrastructure. They state: "One reason for this is that the resettlement of Jews, and possibly of Christians, from the south in the first and second centuries CE caused destruction (archaeologically speaking) of many of the earlier remains" (Meyers and Strange, 1981: 34). Given this, the paucity of material evidence for the first century CE, they attempt to extrapolate as best they can from the late second- and third-century evidence. Therefore, their conclusions about the cultural setting of the Galilee as evinced in archaeological remains would seem particularly germane to our focus on the turn of the third century.

Meyers and Strange see confirmed in the material evidence the oft-made distinction between upper Galilee (with parts of Golan), on the one hand, and lower Galilee and the Jordan Rift valley (including the Sea of Galilee), on the other. Archaeological remains for the latter regions support Michael Avi-Yonah's assertion that "as a result of the [Roman] policy of urbanization most of the non-urban territories were transformed into cities in the course of the second and third centuries" (Avi-Yonah, 1966: 112, cited in Meyers and Strange, 1981: 44). This urbanization probably refers to the Roman policy of replacing the old Ptolemaic system of "nomes," "toparchies," and "komes," mantained by Rome until the latter half of the second century in Palestine, with the more dominant form of urbanization imposed in the east at the outset of the imperial era in regions other than Egypt, Palestine, and southernmost Syria.[11] In advocating this view, Meyers and Strange (1981: 42, cf. n. 41) follow A.H.M. Jones (1931: 81; 1971: 274-76). Commerce and banking, and (no doubt) tax collection for a region of towns and villages would have been organized centrally for the greater district at an 'urban' capital, with the necessary physical and organizational infrastructure installed therein. Small local markets and commercial infrastructure would have been subsumed within, or supplanted by, the centralized urban facilities. I surmise that with these responsibilities, the urban centre also assumed the tasks of regulation. Interestingly, Yoram Tsafrir notes the significant physical expansion from the mid-second century CE of the urban infrastructures of Palestinian (including Lower Galilee and the Jordan Rift valley) cities. These include the building of an expansive colonnaded *cardo* for commerce; basilicas for civic and civil functions; (pagan) Temples for the non-Jewish population (including Roman soldiers); the theatre, odeon, and/or stadium for entertainment; and, of course, synagogues (Tsafrir, 1984).

I propose that the (re)formation of the Patriarchy under Judah I in lower Galilee be reassessed in light of the aforementioned social transformations, so well reflected in the material remains. What would these transformations have meant for local Jewish aristocratic leaders in the towns and villages of an urbanized region? What regulatory functions would now have to be repartitioned between local and urban centres? How would Roman policy with respect to urbanization and Jewish settlements be furthered and best effected through a strong Patriarchy? These are the questions which now seem to come to the fore in light of the changes reflected in the material remains. A systematic attempt to grapple with these questions is obviously beyond what can be achieved in this study. But the questions themselves contain the seeds of their answers, as a set of opening hypotheses to be assessed. And the outlines of some of those answers are contained in further study of the powers of the Patriarchy outlined near the beginning of Part III.

What now of the members of the rabbinic guild or class of retainers? The urbanization of much of Galilee would have instantly increased the need for a retainer class (on both the Jewish and non-Jewish sides) to help effect regulated, centralized processes. In particular, the appointment by the central authority of judges (among them rabbis) to local courts makes perfectly good sense in the con-

---

11.   See my brief description of main structural features of this Roman-style urbanization, above, n. 6.

text of Roman-style urbanization, this in order to harmonize local practice with central standards. Perhaps further research into the substance of third-century rabbinic rulings for the contemporary context, that is, rulings which do not simply review and elaborate upon Mishnah's agenda, will confirm this line of reasoning and fill in the details, as suggested by Shaye Cohen (1992). My purpose here is not to undertake such an exercise. Rather, I propose a particular social transformation in lower Galilee and in the adjacent Jordan Rift valley as an intelligible context for such a study, in the same manner that such a transformation helps render intelligible the development of the rabbinic movement as retainer functionaries in the Patriarch's administration.

IV
Concluding remarks

In closing, the material evidence for Late Roman Galilee provides several positive results which serve to supplement and complement what we have argued from literary evidence. In all, the evidence suggests that members of the rabbinic class were not part of the longstanding local aristocratic leadership in the Galilee. In this, the rabbis are similar to the Patriarchy, with which the social (re)formation of the rabbinic guild or class near the end of the second century is so intimately linked. In addition, the material evidence demonstrates that significantly accelerated processes of Roman-style "urbanization" took hold of the north of Palestine, beginning in the second half of the second century CE. The massive migration of Jews into the Galilee in the same period is also confirmed in the material evidence. The emergence, powers, and responsibilities of the Patriarchate seem intelligible in this context, as does the promotion of the type of class/guild expertise modelled in Mishnah, the formative rabbinic document (honorifically attributed by the rabbis to the Patriarch, "Rabbi" Judah I). In short, the material evidence seems to have helped confirm proposals concerning the location of the rabbis within the social hierarchy and matrix of late second- and third-century Galilee. In this respect, we understand better the social import of their professional expertise as modelled in, and promoted, by Mishnah's rhetoric.

Finally, with this enhanced sense of the social location of the rabbinic guild or class, one might suggest yet another role played by Mishnah in the social formation of the rabbinic movement at the beginning of the third century. Mishnah and its promulgation under the alleged authorship of Judah I might be profitably understood as myth-making. That is, Mishnah provides a myth which serves the social formation of the early rabbinic movement and of the Patriarch's (reputedly) intimate place within the rabbinic movement. We are used to seeing myths in narrative form. But that need not always be the case. Narrative myths link powerful symbolic representations in a sequenced story. Mishnah achieves a similar result without recourse to story. Mishnah's mythology functions to link a number of core symbolic elements: (a) the Temple with its authoritative nomos and leadership; (b) rabbinic guild expertise as represented in Mishnah's rhetoric;

(c) an alleged sequence of named rabbinic tradents spanning the period from the Great Revolt to Judah I; (d) the Patriarchy of Judah I and his alleged predecessors, themselves similarly depicted as linked to the aforementioned, named, rabbinic tradents. The social matrix and situation revealed in the material evidence–traditional local aristocracies existing apart from, and prior to, a well-established Patriarchy and a rabbinic class of retainers, on the one hand, and the forces of Roman-style urbanization, on the other–are suggestive indeed about the social function of such a mythology within the rabbinic movement .

Without a doubt much systematic research must ensue to move from that which is suggested by our inquiry to what would count as having been demonstrated. It is my hope this volume has tempted others, in addition to myself, to undertake such studies.

Appendix

A Comparison of Mishnah Gittin 1:1-2:2 and James 2:1-13 from a Perspective of Greco-Roman Rhetorical Elaboration

Vernon K. Robbins
Emory University, Atlanta, GA, USA

Jack Lightstone's socio-rhetorical comparison of Mishnah Gittin 1:1-2:2 with passages in Tosefta and Semahot exhibits rhetorical practices of interpretation among Rabbis that are a dynamic alternative to, and in certain instances stand in dynamic interaction with, Christian rhetorical practices during the same centuries.[1] Lightstone's insights are based on analysis and interpretation that, from my perspective, reveal substantive dimensions of the repetitive-progressive, social, cultural, and ideological texture of these texts (Robbins, 1966a; 1966b). His demonstration that Mishnah became a rhetorical foundation for Tosefta and Semahot is a highly important conclusion for broader comparative study for two reasons. First, it means that Mishnah played a rhetorical role in third through fifth century rabbinic culture that has similarities with the rhetorical role of the New Testament in third through fifth century Christian culture. Second, it means that Mishnah created rhetorical procedures in relation both to the Hebrew Bible and to broader Jewish tradition in a manner that is a significant alternative to Christian practices during the same period. Both the similarities in function and the differences in rhetorical, social, cultural, and ideological practice are highly informative for interpreters of Judaism and Christianity, and for comparative study of other religions as well.

For a rhetorical interpreter of early Christian literature, Mishnah Gittin 1:1-2:2 stands out as an exemplary transitional text toward Rabbinic culture alongside portions of the New Testament as transitional texts toward Christian culture. One of the characteristics of these transitional texts is the manner in which they appropriate and reconfigure basic rhetorical patterns of elaboration in Greco-Roman culture. In contrast to Lightstone's emphasis (on page 65) on "what I or, in my view, ancient Greek and Latin rhetoricians would recognize as argument" in m. Gittin 1:1-2:2, I would emphasize the distinctive manner in which this text uses and reconfigures conventional patterns of argumentation in Mediterranean society and culture. The *Rhetorica ad Herennium* and the *Progymnasmata* reveal to us how rhetoricians viewed "basic rhetorical elaboration" (the "working out" [*ergasia* or *exergasia* in Greek; *expolitio* in Latin]) of a "topic" or

---

1.   See especially the discussions of strategies of interpretation in Torjesen (1997: 73-88), Boyarin (1999), Hirshman (1996), Cameron (1991), Brown (1992).

"subject" (*topos* in Greek; *locus* or *res* in Latin) (see Robbins, 1993; Mack and Robbins, 1989; Hock and O'Neil, 1986). To exhibit the importance of observing the argumentative qualities of portions of text in the Mishnah, the following discussion will display the pattern of rhetorical elaboration in m. Gittin 1:1-2:2 and compare it with James 2:1-13 in the New Testament.

Mishnah Gittin 1:1-2:2

1. Introduction: Gittin 1:1-2

Theme: 1:1a-b
Result:

1:1a.   One who brings a writ from a Mediterranean province–
b.   it is required that he should say: In my presence it was written and in my presence it was signed [by the witnesses].

In a manner characteristic of rabbinic discourse, the subject or topic of m. Gittin 1:1 is a ruling or law. In this instance, the concern is the validity of a written document brought from a Mediterranean province to the Land of Israel. By comparison, *Rhetorica ad Herennium* IV.xliv.57 intoduces the theme: "The wise man will, on the republic's behalf, shun no peril." (Cicero, *Ad C. Herennium* 371, LCL edition 403; cf. Robbins, 1993: 127). In enthymematic terms, the ruling or law in Gittin 1:1 is a product of inductive reasoning–reasoning from a series of Cases to a general Result.[2] In *Ad Her.* IV.xliv.57, the theme also is supported by inductive reasoning, but the Cases are not presented with the specificity of their presentation in Gittin 1:1 (see below).

2. Rationale: 1:1c-d

Cases:

1:1c.   R. Gamaliel says: Also one who brings [a writ] from Rekem and from Heger [must be able to so declare].
d.   R. Eliezer says: Even [one who brings a writ] from Kefar Luddim to Lud [must be able to so declare].

[Unstated Rule:
If rabbis extend a ruling even further than its basic formulation, then they presuppose the authoritative nature of the ruling they are extending.]

This tractate of Mishnah launches its rhetorical elaboration of the ruling or law by citing two "statements" of Rabbis that present arguments from authoritative testimony which function as Rationales for the Theme.[3] In contrast, early

---

2.   To see Rule/Case/Result analysis of syllogistic argumentation, see Robbins, 1998a; 1998b; 1999).

3.   In Greek, authoritative testimony is a judgment (*krisis*); in Latin, it is a *testimonium* (see Mack and Robbins, 1989: 28-9, 38-9, 41-2, 51-7, 60-1, 93, 100-1, 136-39 *et passim*; Hock & O'Neil, 1986: 176; Robbins, 1993: 126-29); *Rhet ad Her* IV.iii.5-6: "by testimony we establish the truth of the statement, the testimony must accord with the proposition, for otherwise it cannot confirm the proposition." See Cameron (1991: 84): "The repeated allusions to stock examples (historical figures, "good" and "bad" emperors, kingly figures like Cyrus and Alexander), stock virtues, and stock themes form the technical armory of evocation."

Christian (and Greek and Roman) arguments often cite authoritative testimony to "clinch" an argument.[4] The Rationales indicate that R. Gamaliel and R. Eliezer not only presuppose the requirement of a declaration by the person from a Mediterranean province that the writing and signing occurred in the presence of witnesses, but they extend this reasoning to Rekem, Heger, and from Kefar to Lud as well. In other words, their reasoning presupposes the reasoning in the Theme and builds upon it. This means that the Cases function inductively in support of the Result, which is stated as the Theme. Underlying this reasoning is an Unstated Rule something like: "If rabbis extend a ruling even further than its basic formulation, then they presuppose the authoritative nature of the ruling they are extending."

Aristotle (*Rhet.* 1.1.8 [1356b]) asserted that all arguments use either examples or enthymemes (rhetorical syllogisms) to produce logical persuasion. Since m. Gittin begins with a Result followed by two Cases, the reasoning is enthymematic, rather than simply inductive. Hermogenes' *Progymnasmata* presents the Theme of his elaboration in the form of a chreia (a Case).[5] In this instance, the Theme functions as a Case ("Isocrates said that education's root is bitter, its fruit is sweet"), supported by a Rationale that is a general Mediterranean Rule of reasoning ("For the most important affairs generally succeed because of toil, and once they have succeeded, they bring pleasure;" Robbins, 1993: 128-29). *Rhet ad Her* IV.xliii.56-xliv.57 functions more like m. Gittin, since the Theme is a Result ("The wise man will, on the republic's behalf, shun no peril") and the Rationales are generalized Cases: (a) "because it may often happen that if a man has been loath to perish for his country it will be necessary for him to perish for her;" (b) "since it is from our country that we receive all our advantages, no disadvantage incurred on her behalf is to be regarded as severe" (Robbins, 1993: 127).

But there is a major difference between m. Gittin and *Rhet ad Her* IV.xliii.56-xliv.57. In each instance, the Rationale in *Rhet ad Her* itself is argumentative, or almost argumentative, while in m. Gittin, the Rationales simply are assertions based on authoritative testimony. The first Rationale (a) in *Rhet ad Her* contains an "if . . . (then) . . ." statement, which is "not quite an argument, but almost" (Hurley, 1985: 14-17). The second Rationale (b) in *Rhet ad Her* presents a Case/Result enthymeme, with "since" introducing the Case. m. Gittin simply makes each Case assertive, but, as indicated at the bottom of the display above, the sequence of the Theme and the two Cases evokes or presupposes an unstated Rule that: 'If rabbis extend a ruling even further than its basic formulation, then they presuppose the authoritative nature of the ruling they are extending.' This

---

4.   For Hermogenes' use, see Hock & O'Neil (1986: 177), Robbins (1993: 128-29); for *Rhet ad Her* IV.xliv.57, see Robbins (1993: 127); for Christian use, see Mack and Robbins (1989: 132-33, and 204-7 for qualifying remarks.

5.   A chreia is "a brief statement or action attributed with aptness to a definite person or something analogous to a person;" see Hock & O'Neil (1986: 83); cf. Mack and Robbins (1989: 11). For Hermogenes' rhetorical elaboration of a chreia rather than as an unattributed theme, see Hock & O'Neil (1986: 177); cf. Mack and Robbins (1989: 51-2) and Robbins (1993: 128-29).

means that the opening of m. Gittin is enthymematic, rather than simply based on example.

3. Statement from the Opposite: 1:1e
Case:

1:1e.   And sages say: It is not required that he should say: In my presence it was written,
         and in my presence it was signed [by the witnesses]–
         except him who brings [a writ] from a Mediterranean province
         and him who takes [a writ to a Mediterranean province].

As is customary in Greco-Roman elaboration, Gittin 1:1e presents a statement from the Opposite after stating the Theme supported by Rationales. The purpose of stating the Opposite is to test the truth of the positive form of the statement.[6] The statement from the Opposite in 1:1e is "not required," in contrast to "required" in 1:1a-d. Stating it in the form of the Opposite produces an "except" clause that restates "bringing a writ from a Mediterranean province" in the Theme, but it also elicits an additional assertion about "bringing a writ from a Mediterranean province" as well.

Hermogenes' argument from the Opposite, "For ordinary affairs do not need toil, and they have an outcome that is entirely without pleasure; but serious affairs have the opposite outcome," reverses every item in the Rationale that immediately precedes it: "For the most important affairs generally succeed because of toil, and once they have succeeded, they bring pleasure" (Robbins, 1993: 129).[7] Here the Opposites are "ordinary affairs/most important affairs," "do not need toil to succeed/succeed because of toil," "entirely without pleasure/bring pleasure." The Opposite also creates the opportunity to restate the Theme in a succinct manner: "serious affairs have the opposite outcome." Thus, in Hermogenes' formulation, the Opposite uses the language that the Rationale introduced, and there is no addition of an item beyond those in the Rationale.

The argument from the Opposite in *Rhet ad Her* IV.xliv.57 has more of a relationship to Gittin 1:1e, since the statement of the Opposite creates the context for a Restatement of the Theme with additional Reasons (Robbins, 1993: 127). *Rhet ad Her* begins the Opposite with: "They who flee from the peril to be undergone on behalf of the republic act foolishly, for they cannot avoid the disadvantages, and are found guilty of ingratitude towards the state." This formulation reverses the two major topics of the Theme: "flee from the peril/will shun no peril" and "wise man/act foolishly." But then it adds a rationale: "for they cannot

---

6.   In Aristotle's terms, "one should look to see if the opposite [predicate] is true of the opposite [subject], [thus] refuting the argument if it is not, confirming it if it it is" (*Rhet* 2.23.1); see Fahnestock (2000: 176). I am indebted to Carol Poster for calling my attention to this essay. .

7.   *Rhet ad Her* IV.xliii.56-xliv.57 also presents an argument based on opposites: (a) those who flee from peril/those who shun no peril; (b) those who act wisely/those who act foolishly; (c) what is received from nature/what one gives back to nature; (d) those who achieve manliness and honor/those who live in disgrace and cowardice; see Robbins (1993: 127).

avoid the disadvantages, and are found guilty of ingratitude towards the state." This clause adds "cannot avoid" and "are found guilty" to the Theme. In addition, this statement of the Opposite supported by Rationales creates the context for a Restatement of the Theme in embellished form that adds: (a) render homage due; (b) die "for"/die "with"; (c) unjust to give back to nature/not give back to country; (d) die with manliness and honor/live in disgrace and cowardice; (e) face danger for kin/refuse to risk for the republic, which embraces that holy name of fatherland as well (Robbins, 1993: 127). As we see below, the use of the statement of the Opposite to introduce a Restatement of the Theme with Additions has a close kinship with the sequence in Gittin 1:1e-1:2.

4. Restatement of Theme with Addition and Analogy: 1:1f-1:2
Addition:
Result:

1:1f.   And one who brings [a writ] from province to province in the Mediterranean provinces–

g.   it is required that he should say: In my presence it was written and in my presence it was signed [by the witnesses].

Case:

1:1h.   R. Simeon b. Gamaliel says: Even from district to district [within a single Mediterranean province must make such a declaration].

Addition and Analogy:
Cases:

1:2a.   Rabbi Judah says: [One must make the declaration if taking a writ]:

b.   from Rekem to the East, and Rekem is like the East;

c.   from Ashqalon to the South, and Ashqalon is like the South;

d.   from Akko to the North, and Akko is like the North.

e.   R. Meir says: Akko is like the Land of Israel with respect to writs.

After presenting the Theme supported by Rationales, it is common in Greco-Roman argumentation, as we saw above in *Rhet ad Her* IV.xliv.57, to use a statement of the Opposite as a context for a Restatement of the Theme that introduces substantive new topics. This is what occurs in Gittin 1:1e-2a. Gittin 1:1f begins a process of "addition" to the topic in the Theme of "bringing from a Mediterranean province" and the topic in the Opposite of "taking to a Mediterranean province" (1:1e). The Restatement of the Theme, with its Rationales, adds: (a) from province to province in the Mediterranean provinces; (b) from district to district within a single Mediterranean province; (c) from Rekem to the East; (d) from Ashqalon to the South; and (e) from Akko to the North. As Lightstone observes, one of the most salient activities in Mishnaic rhetoric is the creation of "lists." In the Restatement, new items in a list begin to emerge (1:1f) and take fully the form of a list in 1:2a.

Immediately after the statement of the Opposite in Greco-Roman argumentation, it is common to present an argument from Analogy. This argument features the use of "just as . . . so," ". . . is like . . .," or a description that evokes a comparison with some new item (Mack and Robbins, 1989: 54-7). The purpose is to persuade not only by testing differences but also by introducing similarities. In an uncanny way, Gittin 1:2A participates in the conventional sequence from the

Opposite to Analogy as it introduces "Rekem is like the East," "Ashqalon is like the South," "Akko is like the North," and "Akko is like the Land of Israel." In contrast to Greco-Roman argumentation, there is no attempt in Gittin to "persuade" through an argument that one thing "is like" another. The inclusion of assertions of likeness after a formulation of the Opposite, however, is noticeable when this Mishnaic rhetoric is compared with conventional rhetorical sequences in Greco-Roman argumentation. When the statements about likeness lead to an assertion about "the Land of Israel," which is the first time this phrase occurs in the elaboration, the sequence has created a natural transition to the body of the argument, which gives serious consideration to situations within the Land of Israel as well as in the Mediterranean provinces. It is remarkable, though I think little or nothing should be made of it, that the Restatement of the Theme in the context of the Opposite in *Rhet ad Her* IV.xliv.57 reaches its climax in a statement about "that most holy name of the fatherland." In turn, the final Rationale (Case) in the Restatement in Gittin 1:2E introduces "the Land of Israel" as a transition to the first statement (1:3a) in the Argument.

5. Argument (Probatio): Gittin 1:3-6
Reintroduction of the Opposite as a Context for Contraries: 1:3
Result:

1:3a.	One who brings a writ within the Land of Israel–
b.	it is not required that he should say: In my presence it was written and in my presence it was signed [by the witnesses].

Condition:

c.	If there are challengers to it[s validity], it[s validity] shall stand upon [the authentication of] it[s witnesses'] signatures.

Result:

d.	One who brings a writ from a Mediterranean province,
e.	and cannot say: In my presence it was written, and in my presence it was signed [by witnesses]–

Condition:

f.	if there are upon it [the signatures of] witnesses, it[s validity] shall stand upon [the authentication of] it[s witnesses'] signatures.

Once Greco-Roman argumentation has introduced the topic through a sequence of Theme, Rationales, Opposite, and Restatement, the elaboration moves to the body of the argument, which features Analogy, example, and authoritative ancient testimony (Robbins, 1993: 127-30). As we have seen above, Gittin 1:2 introduces authoritative ancient testimonies as Rationales throughout the beginning, and it introduces Analogy in the Restatement of the Theme. Gittin 1:3 begins the Argument by reintroducing the Opposite ("not required to say") in relation to "bringing a writ within the Land of Israel," and brings in the variation of "cannot say" in relation to "bringing a writ from a Mediterranean province." This move creates a context for a sequence of conditional statements ("if-then") that changes one item in the assertion ("challengers to its validity"/"upon it the signatures of witnesses"). These variations produce a rhetorical environment for negotiating Contraries that extends throughout the body of the argument into the Conclusion.

Contraries are different from Opposites by being "alternatives," things that are different rather than contradictory. There is only one Opposite to a positive assertion (e.g., required/not required),[8] but there are many Contraries to it.[9] In Gittin 1:3, the principle of "addition," which emerged clearly in the list in 1:2, leads to a sequence of negative statements that are Contraries" rather than Opposites. Here we see a primary dimension of Mishnaic rhetoric. Lightstone has keenly observed, as noted above, that Rabbis were "Masters of lists." I would emphasize that they were Masters of "unlimited lists of Contraries in contexts of limited lists of Opposites." The ability of the Rabbis to create Opposites is highly impressive, but this is a widespread ability throughout Mediterranean discourse, and perhaps throughout the world. What is truly impressive, in my view, is their ability to create seemingly unlimited lists of Contraries in contexts of limited lists of Opposites.

As noted above, Gittin 1:3 begins the programmatic exploration of Contraries with a sequence that produces two conditional assertions ("if-[then]"). These assertions enable the formulation of multiple conditions in which something "is" or "is not" required. In 1:3A it is "not required" to say, but in 1:3E they are "not able" to say. Within these alternatives, its validity will stand upon authentication of signatures either "if there are challengers" or "if there are signatures" in relation to "within the Land of Israel" or "from a Mediterranean province." At this point, then, the argumentation is moving decisively beyond Opposites" into highly complex lists of Contraries. Every statement of a Contrary for the remainder of the elaboration can be a context for exploring some kind of complexity. Gittin 1:1-2 features one major Opposite ("required/not required") and one lesser Opposite ("bring from/take to"). Gittin 1:3 introduces a new Opposite ("within the Land of Israel/from a Mediterranean province") as a context for exploring Contraries of various kinds. Interestingly enough, once "the Land of Israel" has been presented in this Opposite manner, there is no need for it to appear throughout the remainder of the elaboration, since what is "required" in the Theme is "not required" for the Land of Israel.

6. Equation of Specific Alternatives: 1:4
Result:
1:4a.   One [and] the same are writs [of divorce] of women and manumission papers of slaves;
Case:
b.   they equated [them] with regard to one who takes [them to a Mediterranean province] and with regard to one who brings [them from a Mediterranean province].
Rule:
c.   And this is one of the ways [only] that they equated writs [of divorce] of women with manumission papers of slaves.

---

8.   Aristotle called this "affirmation/negation" (*Categories* 17a); see Fahnestock (2000: 176).
9.   Aristotle described three kinds in *Categories* 11b): (1) contraries (hot/cold); (2) privation/possession pairs (blindness/sight); and (3) relatives (double/half); see Fahnestock (2000: 176).

Once the body of the argument has been launched with the assertion that what is "required" when a writ is brought from a Mediterranean province is "not required" when it is brought within the Land of Israel, the argumentation moves on to other alternatives (Contraries). Gittin 1:4 explores the relation of writs of divorce of women with manumission papers of slaves. These are Contraries, because there are other kinds of writs besides manumission papers that are different from a writ of divorce.[10] Gittin 1:4 asserts that these Contraries are alike in regard to "bringing from" a Mediterranean province (the Theme) and "taking to" a Mediterranean province (introduced in the Opposite: 1:1e). As 1:4 makes this transition, it seems to me to contain a distinctive rhetorical move in the context of Mediterranean argumentation. It is common in Greco-Roman argumentation to introduce a "divisio" near the beginning of the argument, which may include an "enumeration" and/or "exposition" of the topics the argument will discuss (*Rhet ad Her* I.x.17). In contrast, 1:4 allows the elaboration to deal with "two topics" at the same time. This seems to be a move consistent with the "complexity of Contraries" the discourse establishes in 1:1-3.

7. Negotiating Specific Cases: 1:5-6

Result/Ruling:

1:5a.	Any writ [of divorce] that has upon it [the signature of] a Samaritan witness
b.	is unfit,
c.	except for writs [of divorce] of women and manumission papers of slaves.

Case/Rationale (Example):

1:5d.	It once happened that they brought before R. Gamaliel in Kefar Otnai a writ [of divorce] of a woman,
e.	and its witnesses were Samaritan witnesses,
f.	and he declared [it] fit.

Result/Ruling:

g.	Any bonds issuing from [court] bureaus of the gentiles–
h.	even though their signatories are gentiles–
i.	are fit,
j.	except for writs [of divorce] of women and manumission papers of slaves.

Contrary Case/Rationale (Testimony):

1:5k.	R. Simeon says: Also these are fit.

Negotiating Case (Testimony):

l.	They specified [that the latter were unfit] only when they were done in a nonprofessional tribunal.

Result/Ruling (Testimony):

1:6a.	One who says: Give this writ [of divorce] to my wife and this manumission bond to my slave–
b.	if he desired to retract with respect to both of them, he may retract, the words of R. Meir.

---

10. In Aristotle's terms, these contraries would be "relatives" (*Categories* 11b); see Fahnestock, 2000: 176.

Contrary Result/Ruling:

c.   But sages say: With respect to writs [of divorce] of women, [he may retract]; however not with respect to manumission papers of slaves,

Case/Rationale:

d.   because they benefit one when not in his [or her] presence, but they obligate him [or her] only in his [or her] presence;

Confirmation of Rationale:

e.   since if he should desire not to feed his slave, he is allowed, but not to feed his wife, he is not allowed.

f.   He said to them: But lo he renders unfit his slave for the [eating of] heave offering [if the owner is a priest], just as he renders unfit his wife.

Underlying Rule:

g.   They said to him: Because he is his property [and she is not].

Result/Ruling:

h.   One who says: Give this writ [of divorce] to my wife and this manumission bond to my slave,

i.   and he died–

j.   they may not give [either] after [the person's] death.

Result/Ruling:

k.   [One who says:] Give a maneh to such-and-such person,

l.   and he died–

m.   they may give [the maneh] after [the person's] death.

Gittin 1:5-6 moves into the specialty of Mishnaic rhetoric: negotiating highly complex, contrary phenomena in a context of a limited set of Opposites. In this context, Gittin 1:5-6 uses exception clauses, an example, "even though" clauses, additional arguments from the Opposite, "if-then" clauses, and "because" clauses. In other words, this section of the elaboration uses various argumentative tools to negotiate multiple kinds of Contraries that accompany different kinds of situations.

Gittin 1:5 introduces a new Opposite, "unfit/fit," and negotiates different situations with exception clauses (1:5c, j), an argument from example (1:5d), and an "even though" clause (1:5h). Then Gittin 1:6 introduces "give/not give," "retract/not retract," "not in his presence/in his presence," "obligate/not obligate," "allow/not allow," "is property/is not property." In this context, writs of divorce and writs of manumission finally emerge as Opposites ("may retract/may not retract") in 1:6c: a man may retract writs of divorce with women, but he may not retract manumission papers of slaves. This calls forth the highest form of argumentation in Gittin 1:1-2:2. At this point, Gittin 1:6c, d, e, and g present "syllogistic argumentation" accompanied by a confirmation of the Rationale (Case):

Result/Theme:

1:6c.   With respect of writs [of divorce] of women, [he may retract]; however not with respect to manumission papers of slaves.

Case/Rationale:

1:6d.   because [slaves] benefit one when not in his [or her] presence, but they obligate him [or her] only in his [or her] presence.

Confirmation of the Case (Rationale):

1:6e.   since if he should desire not to feed his slave, he is allowed, but not to feed his wife, he is not allowed.

Underlying Rule:

1:6g.   Because he (slave) is his property [and she (wife) is not].

In the midst of argumentation about bringing or taking writs to various regions, the elaboration moves to a climax at the end of the Argument where it discusses retracting or not retracting a writ. At this point, the argumentation distinguishes between writs of divorce and manumission, and presents syllogistic reasoning to support its ruling. In contrast to all previous argumentative sequences, which contain only a Result (Theme) supported by a Case (Rationale), this one not only contains a sequence of Result/Case/Confirmation/Rule, but it includes "because" or "since" at the beginning of its assertions.

My proposal is that this moment of "conventional Greco-Roman" argumentation emerges in Gittin 1:1–2:2 because at this point the issue about divorce of women and manumission of slaves is a "public" issue in Mediterranean society, rather than simply or primarily an "internal" issue within Jewish communities. Both with divorce and with manumission, Jewish people, including Rabbis, come clearly into public view. At this point, the elaboration presents a case that can be defended in public.

In a surprising way, then, the Argument of the elaboration moves from internal issues, where writs of divorce of women and manumission papers of slaves are equated, to a public issue, where writs of divorce and manumission papers are treated differently. The Argument prepared for this outcome in 1:4c where it asserted: "And this is one of the ways [only] that they equated writs of divorce of women with manumission papers of slaves." Once the Argument makes its case for its "public ruling," which distinguishes between writs of divorce and manumission, the elaboration briefly presents only two more rulings (1:6h-m) before moving to a summarizing conclusion.

8. Conclusion: 2:1-2

Cases: 2:1a. One who brings a writ from a Mediterranean province,

b.   and one said: In my presence it was written, however not in my presence was it signed [by the witnesses];

c.   in my presence it was signed [by the witnesses], however not in my presence was it written;

d.   in my presence it was written in its entirety, and in my presence it was signed in part;

e.   in my presence it was written in part, and in my presence it was signed in its entirety–

Result:

f.   [the writ] is unfit.

Case:

g.   One says: In my presence it was written, and one [i.e., another] says: In my presence it was signed—

Result:

h.   [the writ] is unfit.

Case:

i.   Two [bring writ and] say: In our presence it was written, and one says: In my presence it was signed—

Result:

j.   [the writ] is unfit.

Opposite:

k.   And R. Judah declares fit.

Case:

l.   One says: In my presence it was written, and two [i.e., both] say: In our presence it was signed—

Result:

m. [the writ] is fit.

Cases:

2:2a.   It [the writ] was written in the daytime and was signed in the daytime,

b.   [or was written]in the night time and was signed in the night time,

c.   [or was written] in the night time and was signed in the day time—

Result:

d.   [the writ] is fit.

Opposite Case:

e.   [The writ was written] in the daytime and was signed in the night time—

Result:

f.   [the writ] is unfit.

Opposite Result:

g.   R. Simeon declares [such a writ] fit,

Case:

h.   for R. Simeon used to say: All writs that were written in the daytime and were signed in the night time

i.   are unfit,

j.   except for writs [of divorce] of women.

[Unstated Rule:

      Writs of divorce of women are in one way [at least] different from all other kinds of writs.]

These verses present a summary (Resumé) of the overall argument within an oppositional framework of "fit/unfit," returning to the primary topic of the Theme: "One who brings a writ from a Mediterranean province." Gittin 2:1a-h summarizes all the combinations concerning one person bringing a writ that was written or signed either fully or partially in that person's presence, and there is agreement that the writ is unfit. Gittin 2:1i-m summarizes instances where two people are somehow involved, and here there is disagreement if two say it was written in their presence and only one says it was signed in his/her presence. Gittin 2:2a-h summarizes instances where a writ was written or signed in the daytime or night time. The summary includes all kinds of writs until the very last clause where, similar to the sequence of the Argument, it distinguishes writs of divorce of women from other writs. In this instance, it distinguishes writs of divorce not only from manumission papers but from all other kinds of writs: only writs of divorce are fit if they were written in the daytime and signed in the night time. The exploration of lists of Contraries within a limited list of Opposites reaches its end in this final argument, because at this point it has arrived at the opposite end of the spectrum from where the exploration began. Beginning with a major way in which writs of divorce are equated with manumission papers (1:4a-c: "taking them to" and "bringing them from" a Mediterranean province), the exploration has arrived at the one way in which one Rabbi (R. Simeon) was convinced that writs of divorce are different from all other writs. In other words, in the context of long lists of Contraries and Opposites, the elaboration has explored writs of divorce along the entire spectrum of how it is like other writs and how it is different from them.

The entire sequence exhibits the remarkable way in which Mishnaic rhetoric "elaborates" halakic discourse. Overall, as Lightstone observes, the elaboration exhibits a mastery of "list-making" (cf. pp. 63ff.). In addition, our investigation has exhibited a mastery of unlimited lists of Contraries in contexts of limited lists of Opposites. For the "persuasive" function of this Contrary list-making, it is important to see how the unit works through an elaboration process that features rhetorical figures commonly present in Greco-Roman elaboration. The primary issue at stake in the elaboration appears to be the nature of writs of divorce of women. The nature of all other writs is subsidiary to the importance of this kind of writ. Next in importance, however, are manumission papers of slaves. The importance of these writs, it would appear, concerns the manner in which they are, in the final analysis, "public" writs, rather than writs that can remain "internal" to Jewish life and community. With all other kinds of writs, it may be questionable whether a Jewish person could get a "civil" court to accept the case, if he or she disagreed with the ruling of the Rabbis. With divorce and manumission, however, there are issues of property, inheritance, and ownership that a Jewish person might be able to take to a civil court outside Jewish circles of authority. It is informative in this regard that the elaboration features "all writs brought from a Mediterranean province" at the beginning and end. This framework for the Argument in the middle exhibits, in essence, a public concern about the authority of Rabbinic decisions regarding writs of divorce and manumission papers, but most of all writs of divorce, in Mediterranean society. "Bringing a writ from a Mediterranean province" is, then, a prime example of the relation of internal Jewish convictions to values and practices in Mediterranean society. Wittingly or unwittingly, this dynamic resides in the manner in which m. Gittin 1:1-

2:2 initiates and unfolds its elaboration of the Theme of "all writs one brings from a Mediterranean province."

The promise of this analysis for comparative interpretation becomes evident when an interpreter sees the similarities and differences between m. Gittin 1:1-2:2 and a unit like James 2:1-13 in the New Testament. Wesley H. Wachob's recent socio-rhetorical analysis of this passage (Wachob, 2000) provides a good opportunity to compare briefly the results of his investigation, with slight adaptations, to the results of our investigation of m. Gittin 1:1-2:2.

James 2:1-13

1. Introduction: James 2:1-4
Result/Theme: 2:1-4

2:1.   My brethren, show no partiality as you hold the faith of our glorious Lord Jesus Christ.

Despite the concern of the Epistle of James with "religious law," which caused Martin Luther to consider it to be contradictory to "gospel," the nature of early Christian "religious law" discourse is "theological wisdom discourse," rather than "legal discourse." As the elaborations in the Epistle of James progress, therefore, general, theologically-grounded principles emerge, rather than rulings that negotiate Opposites and Contraries in a context of multiple complexities that emerge with specific cases. Nevertheless, there are similarities. Like Gittin 1:1, James 2:1-4 begins with a Theme (Result/ruling) supported by a Rationale (Case/example). James 2:1 does not begin with the same kind of Theme as Gittin 1:1 and *Rhet ad Her* IV.xliv.57, since the theme contains a reference to a specific personage, "our glorious Lord Jesus Christ." James 2:1 also does not begin with a chreia, like Hermogenes' elaboration. Rather, James 2:1 formulates a global ruling that one should "show no partiality" in a context of "holding the faith of our glorious Lord Jesus Christ." As Wachob explains, since the Theme is formulated in negative rather than positive terms, it presents a contrary assertion: "Acts of partiality are contrary to the 'faith of our glorious Lord Jesus Christ'" (Wachob, 2000: 70). This elaboration begins with a Contrary rather than a positive statement of the Theme in Gittin 1:1. Thus, it has more of a relation to the Theme in Hermogenes' elaboration of the chreia attributed to Isocrates, "Education's root is bitter, its fruit is sweet," which presents both a negative and positive side of the issue.

2. Case/Rationale: 2:2-4

2:2.   For if a man with gold rings and in fine clothing comes into your assembly, and a poor man in shabby clothing also comes in,

3.   and you pay attention to the one who wears the fine clothing and say, "Have a seat here, please," while you say to the poor man, "Stand there," or, "Sit at my feet,"

4.   have you not made distinctions among yourselves, and become judges with evil thoughts?

While Gittin 1:1c-d presents two Cases in support of its ruling, James 2:2-4 presents one Case. The Case in James 2:2-4 is not an authoritative testimony but an argument from example, more like the example in Gittin 1:5d-f. The difference is significant. James 2:1-4 proceeds like a special kind of wisdom discourse in the

Mediterranean world, moving toward a global principle rather than toward guidelines for adjudicating a specific instance that has particular complexities. "Whether the social example in James 2.2-3 refers to an actual or hypothetical case simply cannot be conclusively determined" (Wachob, 2000: 75). It is clear, however, that the author "offers it as proof, as the compelling social basis for what he says" (Wachob, 2000: 77). The Case ends in 2:4 with an argument that if people make distinctions on the basis of wealth, they have allowed evil thoughts to guide their judgments. The goal here is not simply to provide a guideline for negotiating a specific case, but it aims at attitudes and convictions that lie behind people's deeds.

3. Argument (Probatio): James 2:5-11
Theological Rule: 2:5

2:5.   Listen, my beloved brothers [and sisters]. Has not God chosen the poor in the world to be rich in faith and heirs of the kingdom which he has promised to those who love him?

Immediately after presenting a ruling (Result) supported by a Case, James 2:5 formulates a Rule that is grounded in the attributes and actions of God. As Wachob indicates, "James 2.5 essentially restates the enthymematic beginning of the argument by capturing and reformulating the reasoning in James 2.1-4." In addition, ". . . the author appears to play on a Jesus-beatitude, reformulating it around certain terms that are key to his persuasive purpose" (Wachob, 2000: 86). If this Rule were not articulated, the reader would presuppose some kind of unstated Rule that includes "holding the faith of our glorious Lord Jesus Christ" (2:1), which could be compared with: "If Rabbis extend a ruling even further than the basic formulation, then they presuppose the authoritative nature of the ruling they are extending" (see above, Gittin 1:1c-d). Instead, the rule reformulates a beatitude that, in other early Christian literature, is a chreia attributed to Jesus. The articulation of the Rule moves the reasoning beyond "the Lord Jesus Christ" to the nature of God. In other words, rather than allowing the reasoning to focus on an exceptional manifestation of holiness in the human realm (like a Rabbi), the reasoning moves in a theological direction toward God and the nature of God's actions. In addition, when James 2:5 refers to "the kingdom which God has promised to those who love God," it interweaves either prophetic or apocalyptic reasoning into wisdom reasoning (Robbins, forthcoming). The discourse evokes the presuppositions of these other modes of reasoning in a vigorous rhetorical manner by couching the assertion in the form of an *interrogatio*, a strong assertion in the form of a question.

4. Case/Argument from the Opposite: 2:6a

6a.   But you have dishonored the poor.

The argument from the Opposite in James 2:6a is an accusation like a prosecutor would present to a judge. As Wachob says, ". . . it argues that the behavior of the elect community toward the poor man is the conspicuous Opposite of God's actions toward the poor in James 2:5" (Wachob, 2000: 87). Thus, rather than presenting and negotiating laws, this discourse is presenting a case like a trial lawyer presents a case before a judge and jury. The discourse in James, then, is personally-directed "public" discourse from beginning to end, in contrast to Gittin 1:1-2:2, which moves into a mode of public discourse only in 1:6c-g.

5. Case/Social Example: 2:6b-7

6b.   Do not the rich oppress you, and do they not drag you into courts?

7.   Do they not blaspheme the honorable name that was pronounced over you?

This argument from example addresses the reader directly in a manner that indicts the person and moves them into self-examination. In addition, "verses 6b-7 expand the understanding of 'acts of partiality' in the theme (2:1) and rationale (2:2-4) by referring this behavior to a broader arena of relationships. The theme and rationale, and even the argument from the Opposite (2:6a) located partialities within the community of 'the elect poor'; the social example here finds 'unjust judgments' against the (elect) poor in the larger spheres of life, in the socio-economic arena (2:6b) and in the arena of religion (2:7)" (Wachob, 2000: 89). Here, then, the discourse has moved away from religious law itself into a rhetorical challenge to make judgments about justice and injustice on the basis of their knowledge of God's attributes and actions. Again, the discourse in James is not "legal" discourse, like we have seen in m. Gittin 1:1-2:2, but "wisdom" discourse that embeds insights from legal discourse into its own reasoning.

6-10. Argument from Judgment, based on written law, in four parts: 2:8-11

6. Result/Theme based on Authoritative Testimony: 2:8

8.   If you really fulfil the royal law, according to the scripture: "You shall love your neighbor as yourself," you do honorably.

7. Result/Argument from the Contrary: 2:9

9.   But if you show partiality, you commit sin and are convicted by the law as transgressors.

8. Rule/Rationale: 2:10

10.   For whoever keeps the whole law but fails in one point has become guilty of all of it (the whole law).

9. Case/Confirmation of Rationale with Authoritative Testimony: 2:11

11.   For the one [who gave the whole law] who said, "Do not commit adultery," also said, "Do not commit murder."

10. Conditional Result:

Now if you do not commit adultery but you do commit murder, you have become a transgressor of the law (= you have become guilty of the whole law) (Wachob, 2000: 102-3).

James 2:8-11 represents the climax of thé Argument in James 2:5-11, much like Gittin 1:6c-g is the climax of the Argument in Gittin 1:3-6. Like the climax in Gittin 1:1c-g, James 2:6-11 presents an argument that contains a Result/Theme, a Confirmation, and a Rule. In other words, both present a fully developed, syllogistic argument. Like Gittin 1:1c-g, James 2:5-11 is concerned to defend a particular interpretation of religious law. James 2:5-11 is concerned to argue that "if you do not commit adultery but you do commit murder, you have become a transgressor of the whole law" (2:11b). On the other hand, Gittin 1:1c-g is concerned to argue that "With respect to writs of divorce of women, he may retract; however not with respect to manumission papers of slaves." Both arguments concern what a person is and is not permitted to do in the domain of religious law. But the discourse in the Epistle of James has moved to another level or argumentation. Its focus is not on particular stipulations of religious law in and of themselves, but upon stipulations of religious law as a guide towards the nature of all of God's law. In other words, the Epistle of James is focused on the nature of God's law as it is embedded in God's wisdom. If a person knows the nature of God's attributes and actions, then a person has an insight into the wisdom of God, and people can decide for or against allowing God's wisdom to inform their own wisdom. For this reason, the argument in James 2:8-11 begins and ends with conditional statements directed personally at the hearer: "if you . . . ." The discourse in James is not simply telling its hearers what a person is required or not required to do, and thus what practices or documents are fit or unfit. The discourse in James is using social reasoning (acting honorably/being convicted by law as a transgressor) to persuade people to do what they are required by religious law (God's law) to do.

11. Conclusion: James 2:12-13
Enthymematic Summary: 2:12-13
Result:
12.   Thus you should speak and thus you should do as those who are to be judged [by God] under the law of freedom.

Rule:
13.   For judgment is without mercy to one who has shown no mercy; but [for one who has shown mercy], mercy triumphs over judgment (Wachob, 2000, 108).

In accord with its nature as wisdom discourse, James 2:1-13 ends with an enthymematic summary that supports its "Result/ruling" about people's actions with a "Rule" about God's mercy that comes from Hebrew Bible prophetic discourse. As Wachob observes, ".... 'mercy' is here, as it is particularly in Jewish and Christian literature, an attribute of God. . . . On the other hand, in the LXX *eleos* is demanded by God of those to whom God shows love (Micah 6:8; Zech. 7:9-10; LXX Jer. 9:23; Hos. 12:7; cf. Dan. 4:27; Sir. 3:30; 40:17; and Tob. 4:9-11)" (Wachob, 2000: 133-34). Rather than, like Gittin 2:1-2, summarizing all the contrary possibilities that may exist as one attempts to determine what is required or not required, and thus what writ is fit or unfit; James 2:12-13 summarizes how a person should speak and act as a result of God's attributes and actions.

References and Selected Bibliography

Alon, G.
    1967-70   מחקרים בתולדות ישראל. 2 vols. Tel Aviv: HaKibbutz HaMeuhad.

    1977   *Jews and Judaism in the Classical World.* Jerusalem: Magnes Press.

    1989   *The Jews in Their Land in the Talmudic Age.* Reprinted: Cambridge, MA and London, GB: Harvard University Press.

Amir, A.S.
    1977   מוסדות ותארים בספרות התלמוד. Jerusalem: Mosad HaRav Kook.

Avi-Yonah, M.
    1966   *The Holy Land from the Persian to the Arab Conquests (536 B.C.E. - C.E. 640).* Grand Rapids: Michigan.

Baras, Z., S. Safrai, M. Stern, and Y. Tsafrir.
    1984   ארץ ישראל מחורבן בית שני ועד הכיבוש המוסלמי. 2 vols. Jerusalem: Yad Yitzhak Ben Zvi.

Ben-Dov, M.
    1981   "Fragmentary Inscription from the Synagogue at Tiberias." In *Ancient Synagogues Revealed*, ed. L.I. Levine, 157-59. Jerusalem: Academic Press and The Israel Exploration Society.

Berger, P.
    1967   *The Sacred Canopy: Elements of a Sociological Theory of Religion.* Garden City, NY: Doubleday.

Berger, P., and T. Luckmann.
    1966   *The Social Construction of Reality: A Treatise in the Sociology of Knowledge.* Garden City, NY: Doubleday.

Binder, D.D.
    1999   *Into the Temple Courts: The Place of Synagogues in the Second Temple Period.* Atlanta, GA: SBL Dissertation Series.

Boyarin, D.
    1999   *Dying for God: Martyrdom and the Making of Christianity and Judaism. Figurae: Reading Medieval Culture.* Stanford, CA: Stanford University Press.

Boyce, M.
    1986   *Zoroastrians, Their Religious Beliefs and Practices.* London and New York: Routledge and Kegan Paul.

Breasted, J.H.
1962   *Ancient Records of Egypt.* 5 vols. New York: Russell and Russell.
1964   *A History of Egypt.* New York: Bantam. Reprint of the 1909 edition.

Brown, P.
1981   *The Cult of the Saints.* Chicago: University of Chicago Press.
1992   *Power and Persuasion in Late Antiquity: Toward a Christian Empire.* Madison, WI: University of Wisconsin Press.

Cameron, A.
1991   *Christianity and the Rhetoric of Empire: The Development of Christian Discourse. Sather Classical Lectures* 55. Berkeley, CA: University of California Press.

Cohen, S.J.D.
1981- 82   "Epigraphical Rabbis." *Jewish Quarterly Review* 72: 1-17.
1987   *From the Maccabees to the Mishnah.* Philadelphia: Westminster Press.
1992   "The Place of the Rabbi in Jewish Society of the Second Century." In *The Galilee in Late Antiquity,* ed. L. Levine, Jerusalem and New York: Yad Yitzhak Ben-Zvi and Jewish Theological Seminary of America.

Cohen, S.J.D., and E.L.Greenstein, eds.
1990   *The State of Jewish Studies. The Jewish Theological Seminary of America.* Detroit: Wayne State University Press.

Crossan, J.D.
1975   *The Dark Interval.* Niles, IL.: Argus.

Dothan, M.
1981   "The Synagogue at Hammath Tiberias," In *Ancient Synagogues Revealed,* ed. L.I. Levine, 63-69. Jerusalem: Academic Press and The Israel Exploration Society.

Douglas, M.
1973   *Natural Symbols.* 2nd ed. London: Barrie and Jenkins.
1975a   "Self-Evidence." In *Implicit Meanings,* ed. M. Douglas. London: RKP.
1975b   "In the Nature of Things." In *Implicit Meanings,* ed. M. Douglas. London: RKP.
1978   *Cultural Bias.* London: Royal Anthropological Society.

Downey, G.
1960   *Constantinople in the Age of Justinian.* Norman: University of Oklahoma Press.

Durkheim, E.
1980   *Emile Durkheim, Contributions to L'Année sociologique,* ed. Y. Nandan. New York: Free Press.

Durkheim, E., and M. Mauss.
1970   *Primitive Classification*. London: RKP.
Edwards, D.
1992   "The Socio-Economic and Cultural Ethos of the Lower Galilee in the First Century." In *The Galilee in Late Antiquity*, ed. L.I. Levine. Jerusalem and New York: Yad Yitzhak Ben-Zvi and Jewish Theological Seminary of America.
Epstein, Y.N.
1964   מבוא לנוסח למשנה. Tel Aviv: Dvir and Magnes Press.
Fahnestock, J.
2000   "Aristotle and Theories of Figuration." In *Rereading Aristotle's Rhetoric*, eds. A.G. Gross and A.E. Walzer. Carbondale, PA and Edwardsville, IL: Southern Illinois University Press.
Fine, S., ed.
1996a   *Sacred Realm: The Emergence of the Synagogue in the Ancient World*. New York: Oxford University Press and Yeshiva University Museum.
Fine, S.
1996b   "From Meeting House to Sacred Realm: Holiness and the Ancient Synagogue." In *Sacred Realm: The Emergence of the Synagogue in the Ancient World*, ed. S. Fine, 21-47. New York: Oxford University Press and Yeshiva University Museum.
1998   *This Holy Place: On the Sanctity of Synagogues During the Greco-Roman Period*. Christianity and Judaism in Antiquity Series. Notre Dame, IN: University of Notre Dame Press.
Fishbane, M.
1985   *Biblical Interpretation in Ancient Israel*. Oxford: Clarendon Press.
Foerster, G.
1981   "A Survey of Ancient Diaspora Synagogues." In *Ancient Synagogues Revealed*, ed. L.I. Levine Jerusalem: Academic Press and The Israel Exploration Society.
1986   "Ancient Synagogues in The Land of Israel (Hebrew)." Reprinted in *The Ancient Synagogues*: Selected Studies *(Hebrew)*, ed. Z. Sarrai, 63-68. Jerusalem: Zalman Shazar Centre.
1992   "Ancient Synagogues in the Galilee." In *The Galilee in Late Antiquity*, ed. L.I. Levine, 289-319. New York and Jerusalem: Yad Yitzhak Ben-Zvi and Jewish Theological Seminary of America. Distributed: Cambridge, MA and London, GB: Harvard University Press.

Frey, J. B.
1952   *Corpus Inscriptionum Judaicarum.* vol. 2. Rome: Pontificio
             Instituto di Archeologia Cristiana.

Freyne, S.
1992   "Urban-Rural Relations in First-Century Galilee: Some
             Suggestions from Literary Sources." In *The Galilee in Late
             Antiquity*, ed. L.I Levine. Jerusalem and New York: Yad
             Yitzhaq Ben-Zvi and Jewish Theological Seminary of
             America.

Gafni, I.
1987   "The Historical Context." In *The Literature of the Sages.
             First Part: Oral Tora, Halakha, Mishna, Tosefta, Talmud,
             External Tractates*, ed. S. Safrai, 1-34. *Compendia Rerum
             Iudaicarum ad Novum Testamentum, Section 2.3.*
             Assen/Maastricht: Van Gorcum and Philadelphia: Fortress
             Press.

Geertz, C.
1966   "Religion as a Cultural System." In *Anthropological
             Approaches to the Study of Religion*, ed. M. Banton.
             London: Tavistock.

Gereboff, J.
1985   "When to Speak, How to Speak, and When Not to Speak:
             Answers from Early Rabbinic Stories." *Semeia* 34.

Goldberg, A.
1987a   "The Mishnah–A Study Book of Halakhah." In *The Litera-
             ture of the Sages. First Part: Oral Tora, Halakha, Mish-
             nah, Tosefta, Talmud, External Tractates*, ed. S. Safrai,
             211-62. *Compendia Rerum Iudaicarum ad Novum
             Testamentum, Section 2.3.* Assen/Maastricht: Van Gorcum
             and Philadelphia: Fortress Press.

1987b   "The Tosefta–Companion to the Mishna." In *The Literature
             of the Sages. First Part: Oral Tora, Halakha, Mishnah,
             Tosefta, Talmud, External Tractates*, ed. S. Safrai, 283-
             301. *Compendia Rerum Iudaicarum ad Novum
             Testamentum, Section 2.3.* Assen/Maastricht: Van Gorcum
             and Philadelphia: Fortress Press.

Goldenberg, R.
1977   "The Deposition of Gamiliel." In *Persons and Institutions
             in Early Rabbinic Judaism*, ed. W.S. Green. vol. 1. Mis-
             soula, MT: Scholars Press.

Goodblatt, D.
1975   *Rabbinic Institutions in Sassanian Babylonia.* Leiden: E.J.
             Brill.

1994   *The Monarchic Principle: Studies in Jewish Self-
             Government in Antiquity.* Tübingen: J.C.B. Mohr (Paul
             Siebeck).

Goodenough, E.R.
    1956-68   *Jewish Symbols in the Graeco-roman Period.* 12 vols. New York: Pantheon.

Goodman, M.
    1983   *State and Society in Roman Galilee, A.D. 132-212.* Totowa NJ: Rowman and Allanheld for the Oxford Centre for Postgraduate Studies.
    1992   "The Roman State and the Jewish Patriarch in the Third Century." In *The Galilee in Late Antiquity*, ed. L.I Levine. Jerusalem and New York: Yad Yitzhak Ben-Zvi and Jewish Theological Seminary of America.

Goody, J.R.
    1968   *Literacy in Traditional Societies.* London: Cambridge University Press.
    1986   *The Logic of Writing and the Organization of Society.* New York: Cambridge University Press.
    1987   *The Interface between Written and Oral.* New York: Cambridge University Press.

Goody, J.R., and I. Watt.
    1985   "The Consequences of Literacy." *Comparative Studies in Society and History.* vol. 5. 1962-63, 304-45. Reprinted 1985 in *Language and Social Context*, ed. P.P. Giglioli, 311-57. Harmondsworth, Middlesex, Great Britain: Penguin.

Grabbe, L.
    1992   *Judaism from Cyrus to Hadrian.* 2 vols. Minneapolis: Fortress Press.

Green, W.S.
    1979   "What's in a Name? The Question of Rabbinic Biography." In *Approaches to the Study of Ancient Judaism*, ed. W.S. Green. vol. 1. Missoula: Scholars Press.
    1983   "Reading the Writing of Rabbinism: Toward an Interpretation of Rabbinic Literature." *JAAR* 51.

Gumperz, J.
    1985   "The Speech Community." In *International Encyclopaedia of the Social Sciences*, 381-86. New York: Macmillan, 1968. Reprinted 1985 in *Language and Social Context*, ed. P.P. Giglioli, 219-31. Harmondsworth, Middlesex, Great Britain: Penguin.

Harris, J.R.
    1971   *The Legacy of Egypt.* 2nd ed. London: Oxford University Press.

Hezser, C.
    1997   *The Social Structure of the Rabbinic Movement in Roman Palestine.* Texte und Studien zum Antiken Judentum 66. Tubingen: Mohr Siebeck.

Hirshman, M.G.
    1996   *A Rivalry of Genius: Jewish and Christian Biblical Inter-
                    pretation in Late Antiquity*, trans. B. Stein. *SUNY Series in
                    Judaica: Hermeneutics, Mysticism, and Religion.* Albany,
                    NY: State University of New York Press.
Hock, R.F. and E.N. O'Neil, eds.
    1986   *The Chreia in Ancient Rhetoric.* Vol. 1 of *The Progymnas-
                    mata.* Atlanta, GA: Scholars Press.
Hoffman, D.
    1977   *The First Mishna and the Controversies of the Tannaim.* P.
                    Forchheimer, trans. New York: Maurosho Publications.
                    Distributed by Sepher-Hermon Press.
Hurley, P.J.
    1985   *A Concise Introduction to Logic.* 2nd ed. Belmont, CA:
                    Wadsworth.
Jones, A.H.M.
    1931   "The Urbanization of Palestine." *Journal of Roman Studies*
                    21.
    1949   *The Greek City.* London: Oxford University Press.
    1971   *The Cities of the Eastern Roman Provinces.* 2nd ed.
                    Oxford: Clarendon.
Kant, L.H.
    1987   "Jewish Inscription in Greek and Latin." In *Aufstieg und
                    Niedergang der rumischen Welt*, II.20.2, ed. H. Temporini
                    and W. Haase, 671-713. Berlin and New York: de Gruyter.
Kloner, A.
    1981   "Ancient Synagogues in Israel: An Archeological Survey."
                    In *Ancient Synagogues Revealed*, ed. L.I. Levine, 11-18.
                    Jerusalem: Academic Press and The Israel Exploration
                    Society.
Kraabel, A.T.
    1981   "The Societal System of Six Diaspora Synagogues." In
                    Ancient Synagogues: The State of Research, ed. J. Gutman,
                    79-91. Brown Judaic Studies 22. Chico CA: Scholars Press.
Kraeling, Carl, H.
    1979   *The Synagogue. The Excavations at Dura Europos. Final
                    Report VIII, Part I.* New Haven: Yale University Press.
Lerner, M.B.
    1987   "The Tractate Avot." In *The Literature of the Sages. First
                    Part: Oral Tora, Halakha, Mishnah, Tosefta, Talmud,
                    External Tractates.* ed. S. Safrai, 263-81. *Compendia
                    Rerum Iudaicarum ad Novum Testamentum, Section 2. 3.*
                    Assen/Maastricht: Van Gorcum and Philadelphia: Fortress
                    Press.

Levine, L.I.
  1979   "The Jewish Patriarch (Nasi) in Third Century Palestine."
              In *Aufstieg und Niedergang der rumischen Welt,* II.19.2,
              ed. H. Temporini and W. Haase, 649-88. Berlin and New
              York: de Gruyter.
  1981   "Ancient Synagogues–An Historical Introduction." In
              Ancient Synagogues Revealed, ed. L.I.Levine, 1-10.
              Jerusalem: Academic Press and The Israel Exploration
              Society.
  1985   מעמד החכמים בארץ ישראל בתקופת התלמוד. Jerusalem: Yad
              Izhak Ben-Zvi.
  1992   "The Sages and the Synagogue in Late Antiquity: The
              Evidence of the Galilee." In *The Galilee in Late Antiquity,*
              ed. L.I. Levine. Jerusalem and New York: Yad Yitzhak
              Ben-Zvi and Jewish Theological Seminary of America.
  1996   "The Status of the Patriarch in the Third and Fourth
              Centuries: Sources and Methodology." *Journal of Jewish
              Studies* 47:1-32.
Lifshitz, B.
  1967   *Donateurs et Fondateurs dans les Synagogues Juives.*
              Cahiers de la Biblique 7. Paris: Gabalda.
Lightstone, J.
  1979   *Yose the Galilean: Traditions in Mishnah-Tosefta.* Leiden:
              E.J. Brill.
  1983   "Form as Meaning in the Halakic Midrash." *Semeia* 27.
  1984   *The Commerce of the Sacred: Mediation of the Divine
              among Jews in the Graeco-Roman Diaspora.* Chico:
              Scholars Press.
  1985   "When Speech Is No Speech: The Problem of Early Rab-
              binic Rhetoric as Discourse." *Semeia* 34:54-55.
  1988   *Society, the Sacred, and Scripture in Ancient Judaism.*
              Waterloo, ON: Wilfrid Laurier University Press.
  1990   "Names without Lives: Why No Lives of the Rabbis in Ear-
              liest Rabbinic Literature?" *Sciences religieuses/Studies in
              Religion* 19,1:43-57.
  1991   "The Modern Study of Ancient Judaism: Scholarship and
              Contemporary North American Jewish Identity." In
              *Religious Studies: Issues Prospects and Proposals. Univer-
              sity of Manitoba Studies in Religion 2,* ed. L. Hurtado and
              K. Kloestermaier, 211-24. Atlanta: Scholars Press.
  1992   "The Sociological Study of Ancient Judaic Groups and
              Their Texts: Prolegommena." In *Essays in the Social
              Scientific Study of Judaism and Jewish Society,* ed. S.
              Schoenfeld, et al. vol. II. New York: Ktav Publishing.
  1993   "The Institutionalization of the Rabbinic Academy in Late
              Sassanid Babylonia and the Redaction of the Babylonian

Talmud." *Sciences religieuses/Studies in Religion* 22,2:167-86.

1994   *The Rhetoric of the Babylonian Talmud, Its Social Meaning and Context.* Waterloo, ON: Wilfrid Laurier University Press.

1995a   "The Rhetoric of the Mishnah and the Babylonian Talmud: From Rabbinic Priestly Scribes to Scholastic Rabbis." *Historical Reflections* 22,1:1-27.

1995b   "Form, Formularies and Meaning in the Babylonian Talmud: The Case of Bekorot 2a-b." In *Approaches to Ancient Judaism. New Series*, ed. J. Neusner, 3-31. vol. 7. Atlanta: Scholars Press.

1997   "Whence the Rabbis?" *Sciences religieuses/Studies in Religion* 26,3:275-95.

Maccoby, H.
1986   "The Mishnah: Methods of Interpretation." *Midstream*, October, 41.

Mack, B.L.
1995   "On Redescribing Christian Origins." Paper presented to the annual meeting of the Society of Biblical Literature, Philadelphia.

1990   *Rhetoric and the New Testament.* Minneapolis: Fortress Press.

Mack, B.L., and V.K. Robbins.
1989   *Patterns of Persuasion in the Gospels.* Sonoma, CA: Polebridge Press.

Matheson, P.E, trans.
1940   *The Discourses of Epictetus.* In *The Stoic and Epicurean Philosophers*, ed. W.J. Oates, 282-83. New York: Random House.

Melamed, E.Z.
1988   מדרשי הלכה של התנאים בתלמוד בבלי. Jerusalem: Magnes Press.

Meyers, E.M., and J.F. Strange
1981   *Archaeology, the Rabbis and Early Christianity.* Nashville: Abingdon.

Naveh, J.
1981   "Ancient Synagogues Inscriptions." In *Ancient Synagogues Revealed*, ed. L.I. Levine, 133-39. Jerusalem: Academic Press and The Israel Exploration Society.

Neusner, J.
1970   *Development of a Legend.* Leiden: E.J. Brill.
1971   *The Rabbinic Traditions about the Pharisees before AD 70.* 3 vols. Leiden: E.J. Brill.
1973   *Eliezer ben Hyrcanus.* Leiden: E.J. Brill.

1976-79	*A History of the Mishnaic Law of Purities.* 22 vols. Leiden: E.J. Brill.
1977	*A History of the Mishnaic Law of Purities, Part 21,* Formulation and Redaction. Leiden: E.J. Brill.
1981	*Judaism, the Evidence of the Mishnah.* Chicago: University of Chicago Press.
1983a	*Midrash in Context.* Philadelphia: Fortress Press.
1983b	"Judaism and Society." In *Take Judaism, for Example,* ed. J. Neusner. Chicago: University of Chicago Press.
1983c	*Judaism in Society: The Evidence of the Yerushalmi.* Chicago: University of Chicago Press.
1985a	*The Memorized Torah: The Mneumonic System of the Torah.* Chico: Scholars Press.
1985b	*Torah: From Scroll to Symbol in Formative Judaism.* Philadelphia: Fortress Press.
1986a	*The Oral Torah.* San Francisco: Harper and Row.
1986b	*Judaism: The Classical Statement, the Evidence of the Bavli.* Chicago: University of Chicago Press.
1986c	*Sifre to Numbers: An American Translation and Explanation.* vol 1: *Sifre to Numbers 1-58.* vol 2: *Sifre to Numbers 59-115.* Atlanta: Scholars Press.
1986d	*Israel and Iran in Talmudic Times.* Lantham, MD and London: University Press of America.
1986e	*Tosefta: Its Structure and Its Sources.* Atlanta: Scholars Press.
1987a	*Oral Tradition in Judaism: The Case of Mishnah.* New York and London: Garland Publishing.
1987b	*The Making of the Mind of Judaism: The Formative Age.* Atlanta: Scholars Press.
1987c	*Sifre to Deuteronomy: An Introduction to the Rhetorical, Logical and Topical Program.* Atlanta: Scholars Press.
1988a	*The Philosophical Mishnah.* vol. 1. *The Initial Probe.* Atlanta: Scholars Press.
1988b	*A Religion of Pots and Pans: Modes of Philosophical and Theological Discourse in Ancient Judaism.* Essays and a Program. Atlanta: Scholars Press.
1988c	*The Systemic Analysis of Judaism.* Atlanta: Scholars Press.
1989a	*Medium and Message in Judaism. First Series.* Atlanta: Scholars Press.
1989b	*The Mishnah: An Introduction.* Northvale, NJ and London: Jason Aronson Press.
1990a	*Making the Classics in Judaism: The Three Stages of Literary Formation.* Atlanta: Scholars Press.
1990b	*The Economics of the Mishnah.* Chicago: University of Chicago Press.

1990c   *Tradition as Selectivity: Scripture, Mishnah, Tosefta and Midrash in the Talmud of Babylonia. The Case of Tractate Arakhin.* Atlanta: Scholars Press.

1990d   *Uniting the Dual Torah: Sifra and the Problem of Mishnah.* Cambridge, UK: Cambridge Univerity Press.

1991a   *Rabbinic Political Theory: Religion and Politics in the Mishnah.* Chicago: University of Chicago Press.

1991b   *The Bavli That Might Have Been: The Tosefta's Theory of Mishnah Commentary Compared with the Bavli's.* Atlanta: Scholars Press.

Neusner, J, ed.
1971b   *The Modern Study of the Mishnah.* Leiden: E.J. Brill.

Neusner, J., and Green W.S.
1989   *Writing with Scripture: The Authority and Uses of the Hebrew Bible in the Torah of Formative Judaism.* Minneapolis: Fortress Press.

Parsons, T.
1954   *Essays in Sociological Theory.* Glencoe, IL: Free Press.

1977   *The Evolution of Societies.* Englewood Cliffs, NJ: Prentice-Hall.

Patte, D.
1990   *Structural Exegesis for New Testament Critics.* Minneapolis: Fortress Press.

Polzin, R.
1977   *Biblical Structuralism. Semeia Studies.* Missoula, MT: Scholars Press.

Porton, G
1979   *The Rabbinic Traditions about Rabbi Ishmael.* vol. 2. Leiden: E.J. Brill.

Radcliffe-Brown, A.R.
1952   *Structure and Function in Primitive Society.* London: Cohen and West Ltd.

Rendsberg, G.A.
1992   "The Galilean Background of Mishnaic Hebrew." In *The Galilee in Late Antiquity*, ed. L.I. Levine. Jerusalem and New York: Yad Yitzhak Ben-Zvi and Jewish Theological Seminary of America.

Robbins, V.K.
1984   *Jesus the Teacher: A Socio-rhetorical Interpretation of Mark.* Philadelphia: Fortress Press.

1993   "Progymnastic Rhetorical Composition and Pre-Gospel Traditions: A New Approach." In *The Synoptic Gospels: Source Criticism and the New Literary Criticism.* ed. C. Focant, 111-47. *BETL* 110. Leuven: Leuven University Press.

1996a   *The Tapestry of Early Christian Discourse: Rhetoric, Society and Ideology.* London: Routledge.

1996b   *Exploring the Texture of Texts: A Guide to Socio-Rhetorical Interpretation.* Valley Forge PA: Trinity Press International.

1998a   "Enthymemic Texture in the Gospel of Thomas." *SBL Seminar Papers* 37:343-66. Atlanta: Scholars Press. Online at www.emory.edu/COLLEGE/RELIGION/faculty/ robbins/enthyeme/emthymeme343.html.

1998b   "From Enthymeme to Theology in Luke 11:1-13." In *Literary Studies in Luke-Acts: A Collection of Essays in Honor of Joseph B. Tyson*, eds. R.P. Thompson and T.E. Phillips, 191-214. Macon, GA.: Mercer University Press. Online at www.emory.edu/COLLEGE/RELIGION/faculty/ robbins/Theology/theology191.html.

1999   "Rhetorical Ritual: Apocalyptic Discourse in Mark 13." In *Vision and Persuasion: Rhetorical Dimensions of Apocalyptic Discourse*, eds. G. Carey and L.G. Bloomquist, 95-121. St. Louis, MO: Chalice.

2002   "Argumentative Textures in Socio-Rhetorical Interpretation." In *Argumentation in the Bible*, eds. A. Eriksson, W. Überlacker and T. Olbricht, Emory Studies in Early Christianity. Harrisburg, PA: Trinity Press International.

Safrai, S.
1987a   "Halakha." In *The Literature of the Sages, First Part: Oral Tora, Halakha, Mishnah, Tosefta, Talmud, External Tractates*, ed. S. Safrai, 121-209. *Compendia Rerum Iudaicarum ad Novum Testamentum, Section 2.3.* Assen/Maastricht: Van Gorcum and Philadelphia: Fortress Press.

1987b   "Oral Torah." *In The Literature of the Sages, First Part: Oral Tora, Halakha, Mishnah, Tosefta, Talmud, External Tractates*, ed. S. Safrai, 35-119. *Compendia Rerum Iudaicarum ad Novum Testamentum, Section 2.3.* Assen/Maastricht: Van Gorcum and Philadelphia: Fortress Press.

Safrai, S. ed.
1987c   *The Literature of the Sages, First Part: Oral Tora, Halakha, Mishnah, Tosefta, Talmud, External Tractates*, ed. S. Safrai, *Compendia Rerum Iudaicarum ad Novum Testamentum, Section 2.3.* Assen/Maastricht: Van Gorcum and Philadelphia: Fortress Press.

Safrai, Z., ed.
1986   *The Ancient Synagogue: Selected Studies (Hebrew).* Jerusalem: Zalman Shazar Centre.

Saldarini, A.J.
1982   *Scholastic Rabbinism.* Chico, CA: Scholars Press.
1986   "Reconstructions of Rabbinic Judaism." In *Early Judaism and Its Modern Interpreters*, R.A. Kraft and G.W.E. Nickelsburg, eds. Atlanta, GA: Scholars Press, 437-77.
1988   *Pharisees, Sadducees, Scribes in Palestinian Society.* Wilmington: Glazier.

Schiffman, L.H.
1992   "Was There a Galilean Halakha?" In *The Galilee in Late Antiquity*, ed. L.I Levine. Jerusalem and New York: Yad Yitzhak Ben-Zvi and Jewish Theological Seminary of America.

Schuerer, E.
1973-87   *The History of the Jewish People in the Age of Jesus Christ.* Revised and edited by G. Vermes and F. Millar. 4 vols. Edinburgh: T and T Clark.

Schwab, M. and B. Lifshitz, eds.
1974   *Beth She`arim. vol. 2. The Greek Inscription.* New Brunswick NJ: Rutgers.

Smith, J.Z.
1978   "The Temple and the Magician." In *Map Is Not Territory*, ed. J. Z. Smith. Leiden: E.J. Brill.
1982   *Imagining Religion: From Babylon to Jonestown.* Chicago: University of Chicago Press.

Sussman, J.
1981   "The Inscription in the Synagogue at Rehob." In *Ancient Synagoue Revealed*, ed. L.I. Levine, 146-53. Jerusalem: Academic Press and The Israel Exploration Society.

Torjesen, Karen Jo
1997   "You Are the Christ: Five Portraits of Jesus from the Early Church." In *Jesus at 2000*, ed. M.J. Borg, 73-88. Boulder CO: Westview.

Tsafrir, Y.
1984   *The Land of Israel from the Destruction of the Second Temple to Muslim Conquest. II.* Archaeology and Art (Hebrew). Jerusalem: Yad Yitzhak Ben- Zvi.

Urbach, E.E.
1958   תרביץ "הדרשה כיסוד ההלכה ובעיית הסופרים" 27:166-82.
1984   ההלכה: מקורותיה והתפתחותה. Tel Aviv: Masada Press.

Urbach E.E., Y. Susman, D. Rosenthal, S. Friedman, S. Hablin, D. Sperber, D. Boyarin, Y. Ta-Shma, and S. Lieberman,
1983   מחקרים בספרות התלמודית. יום עיון לרגל מלאת שמונים שנה לשאול ליברמן. Jerusalem: Israel Academy of Sciences and Humanities.

Urman, D.
1981 "Jewish Inscriptions from the Village of Dabbura in the Golan." In *Ancient Synagogues Revealed*, ed. L.I. Levine, 154-56. Jerusalem: Academic Press and The Israel Exploration Society.

Urman, D. and P.V.M. Flesher, eds.
1995 *Ancient Synagogues: Historical Analysis and Archaeological Discovery*. 2 vols. Vol. 47, *Studia Post-Biblica*. New York: E.J. Brill.

Van der Horst, P.W.
1991 *Ancient Jewish Epitaphs*. Kampen, Netherlands: Pharos.

Wachob, W. H.
2000 *The Voice of Jesus in the Social Rhetoric of James*. SNTSMS 106. Cambridge, GB: Cambridge University Press.

Weiss, Z.
1992 "Social Aspects of Burial in Beth She`arim: Archaeological Finds and Talmudic Sources." In *The Galilee in Late Antiquity*, ed. L.I. Levine, 357-71. New York and Jerusalem: Jewish Theological Seminary of America: Distributed: Cambridge, MA and London, GB: Harvard University Press.

Weiss-Halivni, D.
1986 *Midrash, Mishnah, and Gemara: The Jewish Predilection for Justified Law*. Cambridge: Harvard University Press.

Zahavy, T.
1977 *The Traditions of Eleazar ben Azariah*. Missoula, MT: Scholars Press.

Zeitlin, S.
1962 *The Rise and Fall of the Judean State*. 3 vols. Philadelphia: Jewish Publication Society.

Zeitline, I.M.
1984 *Ancient Judaism*. Oxford: Polity Press.

Zlotnick, D.
1966 *Semahot: The Tractate Mourning*. New Haven: Yale University Press.

1988 *The Iron Pillar—Mishnah*. Jerusalem: Mosad Bialik Institute. American Distributor, Ktav Publishing.

General Index

Academy, 11-12, 20, 73, 74, 177
Administration, 1, 27-28, 67-71, 186-91, 196, 198
Aggadic midrash, 173
Antisemantic, 34, 37, 49, 54, 59, 62-63, 86, 130, 164
Aqiva, 5, 11, 76, 84, 95, 96, 126-27, 142, 148
Aramaic, 12, 194-95
Archisynágogos, 190, 195
Architecture, 193
Argument, 20-22, 34, 35, 60, 65-66, 74, 79, 81, 116, 177, 180, 196, 201, 203-16
Aristocracy, 191, 19-96
Aristocratic families, 190, 196
Aristotle, 203
Artifact, 3, 64
Attribution, 5, 65, 185, 194
Authority, 5, 6, 18-21, 26-31, 34, 64-71, 75, 77-80, 116-18, 121, 172-75, 177, 184-85, 190, 192, 194-95, 198, 212
Autonomous, 27, 77, 164, 166, 171
Avi-Yonah, M., 197
Avot, 29, 69, 75-76, 173

Babylonian Talmud, 7, 9, 21, 62, 80, 110, 118, 122, 173
Bar-Kohkba, 187, 192
Bekorot, 62
Bible, 9, 11, 22, 175, 180
Boundaries, 8, 19, 59, 65, 70, 170, 194
Bundahis, 68
Byzantine, 192-94

Caesarea, 192
Canonical, 19, 21, 28, 64, 77, 187
Cases, 25-26, 62, 66-67, 71, 83, 89, 111, 113, 117, 164, 173-75, 179-82, 191, 202-03, 205, 208, 210-14
Christian culture, 201
Christianities/Christianity, 5, 10-11, 201
Cicero, 20, 202
Class, 6, 28, 68, 77, 79, 183, 186, 188-92, 194-99

Cohen, S.J.D., 198
Communities
    Christian, 2
    Diaspora, 189
    Jewish, 190, 195, 210
    Judaic, 21
    Judean, 192
    Local, 190
Concatenating, 33, 64, 81, 110, 164, 166
Courts, 190-91, 196, 198, 215
Criticism, 7, 14, 17, 22
Cult, 1, 13, 19, 67-70, 72, 74, 182

Diachronic, 21, 80, 121
Diatribe, 34
Disciples, 23, 27-28, 69-77, 125, 137-38, 183
Discourse
    Legal, 213, 215
Divisions, 2, 16, 23, 25, 29, 118, 166, 170
Documents, 2-3, 7-9, 12, 14-15, 18, 21, 24, 27, 30, 49, 63, 68, 79-81, 107, 122-23, 164, 167, 170, 174, 177, 189-90, 195, 216
Douglas, M., 183

Early rabbinic rhetoric, 23
Eduyyot, 29
Eliezer, 35, 38, 76, 125, 137, 195, 202, 203
Epigraphs, 195
Essenes, 185
Ethnarch, 191
Ethno-religious community, 187
Exegesis, 175, 180
Extra-guild life, 183, 187

Formations, 21, 177, 183
Formative, 19, 184, 188, 199
Formulae/Formularies, 15, 24, 33-34, 37, 49, 63, 74, 80-81, 86, 110-11, 116, 130, 164, 178
Funerary inscriptions, 195

Series Published by Wilfrid Laurier University Press for the Canadian Corporation for Studies in Religion / Corporation Canadienne des Sciences Religieuses

Editions SR

Comparative Ethics Series / Collection d'Éthique Comparée

Studies in Christianity and Judaism / Études sur le christianisme et le judaïsme

The Study of Religion in Canada /
Sciences Religieuses au Canada

Studies in Women and Religion /
Études sur les femmes et la religion

SR Supplements

Available from:

Wilfrid Laurier University Press

Waterloo, Ontario, Canada   N2L 3C5
Telephone: (519) 884-0710, ext. 6124
Fax: (519) 725-1399
E-mail: press@wlu.ca
World Wide Web: http://www.wlupress.wlu.ca